Salvation Manual

Bible Made Easy through Questions and Answers
Jeremiah

Johnny, Nsikan E.

Grosvenor House
Publishing Limited

This book is published by
Grosvenor House Publishing Ltd
Link House
140 The Broadway, Tolworth, Surrey, KT6 7HT.
www.grosvenorhousepublishing.co.uk

A CIP record for this book
is available from the British Library

Paperback ISBN 978-1-80381-368-4
Hardback ISBN 978-1-80381-369-1
eBook ISBN 978-1-80381-370-7

www.smni.org

*All quoted scriptures are taken from the New Heart English Bible (NHEB),
edited by Wayne A. Mitchell 2007–18.*

TABLE OF CONTENTS

TABLE OF CONTENTS

ACKNOWLEDGEMENT

My heartfelt appreciation goes to the New Heart English Bible (NHEB) team for making God's word available for everyone to use freely and to Wayne A. Mitchell, the editor of the 2018 edition of the Bible I used in this book.

FOREWORD

On a fateful Wednesday afternoon, everything around me seemed to be moving fast, like I was living in a slower dimension than everyone else, but I wasn't bothered at all. My reluctance to attend a church programme a friend had invited me to could be seen in my sluggishness as I dragged my feet to meet him. It had been a hectic day, and I would have preferred to take a break, but it was more difficult to turn down the invitation because I had committed myself with my words to attend the programme. At that instant, the passing of time seemed like my only salvation from my dilemma. Patiently and seemingly unperturbed by the lateness I had caused him, my friend, who was determined to take me with him, had the last smile as we finally approached the venue for the meeting.

I had barely sat in the programme for five minutes when my countenance brightened. This was not a regular church programme. It was an interactive non-denominational Bible studies programme where members of the audience were also given an opportunity to take to the pulpit for a few minutes, preach the gospel from a designated portion of the Bible and be corrected where necessary. It was a place where believers could put aside doctrinal differences and look into the Bible for their souls' salvation and nothing more. More so, it was a training ground where people could gain the needed knowledge and confidence to carry out the great commission of taking the gospel to the ends of the earth. The atmosphere was exhilarating, and in the spur of the moment, I raised my hand, indicating that I would like to contribute to the day's discourse. The pause and stare from the crowd gave me a hunch that I had done something unusual, but it didn't matter because the moderator gave me an opportunity to preach for a few minutes. At the end of my message, he said with a smile, "that was a good message, but you would have to come earlier if you would like to share next time because we select those who would share for the day at the beginning of the programme." The moderator, who was also the organiser, was Mr Nsikan Johnny, the author of this book, and that programme is where our paths crossed. Twelve years down the line and in a divine twist of fate, we have grown from being strangers to brothers in the ministry, and all this while, Mr Nsikan Johnny has not stopped employing ingenious ways to enhance Bible studies and Bible teaching.

One of the struggles many Christians face in the study of the Bible is the ability to notice specific necessary information in each chapter and verse of the scripture. Some believers limit themselves to selected parts of the Bible; they fail to cultivate a taste for the Bible's complete content. The reason for this problem could be a lack of proper Bible study methods or a lack of motivation. Others who are motivated or are passionate about studying the Bible may lose track of the many characters, places, or symbols they come across as they study a chapter of the Bible. They may also find it challenging to connect the dots and grasp or understand the context of a passage and its intended meaning. The Bible should not merely be owned but known in its entirety. Only when the word of God is known can it be believed and obeyed.

Salvation Manual: Bible Made Easy through Questions and Answers is one of the tools Mr Nsikan Johnny has created to aid Bible studies. One thing that fascinates me about the book is that it makes the reader study every chapter of the Bible in two directions; the forward and reverse directions. The chapter of the book of the Bible at the beginning of each chapter of this book is the first point of contact for the reader which they have to read and understand what is contained in the chapter. Following that are questions from the chapter and answers at the end of the questions, with which the reader would test their knowledge of what they had read in that chapter. These questions and answers segment presents the reader with problems which points them back to the Bible for confirmation or further studies (the reverse direction). The approach to Bible studies presented in this book is remarkable as it will take its reader a step above regular Bible reading to be fully grounded in the details of the events and messages in the scriptures.

No Christian can afford to be ignorant of the word of God; it is crucial that we are well-informed and versed in the scriptures. This book is a treasure chest that contains truth and knowledge of the scriptures that is perhaps unknown to you. *Salvation Manual: Bible Made Easy through Questions and Answers* lives up to its title; it will enhance an easy understanding of the Bible and get the reader's attention to the tiniest of details. This book is a tool that can challenge your knowledge of the scripture, serve as a Bible study guide and reveal vital information that might have been overlooked or missed in the course of your study of the scriptures. It will also make it easy for you to have the word of God at your fingertips.

I believe this book will make a valuable contribution to your ability to study and comprehend the scripture; I heartily commend it.

Benjamin E. Ifon

PREFACE

Every believer's desire should be to know God intimately. But this knowledge is not gotten on a platter; we have a role to play. The role is a constant study and application of the word of God. The need to encourage people to study the Bible with an emphasis on salvation is highly essential. The word of God is the only veritable manual for navigating this world full of darkness and ungodliness; hence, there is a need for flexible ways to be designed for studying the Bible without sacrificing its truth.

I took on the project of writing and publishing this book in a bid to solve a problem I once faced in my Bible teaching campaign. I am an advocate for the holistic study of the Bible, and I bring people together weekly to study the Bible. I encourage a chapter-by-chapter systematic study of the Bible where every member of my Bible studies group is required to study one chapter of the Bible daily, in an alternating pattern of two Old Testament chapters before a New Testament chapter. My goal is for people to study the Bible completely without omitting any chapter or verse because *"All Scripture is God-breathed and profitable for teaching, for reproof, for correction, and for training in righteousness, [17] that the person of God may be complete, thoroughly equipped for every good work."* (2 Timothy 3:16–17.)

One of the methods I employ to make people pay more attention to Bible studies in a fun way is Bible quizzes. These Bible quizzes were meant to test people's knowledge of the chapters of the Bible they had read for a period of time. As a result, the questions had to come from every chapter that was read and had to be arranged serially, according to the chapters of the Bible. The plan seemed good to me, and everything was going on fine until it was time to source for questions. I searched the internet for Bible quiz questions and found many, but not as comprehensive as I needed, so I took up the task of setting questions from each chapter I read from the Bible to use for the quiz competitions. I began setting the questions from the book of Jeremiah in the early months of 2020. When I realised how many questions I had in store after setting the questions for a period, I decided that the questions be immortalised in the form of a book beginning from the book of Jeremiah. I am still setting these questions at this moment, and I intend to continue setting them until every chapter of the Bible is covered so that others may benefit from my work and not suffer what I suffered.

This book is helpful for personal Bible studies, for educating others about the Bible and as a source of questions for Bible quiz competitions. Through my experience, I have realised that the benefits of studying the Bible through questions and answers are immense. You may scan through a chapter of the Bible and have a general understanding of what you read, but questions from that chapter would awaken your consciousness to the details you may not have taken note of. This consciousness will make you pay closer attention to details while studying and aid your memory to be more retentive regarding what you have studied. I can assure you that you will hardly go through a chapter or two in this book without observing the book's relevance to an in-depth understanding of the Bible.

Apart from its salvation and educational values, the book also serves as a template for understanding the patterns of quiz questions used for the SMNI New Disciples programme – another programme which God laid in my heart to establish. New Disciples is an offspring of a mother Christian organisation – Salvational Manual Network Initiative. It is a programme that brings contestants together, and the major events in the programme are Bible quizzes and preaching by contestants. The questions asked in the New Disciples programme follow the pattern of the questions in this book, and contestants and observers alike would understand and enjoy the programme better if they had read this book. Possible preaching topics from every chapter are also highlighted in this book in the form of hints that the readers should elaborate on. You can find the commentaries to the hints in my *Topical Exegesis* series.

As you go through this book, you should allow the Holy Spirit to shape your life and transform you to be a Christian approved by God. I challenge you to this new approach to studying the Bible and encourage you to embrace the pattern individually, as a family, as a school or as a Christian fellowship.

INTRODUCTION

Often, students form study groups to help them tackle the challenge of understanding difficult subjects. They engage tools like quizzes, giving out topics for members to research and speak on. Speakers entertain questions from members; both the speaker and the members interact to find solutions to problems. Eventually, the Question-and-Answer (Q&A) sessions benefit both the speakers and the audience. The excitement and down-to-earth nature of the sessions make the students learn in a relaxed atmosphere while applying the academic theories to everyday practical life. For ages, Q&A sessions have remained a great method for learning difficult subjects; the discipline of Bible study is no different. Many believers would testify that many of the Bible lessons they learned when preparing for quizzes and during interactive sessions had stuck with them through the ages. Jeremiah is one of those books some people had mistaken to be less interesting and difficult to understand, probably due to its mournful tone. This book, *Salvation Manual: Bible Made Easy through Questions and Answers for the book of Jeremiah*, seeks to make studying the book of Jeremiah easier by engaging the interactive tool of Q&A.

To a casual reader, the Book of Jeremiah could just be a haphazard collection of sorrowful messages. However, a careful study will reveal that the book opens with God's call and briefing of the young Jeremiah, who went on to declare God's displeasure against sin. The messages were not without repeated calls for repentance. Although God's primary concern was Judah, the state and fate of other nations were not overlooked. The book of Jeremiah teaches us of God's love for His children, His justice against sin and the certainty of His judgement coming upon the unrepentant at the close of the age.

Some Bible students miss details in their Bible studies either because attention was not paid to them or their method of studying did not give allowance to observing all the facts in the narration. In a bid to grasp or have a perfect knowledge of the messages, events, and characters in the Bible, many people use the systematic approach of reading chapter by chapter to ensure no part of the Bible is omitted. Despite this, some characters, messages, or events tend to escape people's notice because of their seeming insignificance or, sometimes, due to the reader's oversight. This book seeks to address the human tendency not to pay attention to all details by approaching the study of the Bible using questions and answers.

Reading, listening, and observations are great tools in acquiring knowledge, but to further exercise the mind in understanding and memorising information, the tool of quizzes has been known to be extremely efficient and productive in serving that purpose. *Salvation Manual: Bible Made Easy through Questions and Answers for the Book of Jeremiah* is one of several books in the *Salvation Manual: Bible Made Easy through Questions and Answers* series. Like other books in the series, it adopts a questions and answers pattern in identifying and breaking down biblical truths for them to not only be easily understood but memorised. In a spectacular method of using questions and answers, it unravels every message, event, and character from all the chapters in the book of Jeremiah. This book consists of fifty-two chapters, one for each chapter of the book of Jeremiah. Questions are asked after each chapter of the book of Jeremiah, and answers to all the questions are provided at the end of the questions. This ensures that no information or events in the book of Jeremiah escape the reader's notice.

The questions and answers are placed at the end of each chapter to assess the degree to which the reader understands the chapter read as well as how much of the details of the chapter they have retained in their memory. The questions and answers pattern of studying is indeed very potent, for people cannot truly ascertain if they have learnt and memorised what they have studied if they are not questioned or examined. An average or poor score on a chapter test would quickly reveal the need for the reader to carry out another chapter study for a stronger grasp of it until they can pass the test. Carrying out this exercise from chapter to chapter would invariably ensure a profound knowledge of the entire book of Jeremiah.

The questions in *Salvation Manual: Bible Made Easy Through Questions And Answers for the Book of Jeremiah* are of several categories based on their difficulty levels. There are questions designed to assess the reader's general knowledge of chapters of the book of Jeremiah; these sorts of questions would help the reader grasp every essential detail and have a profound knowledge of the entire book. Some questions would quiz the reader on their knowledge of some Bible verses in the chapters of the book of Jeremiah; these sorts of questions would induce the reader to have some notable verses in the book memorised. Some questions would quiz the reader on several aspects of the book of Jeremiah that relate to other parts of the Bible; these sorts of questions would help the reader have a holistic knowledge of the entire Bible. All categories of questions are designed to aid the reader in identifying aspects of the chapters missed during the study to ensure little or nothing escapes their understanding or memory.

This book will aid readers in fully grasping the messages and events of the entire book of Jeremiah. Not only will their understanding aid their relationship with God and ensure their soul's salvation, but they would be able to teach others profoundly about the book of Jeremiah. Every believer should be well-equipped with Bible knowledge. Good knowledge of the Bible empowers a believer to teach and preach with conviction without the fear of an inability to explain certain events or answer some questions in the Bible when confronted with one. Hints from preaching questions in the book would guide readers to the messages embedded in those verses or events from which the question hints were drafted, which the readers might not have observed at a glance. Having this book is one of the good decisions a person could make. Enjoy your journey.

The different kinds of questions in this book are:

1. Regular questions: These questions are labelled according to their difficulty levels as "a", "b", "b1", "b2" and "c", where "a" questions are the simplest and "c" questions are the most difficult.

2. Context questions: These questions are labelled "CTX" but simpler contexts are labelled "CTX*s*".

3. "Complete the following": A verse of the Bible will be given, and the reader is expected to quote the following verse or verses. These questions are labelled according to their difficulty levels as "CPA", "CPB", and "CPC", where "CPA" is the simplest and "CPC" is the most difficult.

    Where the reader is expected to quote more than a verse, the number of verses to be quoted will be added to indicate that. For example, a CPB question with two verses to be quoted will be labelled as "CPB2", and a CPC question with three verses to be quoted will be labelled "CPC3".

4. Tie questions: These are questions that are intended for use in a quiz competition to break ties between contestants. They are labelled as "Tie".

5. Commentary or Preaching questions: These questions offer the Bible verses from which the reader is required to preach or write a commentary. They are labelled as "CMA", "CMB", and "CMC", according to how easy it is to draw a salvation message from the given Bible passage. Questions labelled "CMA" are the easiest, while "CMC" are the most difficult.

    Note: Some answers have sections that are demarcated with brackets. These brackets indicate that the enclosed part is additional information, which, whether said or not, does not affect the answer.

CHAPTER 1

JEREMIAH CHAPTER 1

"The words of Jeremiah the son of Hilkiah, of the priests who were in Anathoth in the land of Benjamin: [2]*to whom the word of the LORD came in the days of Josiah the son of Amon, king of Judah, in the thirteenth year of his reign.* [3]*It came also in the days of Jehoiakim the son of Josiah, king of Judah, to the end of the eleventh year of Zedekiah, the son of Josiah, king of Judah, to the carrying away of Jerusalem captive in the fifth month.* [4]*Now the word of the LORD came to me, saying,* [5]*"Before I formed you in the belly, I knew you. Before you came forth out of the womb, I sanctified you. I have appointed you a prophet to the nations."* [6]*Then I said, "Ah, Lord GOD. Look, I do not know how to speak; for I am a child."* [7]*But the LORD said to me, "Do not say, 'I am a child;' for to whoever I shall send you, you shall go, and whatever I shall command you, you shall speak.* [8]*Do not be afraid because of them; for I am with you to deliver you," says the LORD.* [9]*Then the LORD put forth his hand, and touched my mouth; and the LORD said to me, "Look, I have put my words in your mouth.* [10]*Look, I have this day set you over the nations and over the kingdoms, to pluck up and to break down and to destroy and to overthrow, to build and to plant."* [11]*Moreover the word of the LORD came to me, saying, "Jeremiah, what do you see?" I said, "I see a branch of an almond tree."* [12]*Then the LORD said to me, "You have seen well; for I watch over my word to perform it."* [13]*The word of the LORD came to me the second time, saying, "What do you see?" I said, "I see a boiling caldron; and it is tipping away from the north."* [14]*Then the LORD said to me, "Out of the north evil will*

break out on all the inhabitants of the land. ¹⁵For, look, I will call all the families of the kingdoms of the north," says the LORD; "and they shall come, and they shall each set his throne at the entrance of the gates of Jerusalem, and against all its walls all around, and against all the cities of Judah. ¹⁶I will utter my judgments against them touching all their wickedness, in that they have forsaken me, and have burned incense to other gods, and worshiped the works of their own hands. ¹⁷"You therefore put your belt on your waist, arise, and speak to them all that I command you. Do not be dismayed at them, lest I dismay you before them. ¹⁸For, look, I have made you this day a fortified city, and an iron pillar, and bronze walls, against the whole land, against the kings of Judah, against its princes, against its priests, and against the people of the land. ¹⁹They will fight against you; but they will not prevail against you; for I am with you," says the LORD, "to deliver you.""

QUESTIONS

QUESTION 1   a

According to Jeremiah chapter 1:

Who is the author of the book of Jeremiah?

QUESTION 2   b

According to Jeremiah chapter 1:

Who was Jeremiah's father, what was his occupation and what town was he from?

QUESTION 3   b

According to Jeremiah chapter 1:

Who was king in Judah when the Lord first gave messages to Jeremiah, and in what year of his reign was it?

QUESTION 4   a

According to Jeremiah chapter 1:

What year of King Zedekiah's reign were the people of Jerusalem taken as captives to Babylon?

QUESTION 5   b2

Jeremiah prophesied during the reign of several kings in Judah:

How many were they, and what are their names?

QUESTION 6   CTXs

"Before I formed you in the belly, I knew you...."

Give the context of the above quote:

Who said it, to who, and under what circumstance?

QUESTION 7   a

According to Jeremiah chapter 1, when the Lord called Jeremiah to be His prophet, Jeremiah was reluctant:

What was his excuse?

QUESTION 8   CPB

Jeremiah chapter 1:7–8 says,

"But the LORD said to me, "Do not say, 'I am a child;' for to whoever I shall send you, you shall go, and whatever I shall command you, you shall speak.""

Complete verse 8.

QUESTION 9   a

According to Jeremiah chapter 1, before God said He had put His words in Jeremiah's mouth:

What did He do to Jeremiah?

QUESTION 10   a

According to Jeremiah chapter 1:

What was Jeremiah's first vision?

QUESTION 11   b

According to Jeremiah chapter 1, when the Lord asked Jeremiah, "what do you see?":

What did Jeremiah say he saw in the first instance, and what was the Lord's response?

QUESTION 12   b

According to Jeremiah chapter 1, when God asked Jeremiah what he saw for the second time:

What did Jeremiah say he saw?

QUESTION 13   a

Jeremiah chapter 1:15 says, *"For, look, I will call all the families of the kingdoms of the north," says the LORD...."*

Which kingdom of the north is the above passage talking about?

QUESTION 14   b1

According to Jeremiah chapter 1:

From where did God say that evil or terror would break out on the inhabitants of the land of Judah and why?

QUESTION 15   CPC 2

Jeremiah chapter 1:17–19 says,

""You therefore put your belt on your waist, arise, and speak to them all that I command you. Do not be dismayed at them, lest I dismay you before them."

Complete verses 18 and 19.

QUESTION 16   **CTX**

"They will fight against you; but they will not prevail against you"

Give the context of the above quote:

Who said it, to who, and under what circumstance?

QUESTION 17   **CMB**

Read Jeremiah chapter 1:4–10, preach or write a commentary on the passage with focus on verse 6 and with emphasis on salvation.

QUESTION 18   **CMB**

Read Jeremiah chapter 1:16, preach or write a commentary on the passage with emphasis on salvation.

QUESTION 19   **CMB**

Read Jeremiah chapter 1:17–19, preach or write a commentary on the passage with emphasis on salvation.

ANSWERS

ANSWER TO QUESTION 1   **a**

Prophet Jeremiah (Jeremiah 1:1).

ANSWER TO QUESTION 2   **b**

- Hilkiah
- He was a priest
- He was from Anathoth in the land of Benjamin (Jeremiah 1:1).

ANSWER TO QUESTION 3   **b**

- King Josiah
- The 13th year of his reign (Jeremiah 1:2).

ANSWER TO QUESTION 4   **a**

Eleventh (11th) year (Jeremiah 1:3).

ANSWER TO QUESTION 5   b2

- 5 Kings
- The names of the kings are:
  1. King Josiah
  2. King Jehoahaz/Shallum
  3. King Jehoiakim/Eliakim
  4. King Jehoiachin/Jeconiah
  5. King Zedekiah/Mattaniah (Jeremiah 1:1–3, 2 Kings 23:31, 24:1–8).

ANSWER TO QUESTION 6   CTXs

- God
- To Prophet Jeremiah
- When God called him to be His prophet (Jeremiah 1:5).

ANSWER TO QUESTION 7   a

His excuse was that he would not be able to speak for God because he was a child (Jeremiah 1:6).

ANSWER TO QUESTION 8   CPB

"""⁸Do not be afraid because of them; for I am with you to deliver you," says the LORD." (Jeremiah 1:8.)

ANSWER TO QUESTION 9   a

He touched Jeremiah's mouth (Jeremiah 1:9).

ANSWER TO QUESTION 10   a

He saw the branch of an almond tree (Jeremiah 1:11).

ANSWER TO QUESTION 11   b

- He saw a branch of an almond tree
- The Lord's response: *"You have seen well; for I watch over my word to perform it."* (Jeremiah 1:11–12.)

ANSWER TO QUESTION 12   b

A boiling caldron or pot or seething pot tipping away from the North (Jeremiah 1:13).

ANSWER TO QUESTION 13   a

Babylon.

ANSWER TO QUESTION 14   b1

- From the North
- Because they have forsaken the Lord, burned incense to other gods, and worshipped the works of their own hands (Jeremiah 1:14–16).

ANSWER TO QUESTION 15   CPC 2

"18 For, look, I have made you this day a fortified city, and an iron pillar, and bronze walls, against the whole land, against the kings of Judah, against its princes, against its priests, and against the people of the land. 19 They will fight against you; but they will not prevail against you; for I am with you," says the LORD, "to deliver you."" (Jeremiah 1:18–19.)

ANSWER TO QUESTION 16   CTX

- God
- To Prophet Jeremiah
- When God commissioned Jeremiah to be His prophet to the people of Judah and encouraged him to be courageous to deliver the message He would send him (Jeremiah 1:19).

HINT TO QUESTION 17   CMB

God's call to Jeremiah was greeted with an excuse of him being a child and his inability to speak. In response to his excuse, God encouraged him not to be afraid and assured him of His presence, and without further hesitation, Jeremiah carried out his task. Some people who God had positioned to be great ministers fall back due to their fears and limitations, which they use as excuses. But those that summon up the courage to follow through on the given assignment always excel.

HINT TO QUESTION 18   CMB

As a consequence of Judah's sins, God said He would judge and punish them. God's judgement comes upon His children who turn away from Him in rebellion. We should not place ourselves in a position to incur God's judgement.

HINT TO QUESTION 19   CMB

One truth about God is that He never forsakes those who He sends on a given assignment. In the verses under consideration, He once again reiterates His promise to be with Jeremiah to deliver him from any form of opposition. God will never forsake us while we are doing His work. He will always be with us to protect, strengthen and guide us. But when we rebel against Him, He will forsake us, and we may be destroyed.

CHAPTER 2

JEREMIAH CHAPTER 2

"The word of the LORD came to me, saying, [2] "Go, and cry in the ears of Jerusalem, saying, 'Thus says the LORD, "I remember you, the devotion of your youth, the love of your weddings; how you went after me in the wilderness, in a land that was not sown. [3] Israel was holiness to the LORD, the first fruits of his increase. All who devour him shall be held guilty. Evil shall come on them,"' says the LORD." [4] Hear the word of the LORD, O house of Jacob, and all the families of the house of Israel. [5] Thus says the LORD, "What unrighteousness have your fathers found in me, that they have gone far from me, and have walked after vanity, and are become vain? [6] Neither did they say, 'Where is the LORD who brought us up out of the land of Egypt, who led us through the wilderness, through a land of deserts and of pits, through a land of drought and of the shadow of death, through a land that none passed through, and where no man lived?' [7] I brought you into a plentiful land, to eat its fruit and its goodness; but when you entered, you defiled my land, and made my heritage an abomination. [8] The priests did not say, 'Where is the LORD?' And those who handle the law did not know me. The rulers also transgressed against me, and the prophets prophesied by Baal, and walked after things that do not profit. [9] "Therefore I will yet contend with you," says the LORD, "and I will contend with your children's children. [10] For pass over to the islands of Kittim, and see; and send to Kedar, and consider diligently; and see if there has been such a thing. [11] Has a nation changed its gods, which really are no gods? But my people have changed their glory for that which

does not profit. ¹²"Be astonished, you heavens, at this, and be
horribly afraid. Be very desolate," says the LORD. ¹³"For my
people have committed two evils: they have forsaken me, the spring
of living waters, and cut them out cisterns, broken cisterns, that
can hold no water. ¹⁴Is Israel a servant? Is he a native-born slave?
Why has he become a prey? ¹⁵The young lions have roared at him,
and yelled. They have made his land waste. His cities are burned
up, without inhabitant. ¹⁶The children of Memphis and Tahpanhes
have also shaved the crown of your head. ¹⁷"Haven't you brought
this on yourself, in that you have forsaken the LORD your God,
when he led you by the way? ¹⁸Now what have you to do in the way
to Egypt, to drink the waters of the Shihor? Or what have you to do
in the way to Assyria, to drink the waters of the River? ¹⁹"Your
own wickedness shall correct you, and your backsliding shall
reprove you. Know therefore and see that it is an evil thing and
bitter that you have forsaken the LORD your God, and that my
fear is not in you," says the Lord, GOD of hosts. ²⁰"For of old time
I have broken your yoke, and burst your bonds; and you said,
'I will not serve;' for on every high hill and under every green tree
you bowed yourself, playing the prostitute. ²¹Yet I had planted you
a noble vine, wholly a right seed. How then have you turned into
the degenerate branches of a foreign vine to me? ²²For though you
wash yourself with lye, and use much soap, yet your iniquity is
marked before me," says the Lord GOD. ²³"How can you say,
'I am not defiled. I have not gone after the Baals'? See your way in
the valley. Know what you have done. You are a swift dromedary
traversing her ways; ²⁴a wild donkey used to the wilderness, that
snuffs up the wind in her desire. When she is in heat, who can turn
her away? All those who seek her will not weary themselves. In her
month, they will find her. ²⁵"Withhold your foot from being
unshod, and your throat from thirst. But you said, 'It is in vain.
No, for I have loved strangers, and I will go after them.' ²⁶As the
thief is ashamed when he is found, so is the house of Israel
ashamed; they, their kings, their officials, and their priests, and
their prophets; ²⁷who tell wood, 'You are my father;' and a stone,
'You have brought me out:' for they have turned their back to me,

*and not their face; but in the time of their trouble they will say, 'Arise, and save us.' *²⁸*"But where are your gods that you have made for yourselves? Let them arise, if they can save you in the time of your trouble. For according to the number of your cities are your gods, Judah. And according to the number of the streets of Jerusalem they were sacrificing to Baal. *²⁹*"Why will you contend with me? You all have transgressed against me," says the LORD. *³⁰*"I have struck your children in vain. They received no correction. Your own sword has devoured your prophets, like a destroying lion. *³¹*Generation, consider the word of the LORD. Have I been a wilderness to Israel? Or a land of thick darkness? Why do my people say, 'We have broken loose. We will come to you no more?' *³²*"Can a virgin forget her ornaments, or a bride her attire? Yet my people have forgotten me for days without number. *³³*How well you prepare your way to seek love. Therefore you have taught even the wicked women your ways. *³⁴*Also the blood of the souls of the innocent poor is found in your skirts. You did not find them breaking in; but it is because of all these things. *³⁵*"Yet you said, ' I am innocent. Surely his anger has turned away from me.' "Look, I will judge you, because you say, 'I have not sinned.' *³⁶*Why do you go about so much to change your way? You will be ashamed of Egypt also, as you were ashamed of Assyria. *³⁷*From there also you shall go forth, with your hands on your head; for the LORD has rejected those in whom you trust, and you shall not prosper with them."""*

QUESTIONS

QUESTION 1   CTX

"I remember you, the devotion of your youth, the love of your weddings; how you went after me in the wilderness...."

Give the context of the above quote:

Who said it, to who, and under what circumstance?

QUESTION 2   **CTX**

"Israel was holiness to the LORD, the first fruits of his increase...."

Give the context of the above quote:

Who said it, to who, and under what circumstance?

QUESTION 3   **CPC**

Jeremiah chapter 2:5–6 says,

"Thus says the LORD, "What unrighteousness have your fathers found in me, that they have gone far from me, and have walked after vanity, and are become vain?""

Complete verse 6.

QUESTION 4   **CTX**

"Neither did they say, 'Where is the LORD who brought us up out of the land of Egypt, who led us through the wilderness...."

Give the context of the above quote:

Who said it, to who, and under what circumstance?

QUESTION 5   **CPC**

Jeremiah chapter 2:7–8 says,

"I brought you into a plentiful land, to eat its fruit and its goodness; but when you entered, you defiled my land, and made my heritage an abomination."

Complete verse 8.

QUESTION 6   **CPB**

Jeremiah chapter 2:10–11 says,

"For pass over to the islands of Kittim, and see; and send to Kedar, and consider diligently; and see if there has been such a thing."

Complete verse 11.

QUESTION 7   b

In Jeremiah chapter 2:13, when the Lord was complaining against His people, He said: *"For my people have committed two evils...."*

According to the passage, what were the two evils committed by the people of Israel?

QUESTION 8   CPB

Jeremiah chapter 2:16–17 says,

"The children of Memphis and Tahpanhes have also shaved the crown of your head."

Complete verse 17.

QUESTION 9   CPC

Jeremiah chapter 2:18–19 says,

"Now what have you to do in the way to Egypt, to drink the waters of the Shihor? Or what have you to do in the way to Assyria, to drink the waters of the River?"

Complete verse 19.

QUESTION 10   CTX

"Your own wickedness shall correct you, and your backsliding shall reprove you."

Give the context of the above quote:

Who said it, to who, and under what circumstance?

QUESTION 11   CPB

Jeremiah chapter 2:21–22 says,

"Yet I had planted you a noble vine, wholly a right seed. How then have you turned into the degenerate branches of a foreign vine to me?"

Complete verse 22.

QUESTION 12   **CTX**

"You are a swift dromedary traversing her ways."

Give the context of the above quote:

Who said it, to who, and under what circumstance?

QUESTION 13   **CTX**

"As the thief is ashamed when he is found, so is the house of Israel ashamed...."

Give the context of the above quote:

Who said it, to who, and under what circumstance?

QUESTION 14   **CPC**

Jeremiah chapter 2:26–27 says,

"As the thief is ashamed when he is found, so is the house of Israel ashamed; they, their kings, their officials, and their priests, and their prophets."

Complete verse 27.

QUESTION 15   **CTX**

"who tell wood, 'You are my father;' and a stone, 'You have brought me out....'"

Give the context of the above quote:

Who said it, to who, and under what circumstance?

QUESTION 16   **CTX**

"For according to the number of your cities are your gods, Judah...."

Give the context of the above quote:

Who said it, to who, and under what circumstance?

QUESTION 17   **CTX**

"Can a virgin forget her ornaments, or a bride her attire?..."

Give the context of the above quote:

Who said it, to who, and under what circumstance?

QUESTION 18   **CTX**

"How well you prepare your way to seek love...."

Give the context of the above quote:

Who said it, to who, and under what circumstance?

QUESTION 19   **CTX**

"Also the blood of the souls of the innocent poor is found in your skirts...."

Give the context of the above quote:

Who said it, to who, and under what circumstance?

QUESTION 20   **CPB**

Jeremiah chapter 2:34–35 says,

"Also the blood of the souls of the innocent poor is found in your skirts. You did not find them breaking in; but it is because of all these things."

Complete verse 35.

QUESTION 21   **CPB**

Jeremiah chapter 2:36–37 says,

"Why do you go about so much to change your way? You will be ashamed of Egypt also, as you were ashamed of Assyria."

Complete verse 37.

QUESTION 22   **CMC**

Read Jeremiah chapter 2:3, preach or write a commentary on the passage with emphasis on salvation.

QUESTION 23   **CMC**

Read Jeremiah chapter 2:19, preach or write a commentary on the passage with emphasis on salvation.

QUESTION 24   **CMB**

Read Jeremiah chapter 2:22–23, preach or write a commentary on the passage with emphasis on salvation.

QUESTION 25   **CMB**

Read Jeremiah chapter 2:26, preach or write a commentary on the passage with emphasis on salvation.

QUESTION 26   **CMB**

Read Jeremiah chapter 2:27, preach or write a commentary on the passage with emphasis on salvation.

QUESTION 27   **CMB**

Read Jeremiah chapter 2:30, preach or write a commentary on the passage with emphasis on salvation.

ANSWERS

ANSWER TO QUESTION 1   CTX

- God, through Prophet Jeremiah
- To the people of Jerusalem
- When He brought up against them a case of their fading love and devotion (Jeremiah 2:2).

ANSWER TO QUESTION 2   CTX

- God, through Prophet Jeremiah
- To the people of Jerusalem

- When the Lord complained against the people for abandoning Him and worshipping other gods (Jeremiah 2:3).

ANSWER TO QUESTION 3   CPC

"⁶ Neither did they say, 'Where is the LORD who brought us up out of the land of Egypt, who led us through the wilderness, through a land of deserts and of pits, through a land of drought and of the shadow of death, through a land that none passed through, and where no man lived?'" (Jeremiah 2:6.)

ANSWER TO QUESTION 4   CTX

- God, through Prophet Jeremiah
- To the people of Israel
- When He brought up against them a case of their fading love and devotion (Jeremiah 2:6).

ANSWER TO QUESTION 5   CPC

"⁸ The priests did not say, 'Where is the LORD?' And those who handle the law did not know me. The rulers also transgressed against me, and the prophets prophesied by Baal, and walked after things that do not profit." (Jeremiah 2:8.)

ANSWER TO QUESTION 6   CPB

"¹¹ Has a nation changed its gods, which really are no gods? But my people have changed their glory for that which does not profit." (Jeremiah 2:11.)

ANSWER TO QUESTION 7   b

- They forsook or abandoned God (the spring of living waters)
- They cut or dug for themselves broken cisterns that could hold no water (Jeremiah 2:13).

ANSWER TO QUESTION 8   CPB

"¹⁷ Haven't you brought this on yourself, in that you have forsaken the LORD your God, when he led you by the way?" (Jeremiah 2:17.)

ANSWER TO QUESTION 9   CPC

"¹⁹Your own wickedness shall correct you, and your backsliding shall reprove you. Know therefore and see that it is an evil thing and bitter that you have forsaken the LORD your God, and that my fear is not in you," says the Lord, GOD of hosts." (Jeremiah 2:19.)

ANSWER TO QUESTION 10   CTX

- God, through Prophet Jeremiah
- To the people of Israel
- When the Lord complained against the people for abandoning Him and worshipping other gods (Jeremiah 2:19).

ANSWER TO QUESTION 11   CPB

" "²²For though you wash yourself with lye, and use much soap, yet your iniquity is marked before me," says the Lord GOD." (Jeremiah 2:22.)

ANSWER TO QUESTION 12   CTX

- God, through Prophet Jeremiah
- To the people of Israel
- When He was talking about Israel's unfaithfulness (Jeremiah 2:23).

ANSWER TO QUESTION 13   CTX

- God, through Prophet Jeremiah
- To the people of Israel
- When the Lord complained against the people for abandoning Him and worshipping other gods (Jeremiah 2:26).

ANSWER TO QUESTION 14   CPC

"²⁷who tell wood, 'You are my father;' and a stone, 'You have brought me out:' for they have turned their back to me, and not their face; but in the time of their trouble they will say, 'Arise, and save us.'" (Jeremiah 2:27.)

ANSWER TO QUESTION 15   CTX

- God, through Prophet Jeremiah
- To the people of Israel
- When He was talking about Israel's unfaithfulness (Jeremiah 2:27).

ANSWER TO QUESTION 16   CTX

- God, through Prophet Jeremiah
- To the people of Israel
- When He was talking about Israel's unfaithfulness (Jeremiah 2:28).

ANSWER TO QUESTION 17   CTX

- God, through Prophet Jeremiah
- To the people of Israel
- When the Lord complained against the people for abandoning Him and worshipping other gods (Jeremiah 2:31–32).

ANSWER TO QUESTION 18   CTX

- God, through Prophet Jeremiah
- To the people of Israel
- When the Lord complained against the people for abandoning Him and worshipping other gods (Jeremiah 2:33).

ANSWER TO QUESTION 19   CTX

- God, through Prophet Jeremiah
- To the people of Israel
- When the Lord complained against the people for abandoning Him and worshipping other gods (Jeremiah 2:34).

ANSWER TO QUESTION 20   CPB

"35 Yet you said, 'I am innocent. Surely his anger has turned away from me. "Look, I will judge you, because you say, 'I have not sinned." (Jeremiah 2:35.)

ANSWER TO QUESTION 21   CPB

"³⁷From there also you shall go forth, with your hands on your head; for the LORD has rejected those in whom you trust, and you shall not prosper with them." (Jeremiah 2:37.)

HINT TO QUESTION 22   CMC

Israel was God's chosen nation and was holy to Him. They were the apple of His eyes and whoever harmed them risked incurring God's wrath on themselves. God always looks out to protect those who believe and trust in Him, just as He did for Israel while they were living in obedience to Him. We should know that when we are holy to the Lord, He will treasure and protect us, and at the same time, we should understand that His protection does not mean we will not come across difficult circumstances. Sometimes even with His protection, we might still find ourselves in unpleasant situations, and in such cases, all we have to do is keep trusting in Him without wavering.

HINT TO QUESTION 23   CMC

Some of the troubles we go through in life result from our own mistakes, as shown in the verse under consideration. If the pains or troubles we go through result from our sins, when we acknowledge our mistakes and run back to God, God has His ways of turning the situation around for our good. At the same time, it is better not to sin than to sin and run back to God because there might be some sins whose physical consequences might have a lasting effect on our lives. It is noteworthy that not all bad situations are caused by our sins; sometimes, God allows us to encounter these seemingly bad situations to bring His plan for us to fulfilment or to test our faith.

HINT TO QUESTION 24   CMB

One thing is sure, as seen in the verses under consideration: no matter how we try to cover up our filthy lifestyle before people, our iniquities can never escape God's eyes. Therefore, the only way to be saved is to repent and live a life of total obedience to God's instructions because there is nothing we can do to cover our sins from Him.

HINT TO QUESTION 25   CMB

Some Christians today feel comfortable living in sin. They only feel ashamed of their sins when exposed, which should not be. A true Christian is not supposed to feel comfortable in sin for any reason. Anybody who feels comfortable in sin needs to go back to God for restoration.

HINT TO QUESTION 26   CMB

The people of Israel turned their back on God by forsaking Him and going after other gods. Many today just like the Israelites, turn their backs on God. Your character and priorities show whether you are turning your back on God or turning your face to Him. You could turn your back on God by living in disobedience to His word.

HINT TO QUESTION 27   CMB

God disciplined the people of Israel by striking their children so they could realise their wrongs and return to God, but they refused to respond to His correction. God's primary purpose in disciplining His children is to correct them when they have begun deviating from the right path. When God disciplines us, we should realise our wrongs, retrace our steps and turn back to Him. We should know that God's discipline is a sign of His love for us.

CHAPTER 3

JEREMIAH CHAPTER 3

"They say, 'If a man puts away his wife, and she goes from him, and become another man's, will he return to her again?' Wouldn't that land be greatly polluted? But you have played the prostitute with many lovers; yet return again to me," says the LORD. ²"Lift up your eyes to the bare heights, and see. Where have you not been lain with? You have sat for them by the ways, as an Arabian in the wilderness. You have polluted the land with your prostitution and with your wickedness. ³Therefore the showers have been withheld, and there has been no latter rain; yet you have a prostitute's forehead, you refused to be ashamed. ⁴Will you not from this time cry to me, 'My Father, you are the guide of my youth?' ⁵"'Will he retain his anger forever? Will he keep it to the end?' Look, you have spoken and have done evil things, and have had your way." ⁶Moreover, the LORD said to me in the days of Josiah the king, "Have you seen that which backsliding Israel has done? She has gone up on every high mountain and under every green tree, and there has played the prostitute. I said after she had done all these things, 'She will return to me;' but she did not return; and her treacherous sister Judah saw it. ⁸She saw that for all the causes for which faithless Israel had committed adultery, I had put her away and given her a bill of divorce, yet treacherous Judah, her sister, did not fear; but she also went and played the prostitute. ⁹And it came to pass, through her casual prostitution, that the land was polluted, and she committed adultery with stone and wood. ¹⁰Yet for all this her treacherous sister, Judah, has not returned to me with her whole heart, but only in pretense," says the LORD. ¹¹The

LORD said to me, "Backsliding Israel has shown herself more righteous than treacherous Judah. [12] Go, and proclaim these words toward the north, and say, 'Return, you backsliding Israel,' says the LORD; 'I will not look in anger on you; for I am merciful,' says the LORD. 'I will not keep anger forever. [13] Only acknowledge your iniquity, that you have transgressed against the LORD your God, and have scattered your ways to the strangers under every green tree, and you have not obeyed my voice,'" says the LORD. [14] "Return, backsliding children," says the LORD; "for I am a husband to you. I will take you one of a city, and two of a family, and I will bring you to Zion. [15] I will give you shepherds according to my heart, who shall feed you with knowledge and understanding. [16] It shall come to pass, when you are multiplied and increased in the land, in those days," says the LORD, "they shall say no more, 'The ark of the covenant of the LORD.' neither shall it come to mind; neither shall they remember it; neither shall they miss it; neither shall it be made any more. [17] At that time they shall call Jerusalem 'The throne of the LORD;' and all the nations shall be gathered to it, to the name of the LORD, to Jerusalem. Neither shall they walk any more after the stubbornness of their evil heart. [18] In those days the house of Judah shall walk with the house of Israel, and they shall come together out of the land of the north to the land that I gave for an inheritance to your fathers. [19] "But I said, 'How I would put you among the children, and give you a pleasant land, the most beautiful inheritance of all the nations.' and I said, 'You shall call me "My Father," and shall not turn away from following me.' [20] "Surely as a wife treacherously departs from her husband, so you have dealt treacherously with me, house of Israel," says the LORD. [21] A voice is heard on the bare heights, the weeping and the petitions of the sons of Israel; because they have perverted their way, they have forgotten the LORD their God. [22] "Return, you backsliding children, I will heal your backsliding." "Look, we have come to you; for you are the LORD our God. [23] Truly the hills are a delusion, the tumult on the mountains. Truly the salvation of Israel is in the LORD our God. [24] But the *shameful thing has devoured the labor of our fathers from our youth, their flocks and their herds, their sons and their daughters. ²⁵Let us lie down in our shame, and let our confusion cover us; for we have sinned against the LORD our God, we and our fathers, from our youth even to this day. We have not obeyed the voice of the LORD our God."*

QUESTIONS

QUESTION 1   b2

Jeremiah chapter 3:1 says, *"They say, 'If a man puts away his wife, and she goes from him, and become another man's, will he return to her again?' Wouldn't that land be greatly polluted?..."*

Where in the Bible is the law which addresses God's statement above first given?

QUESTION 2   CPB

Jeremiah chapter 3:2–3 says,

"Lift up your eyes to the bare heights, and see. Where have you not been lain with? You have sat for them by the ways, as an Arabian in the wilderness. You have polluted the land with your prostitution and with your wickedness."

Complete verse 3.

QUESTION 3   b

According to Jeremiah chapter 3:

What was the effect of Israel's idolatrous act on their environment?

QUESTION 4   b

According to Jeremiah chapter 3:

Mention 2 things the Lord accused Judah of.

QUESTION 5 CTX

"Backsliding Israel has shown herself more righteous than treacherous Judah."

Give the context of the above quote:

Who said it, to who, and under what circumstance?

QUESTION 6 a

Jeremiah chapter 3:8 says, *"She saw that for all the causes for which faithless Israel had committed adultery, I had put her away...."*

What did the Lord mean by Israel's adultery?

QUESTION 7 b

According to Jeremiah chapter 3, when God asked the people of Israel to return to Him for He would not be angry with them forever:

What was the only condition He gave them?

QUESTION 8 CPC

Jeremiah chapter 3:12–13 says,

"Go, and proclaim these words toward the north, and say, 'Return, you backsliding Israel,' says the LORD; 'I will not look in anger on you; for I am merciful,' says the LORD. 'I will not keep anger forever."

Complete verse 13.

QUESTION 9 b1

Jeremiah chapter 3:16 says, *"It shall come to pass, when you are multiplied and increased in the land, in those days,"* says the LORD, *"they shall say no more, 'The ark of the covenant of the LORD.' neither shall it come to mind; neither shall they remember it; neither shall they miss it; neither shall it be made any more."*

Why did God say they would no longer miss or long for the ark?

QUESTION 10   CPB

Jeremiah chapter 3:19–20 says,

"But I said, 'How I would put you among the children, and give you a pleasant land, the most beautiful inheritance of all the nations.' and I said, 'You shall call me "My Father," and shall not turn away from following me.'"

Complete verse 20.

QUESTION 11   CPB

Jeremiah chapter 3:22–23 says,

"Return, you backsliding children, I will heal your backsliding." "Look, we have come to you; for you are the LORD our God."

Complete verse 23.

QUESTION 12   CPC

Jeremiah chapter 3:24–25 says,

"But the shameful thing has devoured the labor of our fathers from our youth, their flocks and their herds, their sons and their daughters."

Complete verse 25.

QUESTION 13   CMC

Read Jeremiah chapter 3:1–5, preach or write a commentary on the passage with emphasis on salvation.

QUESTION 14   CMB

Read Jeremiah chapter 3:12–13, preach or write a commentary on the passage with emphasis on salvation.

QUESTION 15   CMC

Read Jeremiah chapter 3:19–20, preach or write a commentary on the passage with emphasis on salvation.

CHAPTER 3

ANSWERS

ANSWER TO QUESTION 1   b2

Deuteronomy 24:1–4.

ANSWER TO QUESTION 2   CPB

"³ Therefore the showers have been withheld, and there has been no latter rain; yet you have a prostitute's forehead, you refused to be ashamed." (Jeremiah 3:3.)

ANSWER TO QUESTION 3   b

The showers were withheld, and there was no latter rain (Jeremiah 3:3).

ANSWER TO QUESTION 4   b

- Idolatry; they refused to learn from Israel's example
- Judah only pretended to be sorry, but she was not (Jeremiah 3:6–10).

ANSWER TO QUESTION 5   CTX

- God
- To Prophet Jeremiah
- When God sent Jeremiah a message about the restoration of Israel (Jeremiah 3:6–19).

ANSWER TO QUESTION 6   a

Their Idolatry (Jeremiah 3:9).

ANSWER TO QUESTION 7   b

That they should acknowledge their iniquities (Jeremiah 3:12–13).

ANSWER TO QUESTION 8   CPC

"¹³ Only acknowledge your iniquity, that you have transgressed against the LORD your God, and have scattered your ways to the strangers under every green tree, and you have not obeyed my voice,'" says the LORD." (Jeremiah 3:13.)

ANSWER TO QUESTION 9   b1

Because the presence of God will be in God's people (Ezekiel 36:27). (This was fulfilled after the death of Jesus Christ).

ANSWER TO QUESTION 10   CPB

"20"Surely as a wife treacherously departs from her husband, so you have dealt treacherously with me, house of Israel," says the LORD." (Jeremiah 3:20.)

ANSWER TO QUESTION 11   CPB

"23Truly the hills are a delusion, the tumult on the mountains. Truly the Salvation of Israel is in the LORD our God." (Jeremiah 3:23.)

ANSWER TO QUESTION 12   CPC

"25Let us lie down in our shame, and let our confusion cover us; for we have sinned against the LORD our God, we and our fathers, from our youth even to this day. We have not obeyed the voice of the LORD our God." (Jeremiah 3:25.)

HINT TO QUESTION 13   CMC

Faithfulness is the requirement to have a fruitful relationship with God. In those days, the Israelites were unfaithful to God through idolatry, but today, we are unfaithful when we do anything that contradicts the word of God. Our unfaithfulness can be the architect of our problems or challenges; therefore, whenever we go through the consequences of our sins, rather than being stubborn in rebellion, we should go to God sincerely for forgiveness.

HINT TO QUESTION 14   CMB

God is great in mercy. Just as He was willing to forgive and take back Israel if they acknowledged their iniquities, He is always willing to forgive anyone who goes to Him in repentance, regardless of the sin committed. The person only needs to acknowledge their sins, forsake them and ask God for forgiveness.

HINT TO QUESTION 15   CMC

In the verses under consideration, God expressed His desire to give Israel a pleasant land which would be the envy of all nations. However, Israel continually turned away from God as a treacherous wife from her husband. God demands faithfulness from His children. Every demand of God from us in our relationship with Him is for our good; we stand to benefit from everything He commands us to do. If we rebel against God, we are invariably working against ourselves.

CHAPTER 4

JEREMIAH CHAPTER 4

"If you will return, Israel," says the LORD, "if you will return to me, and if you will put away your abominations out of my sight; then you shall not be removed; [2] and you shall swear, 'As the LORD lives,' in truth, in justice, and in righteousness. The nations shall bless themselves in him, and in him shall they glory." [3] For thus says the LORD to the men of Judah and to Jerusalem, "Break up your fallow ground, and do not sow among thorns. [4] Circumcise yourselves to the LORD, and take away the foreskins of your heart, you men of Judah and inhabitants of Jerusalem; lest my wrath go forth like fire, and burn so that none can quench it, because of the evil of your doings. [5] Declare in Judah, and publish in Jerusalem; and say, 'Blow the trumpet in the land.' Cry aloud and say, 'Assemble yourselves. Let us go into the fortified cities.' [6] Set up a standard toward Zion. Flee for safety. Do not wait; for I will bring evil from the north, and a great destruction." [7] A lion is gone up from his thicket, and a destroyer of nations; he is on his way, he is gone forth from his place, to make your land desolate, that your cities be laid waste, without inhabitant. [8] For this clothe yourself with sackcloth, lament and wail; for the fierce anger of the LORD hasn't turned back from us. [9] "It shall happen at that day," says the LORD, "that the heart of the king shall perish, and the heart of the officials; and the priests shall be astonished, and the prophets shall wonder." [10] Then I said, "Ah, Lord GOD. Surely you have greatly deceived this people and Jerusalem, saying, 'You shall have peace;' whereas the sword reaches to the heart." [11] At that time shall it be said to this people and to Jerusalem, "A hot wind from the bare

heights in the wilderness toward the daughter of my people, not to winnow, nor to cleanse; ¹²*a full wind from these shall come for me. Now I will also utter judgments against them." * ¹³*Look, he shall come up as clouds, and his chariots shall be as the whirlwind: his horses are swifter than eagles. Woe to us. For we are ruined.* ¹⁴*Jerusalem, wash your heart from wickedness, that you may be saved. How long shall your evil thoughts lodge within you?* ¹⁵*For a voice declares from Dan, and publishes evil from the hills of Ephraim:* ¹⁶*"Tell the nations; look, publish against Jerusalem, 'Besiegers come from a far country, and raise their voice against the cities of Judah.* ¹⁷*As keepers of a field, they are against her all around, because she has been rebellious against me,'"* *says the LORD.* ¹⁸*"Your way and your doings have brought these things to you. This is your wickedness; for it is bitter, for it reaches to your heart."* ¹⁹*My anguish, my anguish. I am pained at my very heart; my heart is disquieted in me; I can't hold my peace; because you have heard, O my soul, the sound of the trumpet, the alarm of war.* ²⁰*Destruction on destruction is proclaimed; for the whole land is laid waste: suddenly are my tents destroyed, and my curtains in a moment.* ²¹*How long shall I see the standard, and hear the sound of the trumpet?* ²²*"For my people are foolish, they do not know me. They are foolish children, and they have no understanding. They are skillful in doing evil, but to do good they have no knowledge."* ²³*I saw the earth, and, look, it was waste and void; and the heavens, and they had no light.* ²⁴*I saw the mountains, and look, they trembled, and all the hills moved back and forth.* ²⁵*I saw, and look, there was no man, and all the birds of the sky had fled.* ²⁶*I saw, and look, the fruitful field was a wilderness, and all its cities were broken down at the presence of the LORD; before his fierce anger they were destroyed.* ²⁷*For thus says the LORD, "The whole land shall be a desolation; yet I will not make a full end.* ²⁸*For this the earth will mourn, and the heavens above be black; because I have spoken it, I have purposed it, and I have not relented, neither will I turn back from it."* ²⁹*Every city flees for the noise of the horsemen and archers; they go into caves, and they* *hide themselves in the thickets, and climb up on the rocks; every city is forsaken, and not a man dwells in it. [30]You, when you are made desolate, what will you do? Though you clothe yourself with scarlet, though you dress yourselves with ornaments of gold, though you enlarge your eyes with paint, in vain do you make yourself beautiful; your lovers despise you, they seek your life. [31]For I have heard a voice as of a woman in travail, the anguish as of her who brings forth her first child, the voice of the daughter of Zion, who gasps for breath, who spreads her hands, saying, "Woe is me now. For my soul faints before the murderers.""*

QUESTIONS

QUESTION 1   CPB

Jeremiah chapter 4:3–4 says,

"For thus says the LORD to the men of Judah and to Jerusalem, "Break up your fallow ground, and do not sow among thorns."

Complete verse 4.

QUESTION 2   b

Jeremiah chapter 4:7 says, *"A lion is gone up from his thicket, and a destroyer of nations; he is on his way, he is gone forth from his place, to make your land desolate, that your cities be laid waste, without inhabitant."*

Who does the lion in the above passage refer to?

QUESTION 3   CTX

"Surely you have greatly deceived this people and Jerusalem, saying, 'You shall have peace;' whereas the sword reaches to the heart."

Give the context of the above quote:

Who said it, to who, and under what circumstance?

QUESTION 4   CMB

Read Jeremiah chapter 4:3–4, preach or write a commentary on the passage with emphasis on salvation.

QUESTION 5   CMB

Read Jeremiah chapter 4:16–18, preach or write a commentary on the passage with emphasis on salvation.

ANSWERS

ANSWER TO QUESTION 1   CPB

"⁴Circumcise yourselves to the LORD, and take away the foreskins of your heart, you men of Judah and inhabitants of Jerusalem; lest my wrath go forth like fire, and burn so that none can quench it, because of the evil of your doings." (Jeremiah 4:4.)

ANSWER TO QUESTION 2   b

Nebuchadnezzar, king of Babylon.

ANSWER TO QUESTION 3   CTX

- Prophet Jeremiah
- To God
- When he was responding to God's message about the destruction of Jerusalem and Judah (Jeremiah 4:3–10).

HINT TO QUESTION 4   CMB

God called the children of Israel to circumcise their hearts, teaching us that circumcision of the heart is mandatory in our walk with God. We must be born again and renew our hearts daily by studying and practising God's word in order to please Him.

HINT TO QUESTION 5   CMB

God's message of the impending destruction of Jerusalem did not fail to mention the cause of their punishment. He specifically let

His children know that it was their rebellion that brought the punishment against them as a way of correction. As Christians, unpleasant situations in our lives are sometimes corrective measures taken by God to make us discover our wrongs and make amends where necessary. The Bible says that God disciplines the children He loves (Hebrews 12:4–12); therefore, whenever we experience unpleasant situations, before rashly concluding that they are the handiworks of the devil, we should try to stay calm and run a thorough examination on ourselves and see if by any way we might have erred to attract the punishment. When we discover any flaw in us that might have attracted a punishment, it would be best to eradicate it completely by genuinely confessing and forsaking such sins before God, asking Him for the grace to live above it. But when we examine ourselves and discover that the situation is not a result of our sins, we should trust that our God is in control.

For an example of an unpleasant situation caused by the devil but not sin, read Job chapters 1 and 2.

For an example of an unpleasant situation that is not caused by the devil but is God's discipline for sin, read 2 Samuel 12:1–14, focusing on verses 10–14.

For an example of an unpleasant situation that is not caused by sin but ended in glory, read Genesis 37:18–36 with focus on verses 18–28 and Genesis 45:1–15 with focus on verses 4–8.

CHAPTER 5

JEREMIAH CHAPTER 5

"Run back and forth through the streets of Jerusalem, and see now, and know, and seek in the broad places of it, if you can find a man, if there are any who does justly, who seeks truth; and I will pardon her. ²Though they say, 'As the LORD lives;' surely they swear falsely." ³O LORD, do your eyes not look on truth? You have stricken them, but they were not grieved. You have consumed them, but they have refused to receive correction. They have made their faces harder than a rock. They have refused to return. ⁴Then I said, "Surely these are poor. They are foolish; for they do not know the way of the LORD, nor the law of their God. ⁵I will go to the great men, and will speak to them; for they know the way of the LORD, and the law of their God." But these with one accord have broken the yoke, and burst the bonds. ⁶Therefore a lion out of the forest shall kill them, a wolf of the evenings shall destroy them, a leopard shall watch against their cities; everyone who goes out there shall be torn in pieces; because their transgressions are many, and their backsliding is increased. ⁷"How can I pardon you? Your children have forsaken me, and sworn by what are no gods. When I had fed them to the full, they committed adultery, and assembled themselves in troops at the prostitutes' houses. ⁸They were as fed horses roaming at large: everyone neighed after his neighbor's wife. ⁹Shouldn't I punish them for these things?" says the LORD; "and shouldn't my soul be avenged on such a nation as this? ¹⁰"Go up on her walls, and destroy; but do not make a full end. Take away her branches; for they are not the LORD's. ¹¹For the house of Israel

and the house of Judah have dealt very treacherously against me,"
says the LORD. [12] They have denied the LORD, and said, "It is not
he; neither shall evil come on us; neither shall we see sword nor
famine. [13] The prophets shall become wind, and the word is not in
them. Thus shall it be done to them." [14] Therefore thus says the
LORD, the God of hosts, "Because you speak this word, look, I will
make my words in your mouth fire, and this people wood, and it
shall devour them. [15] Look, I will bring a nation on you from far,
house of Israel," says the LORD. "It is a mighty nation. It is an
ancient nation, a nation whose language you do not know, neither
understand what they say. [16] Their quiver is an open tomb, they
are all mighty men. [17] They shall eat up your harvest, and your
bread, which your sons and your daughters should eat. They shall
eat up your flocks and your herds. They shall eat up your vines and
your fig trees. They shall beat down your fortified cities, in which
you trust, with the sword. [18] "But even in those days," says the
LORD, "I will not make a full end with you. [19] It will happen,
when you say, 'Why has the LORD our God done all these things
to us?' Then you shall say to them, 'Thus says the LORD, Just
like you have forsaken me, and served foreign gods in your land, so
you shall serve strangers in a land that is not yours.' [20] "Declare
this in the house of Jacob, and publish it in Judah, saying, [21] 'Hear
now this, foolish people, and without understanding; who have
eyes, and do not see; who have ears, and do not hear: [22] Do you not
fear me?' says the LORD 'Won't you tremble at my presence, who
have placed the sand for the bound of the sea, by a perpetual
decree, that it can't pass it? And though its waves toss themselves,
yet they can't prevail; though they roar, yet they can't pass over it.'
[23] "But this people has a revolting and a rebellious heart; they
have revolted and gone. [24] Neither do they say in their heart,
'Let us now fear the LORD our God, who gives rain, both the
former and the latter, in its season; who preserves to us the
appointed weeks of the harvest.' [25] "Your iniquities have turned
away these things, and your sins have withheld good from you.
[26] For among my people are found wicked men. They watch, as
fowlers lie in wait. They set a trap. They catch men. [27] As a cage is

full of birds, so are their houses full of deceit. Therefore they have become great, and grew rich. ²⁸ They have grown fat. They shine; yes, they excel in deeds of wickedness. They do not plead the cause, the cause of the fatherless, that they may prosper; and they do not judge the right of the needy. ²⁹ "Shall I not punish for these things?" says the LORD. "Shall not my soul be avenged on such a nation as this? ³⁰ "An astonishing and horrible thing has happened in the land. ³¹ The prophets prophesy falsely, and the priests rule by their own authority; and my people love to have it so. What will you do in the end of it?"

QUESTIONS

QUESTION 1   b1

Jeremiah chapter 5:1 says, *"Run back and forth through the streets of Jerusalem, and see now, and know, and seek in the broad places of it, if you can find a man, if there are any who does justly, who seeks truth; and I will pardon her."*

Which other instance in the Bible did God promise to refrain from destroying a city if He could find some righteous people, and what was the least number of righteous people God agreed to spare the city if He found?

QUESTION 2   a

According to Jeremiah chapter 5:

What did God say about the people who said, 'as the Lord lives?'

QUESTION 3   CTX

"But these with one accord have broken the yoke, and burst the bonds."

Give the context of the above quote:

Who said it, to who, and under what circumstance?

QUESTION 4   **b**

According to Jeremiah chapter 5:

What did Jeremiah say everyone who goes out of the city would suffer because of their transgressions?

QUESTION 5   **CPB**

Jeremiah chapter 5:8–9 says,

"They were as fed horses roaming at large: everyone neighed after his neighbor's wife."

Complete verse 9.

QUESTION 6   **b**

Jeremiah chapter 5:14 says, *"Because you speak this word, look, I will make my words in your mouth fire, and this people wood, and it shall devour them."*

Mention two things the people said that made God speak against them in the above scripture.

QUESTION 7   **CPA**

Jeremiah chapter 5:15–16 says,

""Look, I will bring a nation on you from far, house of Israel," says the LORD. "It is a mighty nation. It is an ancient nation, a nation whose language you do not know, neither understand what they say.""

Complete verse 16.

QUESTION 8   **b**

Jeremiah chapter 5:15 says, *"Look, I will bring a nation on you from far, house of Israel," says the LORD...."*

Mention two things the nation from afar would do to Israel when they arrive.

QUESTION 9   **b1**

According to Jeremiah chapter 5:

What reply did God say Jeremiah should give the people of Judah when they asked why the Lord dealt with them?

QUESTION 10   **CTX**

"Hear now this, foolish people, and without understanding...."

Give the context of the above quote:

Who said it, to who, and under what circumstance?

QUESTION 11   **b**

Jeremiah chapter 5:25 says, *"Your iniquities have turned away these things, and your sins have withheld good from you."*

What two things are referred to in the scripture that the people's iniquities turned away?

QUESTION 12   **CPB**

Jeremiah chapter 5:24–25 says,

"Neither do they say in their heart, 'Let us now fear the LORD our God, who gives rain, both the former and the latter, in its season; who preserves to us the appointed weeks of the harvest.'"

Complete verse 25.

QUESTION 13   **CPB**

Jeremiah chapter 5:26–27 says,

"For among my people are found wicked men. They watch, as fowlers lie in wait. They set a trap. They catch men."

Complete verse 27.

QUESTION 14   **CPB**

Jeremiah chapter 5:28–29 says,

"They have grown fat. They shine; yes, they excel in deeds of wickedness. They do not plead the cause, the cause of the fatherless, that they may prosper; and they do not judge the right of the needy."

Complete verse 29.

QUESTION 15   **CPB**

Jeremiah chapter 5:30–31 says,

"An astonishing and horrible thing has happened in the land."

Complete verse 31.

QUESTION 16   **CMB**

Read Jeremiah chapter 5:20–24, preach or write a commentary on the passage with emphasis on salvation.

QUESTION 17   **CMB**

Read Jeremiah chapter 5:26–29, preach or write a commentary on the passage with emphasis on salvation.

QUESTION 18   **CMB**

Read Jeremiah chapter 5:30–31, preach or write a commentary on the passage with emphasis on salvation.

ANSWERS

ANSWER TO QUESTION 1   **b1**

- In the case of Sodom and Gomorrah
- Ten persons (Genesis 18:26–33).

ANSWER TO QUESTION 2   **a**

They swore falsely (Jeremiah 5:2).

ANSWER TO QUESTION 3   CTX

- Prophet Jeremiah
- To himself
- When he went to the leaders or great men to see if they kept the laws of God better than the poor (Jeremiah 5:5).

ANSWER TO NUMBER 4   b

They would be torn to pieces by either a lion, a wolf or a leopard (Jeremiah 5:6).

ANSWER TO QUESTION 5   CPB

"⁹Shouldn't I punish them for these things?" says the LORD; "and shouldn't my soul be avenged on such a nation as this?" (Jeremiah 5:9.)

ANSWER TO QUESTION 6   b

- They said it was not God or God would do nothing; that no evil, harm or disaster would come on them, neither shall they see sword nor famine.
- They said the prophets would become wind, and the word is not in them.

Or

The prophet's prediction would come upon the prophets (Jeremiah 5:12–13).

ANSWER TO QUESTION 7   CPA

"¹⁶Their quiver is an open tomb, they are all mighty men." (Jeremiah 5:16.)

ANSWER TO QUESTION 8   b

- They would eat up their harvest and food (which belongs to their sons and daughters)
- They would devour their sons and daughters
- They would eat up their flocks and herds

- They would eat up their vines and fig trees
- They would destroy their fortified cities with swords (Jeremiah 5:17).

ANSWER TO QUESTION 9   b1

God said Jeremiah should tell them that because they chose to serve foreign gods in their land, they would serve strangers in a land that was not theirs (Jeremiah 5:19).

ANSWER TO QUESTION 10   CTX

- God, through Prophet Jeremiah
- To the people of Israel and Judah
- When He was reprimanding them for their sinfulness which had incurred His wrath upon them (Jeremiah 5:21).

ANSWER TO QUESTION 11   b

- Rain in its due seasons
- Appointed or regular weeks of harvest (Jeremiah 5:24).

ANSWER TO QUESTION 12   CPB

"25 Your iniquities have turned away these things, and your sins have withheld good from you." (Jeremiah 5:25.)

ANSWER TO QUESTION 13   CPB

"27 As a cage is full of birds, so are their houses full of deceit. Therefore they have become great, and grew rich." (Jeremiah 5:27.)

ANSWER TO QUESTION 14   CPB

"29 "Shall I not punish for these things?" says the LORD. "Shall not my soul be avenged on such a nation as this?"" (Jeremiah 5:29.)

ANSWER TO QUESTION 15   CPB

"31 The prophets prophesy falsely, and the priests rule by their own authority; and my people love to have it so. What will you do in the end of it?" (Jeremiah 5:31.)

HINT TO QUESTION 16   CMB

God is a mighty God whom we should revere and obey. We can look at the things He has created and have a glimpse of His power and might. The fact that we cannot see Him physically should not make us act disrespectfully towards Him.

HINT TO QUESTION 17   CMB

God made up His mind to punish Judah for their wickedness. However, before He did that, God listed their acts of wickedness which necessitated the punishment. Judah had carried out those wicked acts and even profited and excelled in them. Wickedness and exploitation might provide wealth and affluence for those who indulge in it. They may be deluded to believe that there is no retribution for their way of life, but the truth is that God's wrath is on those who practice wickedness unless they repent. The fact that God's wrath tarries does not mean it is absent. So everyone involved in wickedness and exploitation should desist from such acts no matter the benefit they seem to enjoy, and no one should envy those who benefit from such acts.

HINT TO QUESTION 18   CMB

The prophets in Judah prophesied falsely, and sadly, the people loved the false prophecies and teachings more than true words from God, which rebuked their sins. When people enjoy listening to false prophecies or teachings, it is a sign of depraved minds. People who are not careful to obey the word of God love to listen to the messages that appeal to their flesh, thereby being prone to patronising false prophets and teachers. False teachings or prophecies will lead people farther from God rather than closer to Him.

CHAPTER 6

JEREMIAH CHAPTER 6

"Flee for safety, you children of Benjamin, out of the midst of Jerusalem, and blow the trumpet in Tekoa, and raise up a signal on Beth Haccherem; for evil looks forth from the north, and a great destruction. ²The comely and delicate one, the daughter of Zion, will I cut off. ³Shepherds with their flocks shall come to her; they shall pitch their tents against her all around; they shall feed everyone in his place." ⁴"Prepare war against her; arise, and let us go up at noon. Woe to us. For the day declines, for the shadows of the evening are stretched out. ⁵Arise, and let us go up by night, and let us destroy her palaces." ⁶For the LORD of hosts said, "Cut down trees, and cast up a mound against Jerusalem. She is the city to be punished; she is full of oppression in the midst of her. ⁷As a well casts forth its waters, so she casts forth her wickedness: violence and destruction is heard in her; before me continually is sickness and wounds. ⁸Be instructed, Jerusalem, lest my soul be alienated from you; lest I make you a desolation, a land not inhabited." ⁹Thus says the LORD of hosts, "They shall thoroughly glean the remnant of Israel like a vine. Pass your hand again as a grape gatherer into the baskets." ¹⁰To whom shall I speak and testify, that they may hear? Look, their ear is uncircumcised, and they can't listen. Look, the word of the LORD has become a reproach to them. They have no delight in it. ¹¹Therefore I am full of the wrath of the LORD. I am weary with holding in. "Pour it out on the children in the street, and on the assembly of young men together; for even the husband with the wife shall be taken, the aged with him who is full of days. ¹²Their houses shall be turned to

others, their fields and their wives together; for I will stretch out my hand on the inhabitants of the land," says the LORD. ¹³"For from their least even to their greatest, everyone is given to covetousness; and from the prophet even to the priest, everyone deals falsely. ¹⁴They have healed also the hurt of my people superficially, saying, 'Peace, peace.' when there is no peace. ¹⁵Were they ashamed when they had committed abomination? No, they were not at all ashamed, neither could they blush. Therefore they shall fall among those who fall; at the time that I visit them, they shall be cast down," says the LORD. ¹⁶Thus says the LORD, "Stand in the ways and see, and ask for the old paths, 'Where is the good way?' and walk in it, and you will find rest for your souls." But they said, "We will not walk in it." ¹⁷"I set watchmen over you, saying, 'Listen to the sound of the trumpet.'" But they said, "We will not listen." ¹⁸"Therefore hear, you nations, and know, congregation, what will happen to them. ¹⁹Hear, earth. 'Look, I will bring disaster on this people, even the fruit of their thoughts, because they have not listened to my words; and as for my law, they have rejected it. ²⁰To what purpose comes there to me frankincense from Sheba, and the sweet cane from a far country? Your burnt offerings are not acceptable, nor your sacrifices pleasing to me.' ²¹Therefore thus says the LORD, 'Look, I will lay stumbling blocks before this people. The fathers and the sons together shall stumble against them. The neighbor and his friend shall perish.' ²²"Thus says the LORD, 'Look, a people comes from the north country. A great nation shall be stirred up from the uttermost parts of the earth. ²³They take hold of bow and spear. They are cruel, and have no mercy. Their voice roars like the sea, and they ride on horses, everyone set in array, as a man to the battle, against you, daughter of Zion.'" ²⁴"We have heard its report; our hands become feeble: anguish has taken hold of us, and pains as of a woman in labor. ²⁵Do not go forth into the field, nor walk by the way; for the sword of the enemy and terror, are on every side." ²⁶"Daughter of my people, clothe yourself with sackcloth, and wallow in ashes. Mourn, as for an only son, most bitter lamentation; for the *destroyer shall suddenly come on us."* ²⁷*"I have made you a tester of metals and a fortress among my people; that you may know and try their way."* ²⁸*"They are all grievous rebels, going about with slanders; they are bronze and iron: they all of them deal corruptly.* ²⁹*The bellows blow fiercely; the lead is consumed of the fire: in vain do they go on refining; for the wicked are not plucked away.* ³⁰*Men will call them 'rejected silver,' because the LORD has rejected them.""*

QUESTIONS

QUESTION 1   b2

Jeremiah chapter 6:1 says, *"Flee for safety, you children of Benjamin, out of the midst of Jerusalem, and blow the trumpet in Tekoa, and raise up a signal on Beth Haccherem; for evil looks forth from the north, and a great destruction."*

Which event in David's family involves someone from Tekoa?

QUESTION 2   a

According to Jeremiah chapter 6:

What did the word of God become to the people of Judah?

QUESTION 3   a

According to Jeremiah chapter 6:

Which people were covetous or given to greed in the land of Judah?

QUESTION 4   b

Jeremiah chapter 6:14 says, *"They have healed also the hurt of my people superficially...."*

How did they heal the hurt of God's people superficially?

QUESTION 5   CTX

"To what purpose comes there to me frankincense from Sheba, and the sweet cane from a far country? Your burnt offerings are not acceptable, nor your sacrifices pleasing to me."

Give the context of the above quote:

Who said it, to who, and under what circumstance?

QUESTION 6   CMB

Read Jeremiah chapter 6:13–14, preach or write a commentary on the passage with emphasis on salvation.

QUESTION 7   CMB

Read Jeremiah chapter 6:16, preach or write a commentary on the passage with emphasis on salvation.

QUESTION 8   CMB

Read Jeremiah chapter 6:19–20, preach or write a commentary on the passage with emphasis on salvation.

ANSWERS

ANSWER TO QUESTION 1   b2

It was when Joab realised how much King David missed Absalom and then arranged for a woman from Tekoa who was considered wise to convince David to bring Absalom back to Jerusalem after being in exile for three years for killing Amnon, who raped his sister (2 Samuel 14:1–20).

ANSWER TO QUESTION 2   a

It became a reproach or an offense (Jeremiah 6:10).

ANSWER TO QUESTION 3   a

Everyone (Jeremiah 6:13).

ANSWER TO QUESTION 4   b

By giving the people a false assurance of peace (Jeremiah 6:14).

ANSWER TO QUESTION 5   CTX

- God, through Prophet Jeremiah
- To the people of Judah
- When God complained about Judah's refusal to return to Him and pronounced an impending punishment for their refusal (Jeremiah 6:19–20).

HINT TO QUESTION 6   CMB

God was against the prophets and the priests of Judah because they gave the people false assurances of peace. God described the situation as superficial healing. The sin of superficially soothing the conscience of the people, which was prevalent in Judah, is still in practice today. Superficially soothing a sinner's conscience does more harm than good. We should be honest and factual in addressing issues of sin. Until the truth of God's word gets to the heart, there is no true peace.

HINT TO QUESTION 7   CMB

On several occasions, God admonished the people of Judah to seek the right path and walk in it. Sadly, they resolved not to walk in God's ways. The path God has ordained for us has been the same throughout the ages. It was good for the saints of old, and it is still good for us today. We are to seek this right path that leads to life and tread it. The path that leads to life is obedience to the word of God.

HINT TO QUESTION 8   CMB

It is surprising that even in their backslidden state, the Judeans were still very religious – making sacrifices and burning expensive incense in the temple. God did not mince words when He made them understand that their sacrifices were meaningless to Him. Obedience has always been what God wants from us. It is greater than sacrifices and offerings. Without obedience, whatever we offer to God is meaningless.

CHAPTER 7

JEREMIAH CHAPTER 7

"The word that came to Jeremiah from the LORD, saying, ² "Stand in the gate of the LORD's house, and proclaim there this word, and say, 'Hear the word of the LORD, all you of Judah, who enter in at these gates to worship the LORD. ³ Thus says the LORD of hosts, the God of Israel, Amend your ways and your doings, and I will cause you to dwell in this place. ⁴Do not trust in lying words, saying, "The LORD's temple, The LORD's temple, The LORD's temple, are these." ⁵For if you thoroughly amend your ways and your doings; if you thoroughly execute justice between a man and his neighbor; ⁶if you do not oppress the foreigner, the fatherless, and the widow, and do not shed innocent blood in this place, neither walk after other gods to your own hurt: ⁷then will I cause you to dwell in this place, in the land that I gave to your fathers, from of old even forevermore. ⁸Look, you trust in lying words, that can't profit. ⁹Will you steal, murder, and commit adultery, and swear falsely, and burn incense to Baal, and walk after other gods that you have not known, ¹⁰and come and stand before me in this house, which is called by my name, and say, "We are delivered"; that you may do all these abominations? ¹¹Is this house, which is called by my name, become a den of robbers in your eyes? Look, I, even I, have seen it, says the LORD. ¹²But go now to my place which was in Shiloh, where I caused my name to dwell at the first, and see what I did to it for the wickedness of my people Israel. ¹³Now, because you have done all these works, says the LORD, and I spoke to you, rising up early and speaking, but you did not hear;

and I called you, but you did not answer: [14]therefore I will do to the house which is called by my name, in which you trust, and to the place which I gave to you and to your fathers, as I did to Shiloh. [15]I will cast you out of my sight, as I have cast out all your brothers, even the whole seed of Ephraim. [16]Therefore do not pray for this people, neither lift up a cry nor prayer for them, neither make intercession to me; for I will not hear you. [17]Do you not see what they do in the cities of Judah and in the streets of Jerusalem? [18]The children gather wood, and the fathers kindle the fire, and the women knead the dough, to make cakes to the queen of heaven, and to pour out drink offerings to other gods, that they may provoke me to anger. [19]Do they provoke me to anger?" says the LORD. "Do they not provoke themselves, to the confusion of their own faces?" [20]Therefore thus says the Lord GOD: "Look, my anger and my wrath shall be poured out on this place, on man, and on animal, and on the trees of the field, and on the fruit of the ground; and it shall burn, and shall not be quenched." [21]Thus says the LORD of hosts, the God of Israel: "Add your burnt offerings to your sacrifices, and eat meat. [22]For I did not speak to your fathers, nor command them in the day that I brought them out of the land of Egypt, concerning burnt offerings or sacrifices: [23]but this thing I commanded them, saying, 'Listen to my voice, and I will be your God, and you shall be my people; and walk in all the way that I command you, that it may be well with you.' [24]But they did not listen nor turn their ear, but walked in their own counsels and in the stubbornness of their evil heart, and went backward, and not forward. [25]Since the day that your fathers came forth out of the land of Egypt to this day, I have sent to you all my servants the prophets, daily rising up early and sending them: [26]yet they did not listen to me, nor inclined their ear, but made their neck stiff: they did worse than their fathers." [27]"You shall speak all these words to them; but they will not listen to you: you shall also call to them; but they will not answer you. [28]You shall tell them, 'This is the nation that has not listened to the voice of the LORD their God, nor received instruction: truth is perished, and is cut off from their mouth. [29]Cut off your hair, and throw it away, and take up a *lamentation on the bare heights; for the LORD has rejected and forsaken the generation of his wrath.'" 30 "For the children of Judah have done that which is evil in my sight," says the LORD: "they have set their abominations in the house which is called by my name, to defile it. 31 They have built the high places of Topheth, which is in the Valley of Ben Hinnom, to burn their sons and their daughters in the fire; which I did not command, nor did it come into my mind. 32 Therefore look, the days come," says the LORD, "that it shall no more be called Topheth, nor The Valley of Ben Hinnom, but The valley of Slaughter: for they shall bury in Topheth, until there is no place to bury. 33 The dead bodies of this people shall be food for the birds of the sky, and for the animals of the earth; and none shall frighten them away. 34 Then will I cause to cease from the cities of Judah, and from the streets of Jerusalem, the voice of mirth and the voice of gladness, the voice of the bridegroom and the voice of the bride; for the land shall become a waste."*

QUESTIONS

QUESTION 1   b2

Jeremiah chapter 7:11 says, *"Is this house, which is called by my name, become a den of robbers in your eyes?..."*

Mention a passage in the New Testament where the above quote was used, and under what circumstance was it used?

QUESTION 2   b1

According to Jeremiah chapter 7, before Judah's exile in Babylon:

Where were the people of Israel?

QUESTION 3   b

Jeremiah chapter 7:15 says, *"I will cast you out of my sight, as I have cast out all your brothers, even the whole seed of Ephraim."*

Who does the seed of Ephraim in the above passage refer to?

QUESTION 4   **CTX**

"Add your burnt offerings to your sacrifices, and eat meat."

Give the context of the above quote:

Who said it, to who, and under what circumstance?

QUESTION 5   **b**

Jeremiah chapter 7:18 says, *"The children gather wood, and the fathers kindle the fire, and the women knead the dough...."*

Why did the people in the above passage do all these?

QUESTION 6   **b**

Jeremiah chapter 7:22 says, *"For I did not speak to your fathers, nor command them in the day that I brought them out of the land of Egypt, concerning burnt offerings or sacrifices."*

What did God say He commanded their fathers instead?

QUESTION 7   **b**

According to Jeremiah chapter 7:

What did the people of Judah do at Topheth or the valley of Ben Hinnom?

QUESTION 8   **b1**

According to Jeremiah chapter 7:

What did God say Topheth shall be called in the future and why?

QUESTION 9   **CMC**

Read Jeremiah chapter 7:3–7, preach or write a commentary on the passage with focus on verse 3 and with emphasis on salvation.

QUESTION 10   **CMC**

Read Jeremiah chapter 7:3–12, preach or write a commentary on the passage with emphasis on salvation.

QUESTION 11   **CMB**

Read Jeremiah chapter 7:16–19, preach or write a commentary on the passage with focus on verse 19 and with emphasis on salvation.

ANSWERS

ANSWER TO QUESTION 1   b2

- Matthew 21:13, Mark 11:17, Luke 19:46, or John 2:16
- When Jesus drove the merchants out of the temple at Jerusalem.

ANSWER TO QUESTION 2   b1

They were exiled to Assyria (2 Kings 17:23).

ANSWER TO QUESTION 3   b

The Northern Kingdom or Israel (Jeremiah 7:15).

ANSWER TO QUESTION 4   CTX

- God, through Prophet Jeremiah
- To the people of Judah
- When God asked Jeremiah not to plead for the people of Judah anymore because of their idolatry and other sins (Jeremiah 7:16–21).

ANSWER TO QUESTION 5   b

To make cakes to the queen of heaven (Jeremiah 7:18).

ANSWER TO QUESTION 6   b

They should listen to Him and walk in all the ways He commanded them

Or

They should obey Him (Jeremiah 7:23).

ANSWER TO QUESTION 7   b

They built high places to burn their sons and daughters in the fire (Jeremiah 7:31).

ANSWER TO QUESTION 8   b1

- Valley of Slaughter
- Because they shall bury until there is no place to bury (Jeremiah 7:32).

HINT TO QUESTION 9   CMC

It was never God's desire to destroy Judah and the temple. This is evident in His admonishment to the Judeans to amend their evil ways. It is never God's desire that His erring children should be destroyed but that they should forsake their sinful ways and return to Him wholeheartedly. It was because of His love for the world and His desire to redeem us that He sent Jesus, His Son, to die and pave the way for our reconciliation.

HINTS TO QUESTION 10   CMC

- God, in His mercies, extended an olive branch, that is, a hand of reconciliation, to the Judeans even in their sin. Instead of embracing such privilege by repenting, they nosedived into the mud of sins in rebellion against God. We should understand that the grace of God and our liberty are not licenses to sin but rather an opportunity for us to retrace our steps, repent and return to God in obedience.
- We should not put our hopes or trust in false teachings, teachings that make us feel at ease while living in disobedience to God.
- Merely professing to be a Christian or participating in church activities cannot save a person. Just as God rebuked the Judeans for living in sin while believing they were saved because of the presence of the temple, everyone who lives in sin, no matter their religious involvement, is not acceptable to God.

HINT TO QUESTION 11   CMB

When we disobey God, and He knows our actions will only bring pain and disaster, He still gets involved to warn us of the path we are taking. This is because of His love for us. He seeks to save us from ourselves by imploring us to desist from actions contrary to His word.

CHAPTER 8

JEREMIAH CHAPTER 8

"At that time," says the LORD, "they shall bring out the bones of the kings of Judah, and the bones of his officials, and the bones of the priests, and the bones of the prophets, and the bones of the inhabitants of Jerusalem, out of their graves; ²and they shall spread them before the sun, and the moon, and all the host of heaven, which they have loved, and which they have served, and after which they have walked, and which they have sought, and which they have worshiped: they shall not be gathered, nor be buried, they shall be for dung on the surface of the earth. ³Death shall be chosen rather than life by all the residue that remain of this evil family, that remain in all the places where I have driven them," says the LORD of hosts. ⁴"Moreover you shall tell them, 'Thus says the LORD: Shall men fall, and not rise up again? Shall one turn away, and not return? ⁵Why then do these people of Jerusalem turn away in perpetual backsliding? They hold fast deceit; they refuse to return. ⁶I listened and heard, but they did not speak what is right: no man repents him of his wickedness, saying, "What have I done?" Everyone turns to his course, as a horse that rushes headlong in the battle. ⁷Yes, the stork in the sky knows her appointed times; and the turtledove and the swallow and the crane observe the time of their coming; but my people do not know the LORD's law. ⁸How can you say, "We are wise, and the law of the LORD is with us?" But, look, the false pen of the scribes has worked falsely. ⁹The wise men are disappointed, they are dismayed and taken: look, they have rejected the word of the LORD; and

what kind of wisdom is in them? [10] Therefore I will give their wives to others, and their fields to those who shall possess them: for everyone from the least even to the greatest is given to covetousness; from the prophet even to the priest every one deals falsely. [11] They have healed the hurt of the daughter of my people slightly, saying, "Peace, peace;" when there is no peace. [12] Were they ashamed when they had committed abomination? No. They were not at all ashamed, neither could they blush: therefore shall they fall among those who fall; in the time of their visitation they shall be cast down, says the LORD. [13] I will utterly consume them, says the LORD: no grapes shall be on the vine, nor figs on the fig tree, and the leaf shall fade; and the things that I have given them shall pass away from them.'" [14] "Why do we sit still? Assemble yourselves, and let us enter into the fortified cities, and let us be silent there; for the LORD our God has put us to silence, and given us water of gall to drink, because we have sinned against the LORD. [15] We looked for peace, but no good came; and for a time of healing, and look, dismay. [16] The snorting of his horses is heard from Dan: at the sound of the neighing of his strong ones the whole land trembles; for they have come, and have devoured the land and all that is in it; the city and those who dwell in it. [17] For, look, I will send serpents, adders, among you, which will not be charmed; and they shall bite you," says the LORD. [18] "Oh that I could comfort myself against sorrow. My heart is faint within me. [19] Look, the voice of the cry of the daughter of my people from a land that is very far off: 'Isn't the LORD in Zion? Isn't her King in her?'" "Why have they provoked me to anger with their engraved images, and with foreign vanities?" [20] "'The harvest is past, the summer is ended, and we are not saved.' [21] For the hurt of the daughter of my people am I hurt: I mourn; dismay has taken hold on me. [22] Is there no balm in Gilead? Is there no physician there? Why then isn't the health of the daughter of my people recovered?"

QUESTIONS

QUESTION 1   CTX

"Shall men fall, and not rise up again? Shall one turn away, and not return?"

Give the context of the above quote:

Who said it, to who, and under what circumstance?

QUESTION 2   CPC

Jeremiah chapter 8:6–7 says,

"I listened and heard, but they did not speak what is right: no man repents him of his wickedness, saying, "What have I done?" Everyone turns to his course, as a horse that rushes headlong in the battle."

Complete verse 7.

QUESTION 3   CPC

Jeremiah chapter 8:12–13 says,

"Were they ashamed when they had committed abomination? No. They were not at all ashamed, neither could they blush: therefore shall they fall among those who fall; in the time of their visitation they shall be cast down, says the LORD."

Complete verse 13.

QUESTION 4   CTX

"Is there no balm in Gilead? Is there no physician there? Why then isn't the health of the daughter of my people recovered?"

Give the context of the above quote:

Who said it, to who, and under what circumstance?

QUESTION 5   **CPB**

Jeremiah chapter 8:18–19 says,

"Oh that I could comfort myself against sorrow. My heart is faint within me."

Complete verse 19.

QUESTION 6   **CPA**

Jeremiah chapter 8:21–22 says,

"For the hurt of the daughter of my people am I hurt: I mourn; dismay has taken hold on me."

Complete verse 22.

QUESTION 7   **CMC**

Read Jeremiah chapter 8:4–6, preach or write a commentary on the passage with emphasis on salvation.

QUESTION 8   **CMB**

Read Jeremiah chapter 8:8–9, preach or write a commentary on the passage with emphasis on salvation.

QUESTION 9   **CMC**

Read Jeremiah chapter 8:22, preach or write a commentary on the passage with emphasis on salvation.

ANSWERS

ANSWER TO QUESTION 1   CTX

- God, through Prophet Jeremiah
- To the people of Judah
- When He was talking about their refusal to repent and turn back to Him (Jeremiah 8:4–5).

ANSWER TO QUESTION 2   CPC

"⁷Yes, the stork in the sky knows her appointed times; and the turtledove and the swallow and the crane observe the time of their coming; but my people do not know the LORD's law." (Jeremiah 8:7.)

ANSWER TO QUESTION 3   CPC

"¹³I will utterly consume them, says the LORD: no grapes shall be on the vine, nor figs on the fig tree, and the leaf shall fade; and the things that I have given them shall pass away from them." (Jeremiah 8:13.)

ANSWER TO QUESTION 4   CTX

- Prophet Jeremiah
- To himself
- When he was lamenting about the impending punishment or suffering of the Judeans (Jeremiah 8:18–22).

ANSWER TO QUESTION 5   CPB

"¹⁹Look, the voice of the cry of the daughter of my people from a land that is very far off: 'Isn't the LORD in Zion? Isn't her King in her?'" "Why have they provoked me to anger with their engraved images, and with foreign vanities?" (Jeremiah 8:19.)

ANSWER TO QUESTION 6   CPA

"²²Is there no balm in Gilead? Is there no physician there? Why then isn't the health of the daughter of my people recovered?" (Jeremiah 8:22.)

HINT TO QUESTION 7   CMC

In His rebuke to the Judeans, God used the allegory of the natural process of people falling and getting up. He then said that, contrarily, His people had backslidden and refused to return to Him. He watched and listened for repentance, but none was forthcoming. God is displeased when we fall into sin, but He is more displeased when we refuse to realise our sins, repent and turn to Him.

HINT TO QUESTION 8   CMB

In their sins, the Judeans falsely believed they were wise and had the law of God. But since they did not live according to the word of God, God questioned their wisdom. There is no wisdom outside God, who is the Source of wisdom. God's word is all we need to be wise. For us to be considered wise, we must ensure that we study and abide by His words. This we must do with an emphasis on salvation because a distorted knowledge of God's word will not make a person wise.

HINT TO QUESTION 9   CMC

The balm in Gilead and the physician refers to the true word of God and the true prophet that the people should have listened to and received healing for their souls. God had sent prophets, but the presence of the prophets does not automatically translate to salvation except if a person consciously obeys the word of God. For us today, the fact that Christ came and died for our sins does not automatically translate to our salvation. For a person to be saved, they have to believe and obey Him.

CHAPTER 9

JEREMIAH CHAPTER 9

"Oh that my head were waters, and my eyes a spring of tears, that I might weep day and night for the slain of the daughter of my people. ²Oh that I had in the wilderness a lodging place of wayfaring men; that I might leave my people, and go from them. For they are all adulterers, an assembly of treacherous men." ³"They bend their tongue, as their bow, for falsehood; and they are grown strong in the land, but not for truth: for they proceed from evil to evil, and they do not know me," says the LORD. ⁴"Everyone be on guard against his neighbor, and do not trust any brother; for every brother is a deceiver, and every neighbor will go about with slanders. ⁵They will deceive everyone his neighbor, and will not speak the truth: they have taught their tongue to speak lies; they weary themselves to commit iniquity. ⁶Your habitation is in the midst of deceit; through deceit they refuse to know me," says the LORD. ⁷Therefore thus says the LORD of hosts, "Look, I will melt them, and try them; for how should I deal with the wickedness of the daughter of my people? ⁸Their tongue is a deadly arrow; it speaks deceit: one speaks peaceably to his neighbor with his mouth, but in his heart he lies in wait for him. ⁹Shall I not visit them for these things?" says the LORD; "shall not my soul be avenged on such a nation as this?" ¹⁰"For the mountains I will take up weeping and wailing, and for the pastures of the wilderness a lamentation, because they are laid waste so that no one passes through; nor can men hear the voice of the cattle. Both the birds of the sky and the animals have fled, they are gone." ¹¹"I will make

Jerusalem heaps, a dwelling place of jackals; and I will make the cities of Judah a desolation, without inhabitant." ¹²"Who is the wise man, that may understand this? Who is he to whom the mouth of the LORD has spoken, that he may declare it? Why is the land perished and burned up like a wilderness, so that none passes through?" ¹³The LORD says, "Because they have forsaken my law which I set before them, and have not obeyed my voice, neither walked in it, ¹⁴but have walked after the stubbornness of their own heart, and after the Baals, which their fathers taught them; ¹⁵therefore thus says the LORD of hosts, the God of Israel, 'Look, I will feed them, even this people, with wormwood, and give them water of gall to drink. ¹⁶I will scatter them also among the nations, whom neither they nor their fathers have known; and I will send the sword after them, until I have consumed them.'" ¹⁷Thus says the LORD of hosts, "Consider, and call for the mourning women, that they may come; and send for the skillful women, that they may come:" ¹⁸"and let them make haste, and take up a wailing for us, that our eyes may run down with tears, and our eyelids gush out with waters. ¹⁹For a voice of wailing is heard out of Zion, 'How are we ruined. We are greatly confounded, because we have forsaken the land, because they have cast down our dwellings.'" ²⁰"Yet hear the word of the LORD, you women, and let your ear receive the word of his mouth; and teach your daughters wailing, and everyone her neighbor lamentation. ²¹'For death has come up into our windows, it is entered into our palaces; to cut off the children from outside, and the young men from the streets.' ²²Speak, 'Thus says the LORD, "The dead bodies of men shall fall as dung on the open field, and as the handful after the harvester; and none shall gather them."'" ²³Thus says the LORD, "Do not let the wise man glory in his wisdom, neither let the mighty man glory in his might, do not let the rich man glory in his riches; ²⁴but let him who boasts boast in this, that he has understanding, and knows me, that I am the LORD who exercises loving kindness, justice, and righteousness, in the earth: for in these things I delight," says the LORD. ²⁵"Look, the days come," says the LORD, "that I will punish all those who are circumcised in *uncircumcision:* ²⁶*Egypt, and Judah, and Edom, and the children of Ammon, and Moab, and all that have the corners of their hair cut off, who dwell in the wilderness; for all the nations are uncircumcised, and all the house of Israel are uncircumcised in heart.""*

QUESTIONS

QUESTION 1   b

According to Jeremiah chapter 9:

What did God describe the tongues of the people of Judah as?

QUESTION 2   b

Jeremiah chapter 9:20 says, *"Yet hear the word of the LORD, you women, and let your ear receive the word of his mouth; and teach your daughters wailing, and everyone her neighbor lamentation."*

Why did God ask the women to teach their daughters how to wail?

QUESTION 3   CPB

Jeremiah chapter 9:23–24 says,

"Thus says the LORD, "Do not let the wise man glory in his wisdom, neither let the mighty man glory in his might, do not let the rich man glory in his riches."

Complete verse 24.

QUESTION 4   CMC

Read Jeremiah chapter 9:3–9, preach or write a commentary on the passage with emphasis on salvation.

QUESTION 5   CMB

Read Jeremiah chapter 9:23–24, preach or write a commentary on the passage with emphasis on salvation.

QUESTION 6   CMB

Read Jeremiah chapter 9:25–26, preach or write a commentary on the passage with emphasis on salvation.

ANSWERS

ANSWER TO QUESTION 1   b

Deadly or poisonous arrows (Jeremiah 9:8).

ANSWER TO QUESTION 2   b

Because death was upon the city (Jeremiah 9:20–21).

ANSWER TO QUESTION 3   CPB

"24but let him who boasts boast in this, that he has understanding, and knows me, that I am the LORD who exercises loving kindness, justice, and righteousness, in the earth: for in these things I delight," says the LORD." (Jeremiah 9:24.)

HINT TO QUESTION 4   CMC

One of the Judeans' sins that brought God's judgement was deceit. God is the same today as He was yesterday, and He would not overlook the sin of deceit today among His children. We can see how displeased He was that the Judeans lived in falsehood; hence, we should refrain from every act of deceit and falsehood.

HINT TO QUESTION 5   CMB

God admonished the people of Judah not to boast in their wisdom, might and riches; rather, they should boast in their understanding and knowledge of the Lord. Our sense of achievement should not be in our wisdom or riches but in our knowledge of God. Wealth and riches will perish with the world, but our knowledge of God is what will preserve our souls forever.

HINT TO QUESTION 6   CMB

Physical circumcision qualified the Israelites to be bonafide people of God, but this was expected to be done without leaving the circumcision of their hearts undone. Lack of fear for God and obedience to His word are peculiar attributes of someone whose heart is uncircumcised. God demands that we circumcise our hearts in order to love Him and obey Him in all our ways.

CHAPTER 10

JEREMIAH CHAPTER 10

*"Hear the word which the LORD speaks to you, house of Israel.
²Thus says the LORD, "Do not learn the way of the nations, and do
not be dismayed at the signs of the sky; for the nations are dismayed
at them. ³For the customs of the peoples are vanity; for one cuts a
tree out of the forest, the work of the hands of the workman with the
axe. ⁴They deck it with silver and with gold; they fasten it with nails
and with hammers, that it not move. ⁵They are like a palm tree, of
turned work, and do not speak: they must be carried, because they
can't go. Do not be afraid of them; for they can't do evil, neither is it
in them to do good." ⁶"There is none like you, LORD; you are great,
and your name is great in might. ⁷Who should not fear you, King of
the nations? For it appertains to you; because among all the wise
men of the nations, and in all their royal estate, there is none like
you. ⁸But they are together brutish and foolish: the instruction of
idols. it is but a stock. ⁹There is silver beaten into plates, which is
brought from Tarshish, and gold from Uphaz, the work of the
artificer and of the hands of the goldsmith; blue and purple for their
clothing; they are all the work of skillful men. ¹⁰But the LORD is the
true God; he is the living God, and an everlasting King: at his wrath
the earth trembles, and the nations are not able to withstand his
indignation. ¹¹You shall say this to them: 'The gods that have not
made the heavens and the earth, these shall perish from the earth,
and from under the heavens.' ¹²He has made the earth by his power,
he has established the world by his wisdom, and by his understanding
has he stretched out the heavens: ¹³when he utters his voice, there is
a tumult of waters in the heavens, and he causes the vapors to*

ascend from the farthest parts of the earth; he makes lightnings for the rain, and brings forth the wind out of his treasuries. ^{14}*Every man has become brutish and without knowledge; every goldsmith is disappointed by his engraved image; for his molten image is falsehood, and there is no breath in them.* ^{15}*They are vanity, a work of delusion: in the time of their visitation they shall perish.* ^{16}*The portion of Jacob is not like these; for he is the former of all things; and Israel is the tribe of his inheritance; the LORD of hosts is his name."* ^{17}*"Gather up your wares out of the land, you who live under siege.* ^{18}*For thus says the LORD, 'Look, I will sling out the inhabitants of the land at this time, and will distress them, that they may feel it.'* ^{19}*Woe is me because of my hurt. My wound is grievous: but I said, 'Truly this is my grief, and I must bear it.'* ^{20}*My tent is destroyed, and all my cords are broken: my children are gone forth from me, and they are no more: there is none to spread my tent any more, and to set up my curtains.* ^{21}*For the shepherds are become brutish, and have not inquired of the LORD: therefore they have not prospered, and all their flocks are scattered.* ^{22}*The voice of news, look, it comes, and a great commotion out of the north country, to make the cities of Judah a desolation, a dwelling place of jackals.* ^{23}*LORD, I know that the way of man is not in himself: it is not in man who walks to direct his steps.* ^{24}*LORD, correct me, but in measure: not in your anger, lest you bring me to nothing.* ^{25}*Pour out your wrath on the nations that do not know you, and on the families that do not call on your name: for they have devoured Jacob, yes, they have devoured him and consumed him, and have laid waste his habitation."*

QUESTIONS

QUESTION 1   b

According to Jeremiah chapter 10:

What did God tell the house of Israel not to be dismayed at or terrified by?

QUESTION 2   **CPB**

Jeremiah chapter 10:6–7 says,

"There is none like you, LORD; you are great, and your name is great in might."

Complete verse 7.

QUESTION 3   **b**

According to Jeremiah chapter 10:

Where did the idol worshippers get the silver and gold they used in making idols?

QUESTION 4   **b**

According to Jeremiah chapter 10:

What colour of dress did the idol worshippers dress their gods with?

QUESTION 5   **CPB**

Jeremiah chapter 10:11–12 says,

"You shall say this to them: 'The gods that have not made the heavens and the earth, these shall perish from the earth, and from under the heavens.'"

Complete verse 12.

QUESTION 6   **CPC 2**

Jeremiah chapter 10:14–16 says,

"Every man has become brutish and without knowledge; every goldsmith is disappointed by his engraved image; for his molten image is falsehood, and there is no breath in them."

Complete verses 15 and 16.

QUESTION 7   **CTX**

"Gather up your wares out of the land, you who live under siege."

Give the context of the above quote:

Who said it, to who, and under what circumstance?

QUESTION 8   **CPC 2**

Jeremiah chapter 10:19–21 says,

"Woe is me because of my hurt. My wound is grievous: but I said, 'Truly this is my grief, and I must bear it.'"

Complete verses 20 and 21.

QUESTION 9   **b**

According to Jeremiah chapter 10:

Which nations did Prophet Jeremiah say God should pour out His fury on?

QUESTION 10   **CMB**

Read Jeremiah chapter 10:1–5, preach or write a commentary on the passage with focus on verses 3–5 and with emphasis on salvation.

QUESTION 11   **CMB**

Read Jeremiah chapter 10:23–24, preach or write a commentary on the passage with emphasis on salvation.

QUESTION 12   **CMB**

Read Jeremiah chapter 10:25, preach or write a commentary on the passage with emphasis on salvation.

ANSWERS

ANSWER TO QUESTION 1   **b**

Signs or predictions of the sky or heavens or stars (Jeremiah 10:2).

ANSWER TO QUESTION 2   CPB

"7Who should not fear you, King of the nations? For it appertains to you; because among all the wise men of the nations, and in all their royal estate, there is none like you." (Jeremiah 10:7.)

ANSWER TO QUESTION 3   b

- Silver from Tarshish
- Gold from Uphaz (Jeremiah 10:9).

ANSWER TO QUESTION 4   b

Royal blue or blue and purple (Jeremiah 10:9).

ANSWER TO QUESTION 5   CPB

"12He has made the earth by his power, he has established the world by his wisdom, and by his understanding has he stretched out the heavens." (Jeremiah 10:12.)

ANSWER TO QUESTION 6   CPC 2

"15They are vanity, a work of delusion: in the time of their visitation they shall perish. 16The portion of Jacob is not like these; for he is the former of all things; and Israel is the tribe of his inheritance; the LORD of hosts is his name." (Jeremiah 10:15–16.)

ANSWER TO QUESTION 7   CTX

- Prophet Jeremiah
- To the people of Judah
- When he was giving them the prophecy of the impending exile of the Judeans by the Babylonians (Jeremiah 10:17).

ANSWER TO QUESTION 8   CPC 2

"20My tent is destroyed, and all my cords are broken: my children are gone forth from me, and they are no more: there is none to spread my tent any more, and to set up my curtains. 21For the shepherds are become brutish, and have not inquired of the LORD: therefore they have not prospered, and all their flocks are scattered." (Jeremiah 10:20–21.)

CHAPTER 10

ANSWER TO QUESTION 9   b

The nations that do not know God or acknowledge Him (Jeremiah 10:25).

HINT TO QUESTION 10   CMB

The Bible here describes idols as worthless objects without any use, powers, or effect, which is true. It is important to note that carved images are ordinary works of art when they are made or produced, but the moment allegiance is given to them, and spiritual acts such as sacrifices, libations, incantations or a combination of these are carried out over them, it attracts the spirit of darkness and the objects are no more the works of art they were but have become a habitation for principalities and powers. Notwithstanding the aforementioned, these principalities and powers are powerless before God and true children of God.

HINT TO QUESTION 11   CMB

Jeremiah recognised human weaknesses and limitations when it has to do with meeting God's perfect standards. So, he called on God to always correct him, howbeit in a measure that would not destroy him. One of the litmus tests of a person with a broken spirit is their willingness to acknowledge their limitations before the Creator of the whole universe. No matter how great we are, we should depend on God for direction in every aspect of our lives. When we err, we should go to God in humility, asking Him to correct us in love as a father would his child.

HINT TO QUESTION 12   CMB

Prophet Jeremiah's prayer of vengeance was acceptable in his time. Believers today should not follow this template as it does not align with the teachings of Christ concerning how we should relate with our enemies.

CHAPTER 11

JEREMIAH CHAPTER 11

"The word that came to Jeremiah from the LORD, saying, ²"Hear

"The word that came to Jeremiah from the LORD, saying, [2]"Hear the words of this covenant, and speak to the men of Judah, and to the inhabitants of Jerusalem; [3]and say to them, 'Thus says the LORD, the God of Israel: "Cursed is the man who doesn't hear the words of this covenant, [4]which I commanded your fathers in the day that I brought them forth out of the land of Egypt, out of the iron furnace, saying, "Obey my voice, and do them, according to all which I command you: so you shall be my people, and I will be your God; [5]that I may establish the oath which I swore to your fathers, to give them a land flowing with milk and honey," as at this day.'" Then I answered, and said, "Amen, LORD." [6]The LORD said to me, "Proclaim all these words in the cities of Judah, and in the streets of Jerusalem, saying, 'Hear the words of this covenant, and do them. [7]For I earnestly protested to your fathers in the day that I brought them up out of the land of Egypt, even to this day, rising early and protesting, saying, Obey my voice. [8]Yet they did not obey, nor turn their ear, but walked everyone in the stubbornness of their evil heart: therefore I brought on them all the words of this covenant, which I commanded them to do, but they did not do them.'" [9]The LORD said to me, "A conspiracy is found among the men of Judah, and among the inhabitants of Jerusalem. [10]They are turned back to the iniquities of their forefathers, who refused to hear my words; and they are gone after other gods to serve them: the house of Israel and the house of Judah have broken my covenant which I made with their fathers.

^{11} Therefore thus says the LORD, 'Look, I will bring disaster on them, which they shall not be able to escape; and they shall cry to me, but I will not listen to them. ^{12} Then shall the cities of Judah and the inhabitants of Jerusalem go and cry to the gods to which they offer incense: but they will not save them at all in the time of their trouble. ^{13} For according to the number of your cities are your gods, Judah; and according to the number of the streets of Jerusalem have you set up altars to the shameful thing, even altars to burn incense to Baal.' ^{14} Therefore do not pray for this people, neither lift up cry nor prayer for them; for I will not hear them in the time that they cry to me at the time of their trouble."

^{15} "What has my beloved to do in my house, since she has done many vile deeds? Can holy meat avert your disaster so that you can rejoice?" ^{16} The LORD called your name, "A green olive tree, beautiful with goodly fruit." With the noise of a great tumult he has kindled fire on it, and its branches are broken. ^{17} For the LORD of hosts, who planted you, has pronounced evil against you, because of the evil of the house of Israel and of the house of Judah, which they have worked for themselves in provoking me to anger by offering incense to Baal." ^{18} The LORD gave me knowledge of it, and I knew it: then you showed me their doings. ^{19} But I was like a gentle lamb that is led to the slaughter; and I did not know that they had devised devices against me, saying, "Let us destroy the tree with its fruit, and let us cut him off from the land of the living, that his name may be no more remembered." ^{20} "But, the LORD of hosts, who judges righteously, who tests the heart and the mind, I shall see your vengeance on them; for to you have I revealed my cause." ^{21} Therefore thus says the LORD concerning the men of Anathoth, who seek my life, saying, "You shall not prophesy in the name of the LORD, that you not die by our hand;" ^{22} therefore thus says the LORD of hosts, "Look, I will punish them: the young men shall die by the sword; their sons and their daughters shall die by famine; ^{23} and there shall be no remnant to them: for I will bring disaster on the men of Anathoth, even the year of their visitation."

QUESTIONS

QUESTION 1   b1

According to Jeremiah chapter 11:

What did God say to the Israelites when He brought them out of Egypt?

QUESTION 2   a

Jeremiah chapter 11:7 says, *"For I earnestly protested to your fathers in the day that I brought them up out of the land of Egypt, even to this day...."*

What did God earnestly protest to the people of Israel?

QUESTION 3   b1

Jeremiah chapter 11:9 says, *"A conspiracy is found among the men of Judah, and among the inhabitants of Jerusalem."*

What conspiracy is the above passage talking about?

QUESTION 4   b1

According to Jeremiah chapter 11:

How many gods and how many altars of Baal did the people of Judah and Jerusalem have?

QUESTION 5   a

According to Jeremiah chapter 11:

What idol or foreign god was mentioned that the people of Judah and Jerusalem worshipped?

QUESTION 6   a

According to Jeremiah chapter 11:

What is the name of the tree God once called the people of Jerusalem and Judah?

QUESTION 7   **a**

According to Jeremiah chapter 11:

How did Jeremiah know about the plot to kill him?

QUESTION 8   **b**

According to Jeremiah chapter 11:

Who was referred to as a gentle lamb being led to the slaughter?

QUESTION 9   **b**

According to Jeremiah chapter 11:

Who were the people that sought to kill Prophet Jeremiah, and why?

QUESTION 10   **b1**

Jeremiah chapter 11 mentions the men of Anathoth:

Which tribe in Israel were they from and where was their portion of land located?

QUESTION 11   **b1**

According to Jeremiah chapter 11, when God said that those who plotted to kill Prophet Jeremiah would have no remnant:

Mention two ways He said that would happen.

QUESTION 12   **CMB**

Read Jeremiah chapter 11:21–23, preach or write a commentary on the passage with emphasis on salvation.

ANSWERS

ANSWER TO QUESTION 1   **b1**

If they obeyed Him and did whatever He commanded them, they would be His people, and He would be their God (Jeremiah 11:2–4).

ANSWER TO QUESTION 2   **a**

To obey His voice (Jeremiah 11:7).

ANSWER TO QUESTION 3   **b1**

The people of Judah and Jerusalem had turned back to the iniquities of their forefathers who refused to hear the words of the Lord and had gone after other gods to serve them (Jeremiah 11:9–10).

ANSWER TO QUESTION 4   **b1**

- Gods as many as the number of their towns
- Altars as many as the streets in Jerusalem (Jeremiah 11:13).

ANSWER TO QUESTION 5   **a**

Baal (Jeremiah 11:13,17).

ANSWER TO QUESTION 6   **a**

The olive tree (Jeremiah 11:16).

ANSWER TO QUESTION 7   **a**

The Lord gave him knowledge of it (Jeremiah 11:18).

ANSWER TO QUESTION 8   **b**

Prophet Jeremiah (Jeremiah 11:19).

ANSWER TO QUESTION 9   **b**

- The men of Anathoth
- Because he prophesied in the Lord's name (Jeremiah 11:21).

ANSWER TO QUESTION 10   **b1**

- They were from the tribe of Levi
- Their portion of land was in the territory of Benjamin (Joshua 21:13–18, 1 Chronicles 6:54–60).

ANSWER TO QUESTION 11   **b1**

- Their young men will die in battle or by the sword.

- Their sons and daughters will die of famine or starve to death (Jeremiah 11:22).

HINT TO QUESTION 12　　CMB

Anathoth was a city of priests. Such a city would be expected to be a good example of accepting and obeying God's word. However, Anathoth manifested the exact opposite of what would be expected of a Levitical community. When people of God go into sin, they tend to oppose the word of God that they are supposed to propagate, and they resist the true ministers God is using to propagate the gospel.

CHAPTER 12

JEREMIAH CHAPTER 12

"You are righteous, LORD, when I contend with you; yet I would reason the cause with you: why does the way of the wicked prosper? Why are they all at ease who deal very treacherously? ²You have planted them, yes, they have taken root; they grow, yes, they bring forth fruit: you are near in their mouth, and far from their heart. ³But you, LORD, know me; you see me, and try my heart toward you: pull them out like sheep for the slaughter, and prepare them for the day of slaughter. ⁴How long shall the land be parched, and the grass of every field wither? For the wickedness of those who dwell in it, the animals are consumed, and the birds; because they said, "He shall not see our latter end." ⁵"If you have run with the footmen, and they have wearied you, then how can you contend with horses? And though in a land of peace you are secure, yet how will you do in the pride of the Jordan? ⁶For even your brothers, and the house of your father, even they have dealt treacherously with you; even they have cried aloud after you: do not believe them, though they speak beautiful words to you. ⁷I have forsaken my house, I have cast off my heritage; I have given the dearly beloved of my soul into the hand of her enemies. ⁸My heritage has become to me as a lion in the forest: she has uttered her voice against me; therefore I have hated her. ⁹Is my heritage to me as a speckled bird of prey? Are the birds of prey against her all around? Go, assemble all the animals of the field, bring them to devour. ¹⁰Many shepherds have destroyed my vineyard, they have trodden my portion under foot, they have made my pleasant portion a desolate wilderness. ¹¹They have made it a desolation; it mourns to me, being desolate; the whole land is made

desolate, because no man lays it to heart. *¹²Destroyers have come on all the bare heights in the wilderness; for the sword of the LORD devours from the one end of the land even to the other end of the land: no flesh has peace. ¹³They have sown wheat, and have reaped thorns; they have put themselves to pain, and profit nothing: and you shall be ashamed of your fruits, because of the fierce anger of the LORD. ¹⁴Thus says the LORD against all my evil neighbors, who touch the inheritance which I have caused my people Israel to inherit: 'look, I will pluck them up from off their land, and will pluck up the house of Judah from among them. ¹⁵It shall happen, after that I have plucked them up, I will return and have compassion on them; and I will bring them again, every man to his heritage, and every man to his land. ¹⁶It shall happen, if they will diligently learn the ways of my people, to swear by my name, "As the LORD lives;" even as they taught my people to swear by Baal; then shall they be built up in the midst of my people. ¹⁷But if they will not hear, then will I pluck up that nation, plucking up and destroying it,'"* says the LORD."

QUESTIONS

QUESTION 1   b

In Jeremiah chapter 12:1, Jeremiah said: *"You are righteous, LORD, when I contend with you; yet I would reason the cause with you...."*

What did Jeremiah reason with God?

QUESTION 2   CTX

"If you have run with the footmen, and they have wearied you, then how can you contend with horses?..."

Give the context of the above quote:

Who said it, to who, and under what circumstance?

QUESTION 3   b

According to Jeremiah chapter 12:

What did God tell Jeremiah about his brothers and family members who have turned against him?

QUESTION 4   CTX

"I have forsaken my house, I have cast off my heritage; I have given the dearly beloved of my soul into the hand of her enemies."

Give the context of the above quote:

Who said it, to who, and under what circumstance?

QUESTION 5   a

Jeremiah chapter 12:10 says, *"Many shepherds have destroyed my vineyard, they have trodden my portion under foot, they have made my pleasant portion a desolate wilderness."*

Who or what is the vineyard in the above verse?

QUESTION 6   CPB

Jeremiah chapter 12:10–11 says,

"Many shepherds have destroyed my vineyard, they have trodden my portion under foot, they have made my pleasant portion a desolate wilderness."

Complete verse 11.

QUESTION 7   b

Jeremiah chapter 12:13 says, *"They have sown wheat, and have reaped thorns...."*

Why did they reap thorns when they sowed wheat?

QUESTION 8   b1

According to Jeremiah chapter 12:

What did God say about Israel's neighbouring nations who reached out for Israel's possession?

QUESTION 9   **CMC**

Read Jeremiah chapter 12:1–4, preach or write a commentary on the passage with emphasis on salvation.

ANSWERS

ANSWER TO QUESTION 1   b

He reasoned why the wicked prospered and treacherous people were at ease (Jeremiah 12:1).

ANSWER TO QUESTION 2   CTX

- God
- To Prophet Jeremiah
- When Prophet Jeremiah complained about the prosperity of the wicked (Jeremiah 12:1–5).

ANSWER TO QUESTION 3   b

He told him not to trust them no matter how pleasantly they spoke (Jeremiah 12:6).

ANSWER TO QUESTION 4   CTX

- God
- To Prophet Jeremiah
- When He was replying to Prophet Jeremiah's complaint about why the wicked are prosperous (Jeremiah 12:7).

ANSWER TO QUESTION 5   a

The people of Judah and Jerusalem (Jeremiah 12:10).

ANSWER TO QUESTION 6   CPB

"¹¹They have made it a desolation; it mourns to me, being desolate; the whole land is made desolate, because no man lays it to heart." (Jeremiah 12:11).

ANSWER TO QUESTION 7   b

Because of the fierce anger of the Lord (Jeremiah 12:13).

ANSWER TO QUESTION 8   b1

God said He would pluck them from their lands but would later bring them back, but He will pluck and destroy the nations who refuse to obey Him (Jeremiah 12:14–17).

HINT TO QUESTION 9   CMC

Jeremiah lamented how the wicked prospered and were at ease. We should note that the prosperity of the wicked does not mean that the justice of God is not active. Every wicked person will face the judgement of God either in this life or in the life to come, or in both. We should not be angry at the prosperity of the wicked; instead, we should pray for their forgiveness and restoration because God is more eager to save them than destroy them.

CHAPTER 13

JEREMIAH CHAPTER 13

"Thus says the LORD to me, "Go, and buy yourself a linen belt, and put it on your waist, and do not put it in water." [2] So I bought a belt according to the word of the LORD, and put it on my waist. [3] The word of the LORD came to me the second time, saying, [4] "Take the belt that you have bought, which is on your waist, and arise, go to the Perath, and hide it there in a cleft of the rock." [5] So I went, and hid it by the Perath, as the LORD commanded me. [6] It happened after many days, that the LORD said to me, "Arise, go to the Perath, and take the belt from there, which I commanded you to hide there." [7] Then I went to the Perath, and dug, and took the belt from the place where I had hidden it; and look, the belt was marred, it was profitable for nothing. [8] Then the word of the LORD came to me, saying, [9] "Thus says the LORD, 'In this way I will mar the pride of Judah, and the great pride of Jerusalem. [10] This evil people, who refuse to hear my words, who walk in the stubbornness of their heart, and are gone after other gods to serve them, and to worship them, shall even be as this belt, which is profitable for nothing. [11] For as the belt clings to the waist of a man, so have I caused to cling to me the whole house of Israel and the whole house of Judah,' says the LORD; 'that they might be my people, for a name, for praise, and for glory. But they would not listen. [12] Therefore you shall speak to them this word: 'Thus says the LORD, the God of Israel, "Every jar shall be filled with wine."' And if they shall say to you, 'Do we not certainly know that every jar shall be filled with wine?' [13] Then you shall tell them, 'Thus says

the LORD, "Look, I will fill all the inhabitants of this land, even the kings who sit on David's throne, and the priests, and the prophets, and all the inhabitants of Jerusalem, with drunkenness. ¹⁴I will dash them one against another, even the fathers and the sons together, says the LORD. I will not pity, nor spare, nor have compassion, that I should not destroy them.""" ¹⁵"Hear, and give ear; do not be proud; for the LORD has spoken. ¹⁶Give glory to the LORD your God, before he causes darkness, and before your feet stumble on the dark mountains, and, while you look for light, he turns it into the shadow of death, and makes it gross darkness. ¹⁷But if you will not hear it, my soul shall weep in secret for your pride; and my eye shall weep bitterly, and run down with tears, because the LORD's flock is taken captive." ¹⁸"Say to the king and to the queen mother, 'Take a lowly seat, for your glorious crowns have come down from your heads. ¹⁹The cities toward the Negev are shut, and there is no one to open them: Judah is carried away into exile, all of it; it is wholly carried away into exile.'" ²⁰"Lift up your eyes, and see those who come from the north: where is the flock that was given you, your beautiful flock? ²¹What will you say, when he shall set over you as head those whom you have yourself taught to be friends to you? Shall not sorrows take hold of you, as of a woman in travail? ²²If you say in your heart, 'Why are these things come on me?' for the greatness of your iniquity are your skirts uncovered, and your heels suffer violence. ²³Can the Ethiopian change his skin, or the leopard his spots? Then may you also do good, who are accustomed to do evil. ²⁴'Therefore I will scatter them, as the stubble that passes away, by the wind of the wilderness. ²⁵This is your lot, the portion measured to you from me,' says the LORD; 'because you have forgotten me, and trusted in falsehood. ²⁶Therefore I will also uncover your skirts on your face, and your shame shall appear. ²⁷I have seen your abominations, even your adulteries, and your neighing, the lewdness of your prostitution, on the hills in the field. Woe to you, Jerusalem. You will not be made clean; how long shall it yet be?'"

CHAPTER 13

QUESTIONS

QUESTION 1   a

According to Jeremiah chapter 13, God instructed Prophet Jeremiah to buy a piece of loincloth or belt:

What fabric was the loincloth or belt to be made of?

QUESTION 2   a

According to Jeremiah chapter 13:

What were the first instructions God gave Jeremiah concerning the loincloth or belt He asked him to buy?

QUESTION 3   b

According to Jeremiah chapter 13:

What was God's second instruction to Jeremiah concerning the loincloth or belt He asked him to buy?

QUESTION 4   a

According to Jeremiah chapter 13:

What happened to the loincloth or belt that God asked Jeremiah to get back from where he hid it?

QUESTION 5   b2

According to Jeremiah chapter 13:

What message did God use the loincloth or belt to pass?

QUESTION 6   CPC

Jeremiah chapter 13:12–13 says,

"Therefore you shall speak to them this word: 'Thus says the LORD, the God of Israel, "Every jar shall be filled with wine."' And if they shall say to you, 'Do we not certainly know that every jar shall be filled with wine?'"

Complete verse 13.

QUESTION 7   **CPC**

Jeremiah chapter 13:15–16 says,

"Hear, and give ear; do not be proud; for the LORD has spoken."

Complete verse 16.

QUESTION 8   **b**

According to Jeremiah chapter 13:

Why did Jeremiah say his eyes shall weep bitterly and run down with tears?

QUESTION 9   **b**

Jeremiah chapter 13:18 says, *"Take a lowly seat, for your glorious crowns have come down from your heads."*

Which two people were the above-quoted statement directed to?

QUESTION 10   **CPB**

Jeremiah chapter 13:22–23 says,

"If you say in your heart, 'Why are these things come on me?' for the greatness of your iniquity are your skirts uncovered, and your heels suffer violence."

Complete verse 23.

QUESTION 11   **CPB**

Jeremiah chapter 13:24–25 says,

"Therefore I will scatter them, as the stubble that passes away, by the wind of the wilderness."

Complete verse 25.

QUESTION 12   **CMB**

Read Jeremiah chapter 13:1–11, preach or write a commentary on the passage with focus on verses 8–11 and with emphasis on salvation.

QUESTION 13   **CMB**

Read Jeremiah chapter 13:8–10 and 15, preach or write a commentary on the passage with focus on verse 15 and with emphasis on salvation.

ANSWERS

ANSWER TO QUESTION 1   **a**

Linen (Jeremiah 13:1).

ANSWER TO QUESTION 2   **a**

To put it on his waist and not to put in water or not to wash it (Jeremiah 13:1).

ANSWER TO QUESTION 3   **b**

God asked him to take it to the Perath or Euphrates and hide it in the cleft or crevice of a rock (Jeremiah 13:4).

ANSWER TO QUESTION 4   **a**

The loincloth or belt was marred and profitable for nothing (Jeremiah 39:7).

ANSWER TO QUESTION 5   **b2**

As the loincloth or belt clings to a man's waist, God also made Israel and Judah cling to Him, but they left Him to worship other gods. And, as the belt was marred, so would God mar the pride of Israel and Judah (Jeremiah 13:8–11).

ANSWER TO QUESTION 6   **CPC**

"13 Then you shall tell them, 'Thus says the LORD, "Look, I will fill all the inhabitants of this land, even the kings who sit on David's throne, and the priests, and the prophets, and all the inhabitants of Jerusalem, with drunkenness."'" (Jeremiah 13:13.)

ANSWER TO QUESTION 7   CPC

"16Give glory to the LORD your God, before he causes darkness, and before your feet stumble on the dark mountains, and, while you look for light, he turns it into the shadow of death, and makes it gross darkness." (Jeremiah 13:16.)

ANSWER TO QUESTION 8   b

Because the Lord's flock is taken captive (Jeremiah 13:17).

ANSWER TO QUESTION 9   b

The King and the Queen Mother (Jeremiah 13:18).

ANSWER TO QUESTION 10   CPB

"23Can the Ethiopian change his skin, or the leopard his spots? Then may you also do good, who are accustomed to do evil." (Jeremiah 13:23).

ANSWER TO QUESTION 11   CPB

"25This is your lot, the portion measured to you from me,' says the LORD; 'because you have forgotten me, and trusted in falsehood.'" (Jeremiah 13:25.)

HINT TO QUESTION 12   CMB

God used the allegory of the belt, which once clung to Jeremiah's waist when it was good but became good for nothing when it was marred, to illustrate how He made Israel cling to Him. However, when they walked stubbornly and refused to obey Him, He marred their pride. God can only draw us close but would not force us to listen to and draw close to Him; God has done His part by drawing us close; we have to do our part by living in obedience to His word. If a person refuses to obey God, God will leave such a person to their peril.

HINT TO QUESTION 13   CMB

The consequences of pride are usually fatal, as seen in God's judgement against Judah and Jerusalem. Pride makes a person glory in 'self,' their achievements, riches, or abilities. It takes a person's heart off God and makes them trust in their guidance, but the end of all prideful people is destruction, as the scripture says. Hence, we must humble ourselves and give all glory to God.

CHAPTER 14

JEREMIAH CHAPTER 14

"The word of the LORD that came to Jeremiah concerning the drought. ²"Judah mourns, and its gates languish, they sit in black on the ground; and the cry of Jerusalem is gone up. ³Their nobles send their little ones to the waters: they come to the cisterns, and find no water; they return with their vessels empty; they are disappointed and confounded, and cover their heads. ⁴Because of the ground which is cracked, because no rain has been in the land, the plowmen are disappointed, they cover their heads. ⁵Yes, the hind also in the field calves, and forsakes her young, because there is no grass. ⁶The wild donkeys stand on the bare heights, they pant for air like jackals; their eyes fail, because there is no herbage." ⁷"Though our iniquities testify against us, work for your name's sake, LORD; for our backslidings are many; we have sinned against you. ⁸Hope of Israel, LORD, its Savior in the time of trouble, why should you be as a foreigner in the land, and as a wayfaring man who turns aside to stay for a night? ⁹Why should you be like a scared man, as a mighty man who can't save? Yet you, LORD, are in the midst of us, and we are called by your name; do not leave us." ¹⁰Thus says the LORD to this people, "Even so have they loved to wander; they have not refrained their feet: therefore the LORD does not accept them; now he will remember their iniquity, and visit their sins." ¹¹The LORD said to me, "Do not pray for this people for their good. ¹²When they fast, I will not hear their cry; and when they offer burnt offering and meal offering, I will not accept them; but I will consume them by the

sword, and by the famine, and by the pestilence." [13] *Then I said, "Ah, Lord GOD. Look, the prophets tell them, 'You shall not see the sword, neither shall you have famine; but I will give you assured peace in this place.'"* [14] *Then the LORD said to me, "The prophets prophesy lies in my name; I did not send them, neither have I commanded them, neither spoke I to them: they prophesy to you a lying vision, and divination, and a thing of nothing, and the deceit of their own heart.* [15] *Therefore thus says the LORD concerning the prophets who prophesy in my name, and I did not send them, yet they say, 'Sword and famine shall not be in this land:' 'By sword and famine shall those prophets be consumed.'* [16] *The people to whom they prophesy shall be cast out in the streets of Jerusalem because of the famine and the sword; and they shall have none to bury them— them, their wives, nor their sons, nor their daughters: for I will pour their wickedness on them."* [17] *"You shall say this word to them, 'Let my eyes run down with tears night and day, and let them not cease; for the virgin daughter of my people is broken with a great breach, with a very grievous wound.* [18] *If I go forth into the field, then, look, the slain with the sword. and if I enter into the city, then, look, those who are sick with famine. For both the prophet and the priest go about in the land, and have no knowledge.'"* [19] *"Have you utterly rejected Judah? Has your soul loathed Zion? Why have you struck us, and there is no healing for us? We looked for peace, but no good came; and for a time of healing, and look, dismay.* [20] *We acknowledge, LORD, our wickedness, and the iniquity of our fathers; for we have sinned against you.* [21] *Do not abhor us, for your name's sake; do not disgrace the throne of your glory: remember, do not break your covenant with us.* [22] *Are there any among the vanities of the nations that can cause rain? Or can the sky give showers? Aren't you he, LORD our God? Therefore we will wait for you; for you have made all these things."*

QUESTIONS

QUESTION 1   b

Jeremiah chapter 14:2 says, *"Judah mourns, and its gates languish, they sit in black on the ground; and the cry of Jerusalem is gone up."*

Why?

QUESTION 2   b

Jeremiah chapter 14:5 says, *"the hind also in the field calves, and forsakes her young...."*

Why did the hind forsake her young?

QUESTION 3   CPC

Jeremiah chapter 14:7–8 says,

"Though our iniquities testify against us, work for your name's sake, LORD; for our backslidings are many; we have sinned against you."

Complete verse 8

QUESTION 4   CPB

Jeremiah chapter 14:11–12 says,

"The LORD said to me, "Do not pray for this people for their good.""

Complete verse 12.

QUESTION 5   CTX

"the prophets tell them, 'You shall not see the sword, neither shall you have famine; but I will give you assured peace in this place.'"

Give the context of the above quote:

Who said it, to who, and under what circumstance?

QUESTION 6   CPC

Jeremiah chapter 14:14–15 says,

"Then the LORD said to me, "The prophets prophesy lies in my name; I did not send them, neither have I commanded them, neither spoke I to them: they prophesy to you a lying vision, and divination, and a thing of nothing, and the deceit of their own heart.""

Complete verse 15.

QUESTION 7   CPB

Jeremiah chapter 14:19–20 says,

"Have you utterly rejected Judah? Has your soul loathed Zion? Why have you struck us, and there is no healing for us? We looked for peace, but no good came; and for a time of healing, and look, dismay."

Complete verse 20.

QUESTION 8   CPC

Jeremiah chapter 14:21–22 says,

"Do not abhor us, for your name's sake; do not disgrace the throne of your glory: remember, do not break your covenant with us."

Complete verse 22.

QUESTION 9   CMB

Read Jeremiah chapter 14:7–12, 19–21, preach or write a commentary on the passage with emphasis on salvation.

QUESTION 10   CMB

Read Jeremiah chapter 14:11–16, preach or write a commentary on the passage with emphasis on salvation.

QUESTION 11   CMC

Read Jeremiah chapter 14:14–16, preach or write a commentary on the passage with emphasis on salvation.

ANSWERS

ANSWER TO QUESTION 1   b

Because the Lord held back the rain (Jeremiah 14:4).

ANSWER TO QUESTION 2   b

Because there was no grass (Jeremiah 14:5).

ANSWER TO QUESTION 3   CPC

"8 Hope of Israel, LORD, its Savior in the time of trouble, why should you be as a foreigner in the land, and as a wayfaring man who turns aside to stay for a night?" (Jeremiah 14:8.)

ANSWER TO QUESTION 4   CPB

"12 When they fast, I will not hear their cry; and when they offer burnt offering and meal offering, I will not accept them; but I will consume them by the sword, and by the famine, and by the pestilence." (Jeremiah 14:12.)

ANSWER TO QUESTION 5   CTX

- Prophet Jeremiah
- To God
- When God asked Jeremiah not to intercede for the people of Judah and Jerusalem (Jeremiah 14:13).

ANSWER TO QUESTION 6   CPC

"15 Therefore thus says the LORD concerning the prophets who prophesy in my name, and I did not send them, yet they say, 'Sword and famine shall not be in this land:' 'By sword and famine shall those prophets be consumed.'" (Jeremiah 14:15.)

ANSWER TO QUESTION 7   CPB

"20 We acknowledge, LORD, our wickedness, and the iniquity of our fathers; for we have sinned against you." (Jeremiah 14:20.)

CHAPTER 14

ANSWER TO QUESTION 8   CPC

"²²Are there any among the vanities of the nations that can cause rain? Or can the sky give showers? Aren't you he, LORD our God? Therefore we will wait for you; for you have made all these things."
(Jeremiah 14:22.)

HINTS TO QUESTION 9   CMB

- Jeremiah's intercession for the people of Judah was for God to have mercy on them and avert their punishment. However, it was obvious that because of the attitude of the people, his prayers seemed not to have an effect. God said He would consume them by the sword, famine and pestilence. The attitude of the people we are interceding for can hamper the result of intercession.
- While it is good to intercede for sinners in their plights, the first and best kind of prayer we can offer to God for sinners is for the salvation of their souls.
- Judah's sin had made God hand them over to their enemies. At this time, God seemed like a weakling and a stranger among His people. It is worthy of note that God is neither a stranger nor a weakling concerning His children's affairs, but their sins can make Him seem so. God always cares for His children's welfare, but we deny ourselves of His care when we turn aside from Him. Sin affects our relationship with God and exposes us to God's punishment. When we go astray, we should turn to God in repentance to obtain mercy.

HINT TO QUESTION 10   CMB

The prophets had prophesied falsely and led the people astray, but God did not only pronounce judgement on the lying prophets but also on those who listened to them. This underscores the need for each person to study the word of God for themselves with an emphasis on salvation so that they will not be led astray.

HINT TO QUESTION 11   CMC

When a blind man leads another blind man, they both fall into a ditch (Matthew 15:14). The verses under consideration have established that God did not send the prophets, the prophets told the people what they wanted to hear, and the people chose to believe their lies.

CHAPTER 15

JEREMIAH CHAPTER 15

"Then the LORD said to me, "Though Moses and Samuel stood before me, yet my mind would not be toward this people: cast them out of my sight, and let them go forth. ²It shall happen, when they tell you, 'Where shall we go forth?' Then you shall tell them, 'Thus says the LORD: "Such as are for death, to death; and such as are for the sword, to the sword; and such as are for the famine, to the famine; and such as are for captivity, to captivity. ³I will appoint over them four kinds, says the LORD: the sword to kill, and the dogs to tear, and the birds of the sky, and the animals of the earth, to devour and to destroy. ⁴I will cause them to be tossed back and forth among all the kingdoms of the earth, because of Manasseh, the son of Hezekiah, king of Judah, for that which he did in Jerusalem. ⁵For who will have pity on you, Jerusalem? Or who will bemoan you? Or who will turn aside to ask of your welfare? ⁶'You have rejected me,' says the LORD, 'you have gone backward:' therefore have I stretched out my hand against you, and destroyed you; I am weary with repenting. ⁷I have winnowed them with a fan in the gates of the land; I have bereaved them of children, I have destroyed my people; they did not return from their ways. ⁸Their widows are increased to me above the sand of the seas; I have brought on them against the mother of the young men a destroyer at noonday; I have made anguish and terror to fall on them suddenly. ⁹She who has borne seven languishes; she has given up the spirit; her sun is gone down while it was yet day; she has been disappointed and confounded: and their residue will I deliver to the sword before their enemies," says the LORD. ¹⁰"Woe is me, my mother, that you have borne me a man of strife and a man of contention to the whole earth. I have not lent, neither have men lent to me; yet everyone of them curses me." ¹¹The LORD said, "Most certainly I will strengthen you for good; most certainly I will cause the enemy to make petition to you in the time of evil and in the time of distress. ¹²Can one break iron, even iron from the north, and bronze? ¹³Your substance and your treasures will I give for a spoil without price, and that for all your sins, even in all your borders. ¹⁴I will make you serve your enemies in a land which you do not know; for a fire is kindled in my anger, which shall burn on you." ¹⁵"LORD, you know; remember me, and visit me, and avenge me of my persecutors; do not take me away in your longsuffering: know that for your sake I have suffered reproach. ¹⁶Your words were found, and I ate them; and your words were to me a joy and the rejoicing of my heart: for I am called by your name, LORD, God of hosts. ¹⁷I did not sit in the assembly of those who make merry, nor rejoiced; I sat alone because of your hand; for you have filled me with indignation. ¹⁸Why is my pain perpetual, and my wound incurable, which refuses to be healed? Will you indeed be to me as a deceitful brook, as waters that fail?" ¹⁹Therefore thus says the LORD, "If you return, then will I bring you again, that you may stand before me; and if you take forth the precious from the vile, you shall be as my mouth: they shall return to you, but you shall not return to them. ²⁰I will make you to this people a fortified bronze wall; and they shall fight against you, but they shall not prevail against you; for I am with you to save you and to deliver you," says the LORD. ²¹"I will deliver you out of the hand of the wicked, and I will redeem you out of the hand of the terrible."

QUESTIONS

QUESTION 1   a

According to Jeremiah chapter 15:

Which two persons did God say even if they stood before Him, His mind would not be towards the people of Judah, or He would not help them?

QUESTION 2   CTX

"Such as are for death, to death; and such as are for the sword, to the sword; and such as are for the famine, to the famine; and such as are for captivity, to captivity."

Give the context of the above quote.

Who said it, to who, and under what circumstance?

QUESTION 3   a

According to Jeremiah chapter 15:

How many kinds of destroyers did God say He would send upon the people of Judah and Jerusalem?

QUESTION 4   b

According to Jeremiah chapter 15:

Name three kinds of destroyers God said He would send upon the people of Judah and Jerusalem.

QUESTION 5   CTX

"For who will have pity on you, Jerusalem? Or who will bemoan you? Or who will turn aside to ask of your welfare?"

Give the context of the above quote:

Who said it, to who, and under what circumstance?

QUESTION 6   b1

According to Jeremiah chapter 15:

Why did God say He would send the destroyers against the people of Judah and toss them among the nations?

QUESTION 7   b1

According to Jeremiah chapter 15:

What reason did God give for deciding to punish the people of Judah and Jerusalem for their sins?

QUESTION 8   a

According to Jeremiah chapter 15:

What did God say will be more than the sands on the seashore?

QUESTION 9   b1

Jeremiah chapter 15:10 says, *"Woe is me, my mother, that you have borne me a man of strife and a man of contention to the whole earth. I have not lent, neither have men lent to me; yet everyone of them curses me."*

Who made the above statement, and what was God's reply to the person?

QUESTION 10   CPB

Jeremiah chapter 15:15–16 says,

"LORD, you know; remember me, and visit me, and avenge me of my persecutors; do not take me away in your longsuffering: know that for your sake I have suffered reproach."

Complete verse 16.

QUESTION 11   b1

According to Jeremiah chapter 15:

Why did Jeremiah not join the people to make merry or rejoice?

QUESTION 12 **b**

Jeremiah chapter 15:19 says, *"Therefore thus says the LORD, "If you return, then will I bring you again, that you may stand before me; and if you take forth the precious from the vile, you shall be as my mouth: they shall return to you, but you shall not return to them."*

Who is the Lord talking to in the above passage?

QUESTION 13 **CMB**

Read Jeremiah chapter 15:10–18, preach or write a commentary on the passage with emphasis on salvation.

ANSWERS

ANSWER TO QUESTION 1 **a**

Moses and Samuel (Jeremiah 15:1).

ANSWER TO QUESTION 2 **CTX**

- God
- To Prophet Jeremiah
- When God told Prophet Jeremiah that even if Moses and Samuel were to plead for the sins of the people of Judah and Jerusalem, He would not listen (and if the people asked where they should go, he should respond to them with the above quote) (Jeremiah 15:1–2).

ANSWER TO QUESTION 3 **a**

Four kinds of destroyers (Jeremiah 15:3).

ANSWER TO QUESTION 4 **b**

- The sword (to kill)
- The dogs (to tear or drag away)
- The birds of the sky or vultures (to devour)

- And the wild animals (to destroy or finish up what is left) (Jeremiah 15:3).

ANSWER TO QUESTION 5   CTX

- God
- To Prophet Jeremiah
- When God was telling Jeremiah what to reply to those who would ask him where they shall go forth (Jeremiah 15:3–5).

ANSWER TO QUESTION 6   b1

Because of the wicked things Manasseh, son of King Hezekiah of Judah, did in Jerusalem (Jeremiah 15:4).

ANSWER TO QUESTION 7   b1

Because He was tired of repenting from His wrath towards them over their sins.

Or

Because He was tired of giving them another chance.

Or

Because He was tired of holding back (Jeremiah 15:6).

ANSWER TO QUESTION 8   a

Widows (Jeremiah 15:8).

ANSWER TO QUESTION 9   b1

- Prophet Jeremiah
- That He (God) will strengthen him (Jeremiah) for good

  Or

  That He (God) will take care of him (Jeremiah) (Jeremiah 15:10).

ANSWER TO QUESTION 10   CPB

"16Your words were found, and I ate them; and your words were to me a joy and the rejoicing of my heart: for I am called by your name, LORD, God of hosts." (Jeremiah 15:16.)

ANSWER TO QUESTION 11   b1

Because God's hand was on him, and God had filled him with indignation (Jeremiah 15:17).

ANSWER TO QUESTION 12   b

Jeremiah (Jeremiah 15:19).

HINT TO QUESTION 13   CMB

Jeremiah lamented the sufferings he was passing through in his ministry and his walk with God. One may expect that as a prophet, God should have shielded him from bitter experiences; however, God only promised to strengthen him. This teaches us that being a Christian does not make us immune to suffering. Children of God may suffer in this world depending on their assignments or purpose in life, but that does not mean God is not with them or they are not on the right path.

CHAPTER 16

JEREMIAH CHAPTER 16

"The word of the LORD came also to me, saying, ²"You shall not take a wife, neither shall you have sons or daughters, in this place. ³For thus says the LORD concerning the sons and concerning the daughters who are born in this place, and concerning their mothers who bore them, and concerning their fathers who became their father in this land: ⁴They shall die grievous deaths: they shall not be lamented, neither shall they be buried; they shall be as dung on the surface of the ground; and they shall be consumed by the sword, and by famine; and their dead bodies shall be food for the birds of the sky, and for the animals of the earth. ⁵For thus says the LORD, 'Do not enter into the house of mourning, neither go to lament, neither bemoan them; for I have taken away my peace from this people, says the LORD, even loving kindness and tender mercies. ⁶Both great and small shall die in this land; they shall not be buried, neither shall men lament for them, nor cut themselves, nor make themselves bald for them; ⁷neither shall men break bread for them in mourning, to comfort them for the dead; neither shall men give them the cup of consolation to drink for their father or for their mother. ⁸You shall not go into the house of feasting to sit with them, to eat and to drink. ⁹For thus says the LORD of hosts, the God of Israel: Look, I will cause to cease out of this place, before your eyes and in your days, the voice of mirth and the voice of gladness, the voice of the bridegroom and the voice of the bride. ¹⁰It shall happen, when you shall show this people all these words, and they shall tell you, 'Why has the LORD

pronounced all this great evil against us? Or what is our iniquity? Or what is our sin that we have committed against the LORD our God?' ¹¹ Then you shall tell them, 'Because your fathers have forsaken me, says the LORD, and have walked after other gods, and have served them, and have worshiped them, and have forsaken me, and have not kept my law; ¹² and you have done evil more than your fathers; for, look, you walk every one after the stubbornness of his evil heart, so that you do not listen to me: ¹³ therefore I will cast you forth out of this land into the land that you have not known, neither you nor your fathers; and there you shall serve other gods day and night; for I will show you no favor.' ¹⁴ Therefore look, the days come," says the LORD, "that it shall no more be said, 'As the LORD lives, who brought up the sons of Israel out of the land of Egypt;' ¹⁵ but, 'As the LORD lives, who brought up the sons of Israel from the land of the north, and from all the countries where he had driven them.' I will bring them again into their land that I gave to their fathers. ¹⁶ Look, I will send for many fishermen," says the LORD, "and they shall fish them up; and afterward I will send for many hunters, and they shall hunt them from every mountain, and from every hill, and out of the clefts of the rocks. ¹⁷ For my eyes are on all their ways; they are not hidden from my face, neither is their iniquity concealed from my eyes. ¹⁸ First I will recompense their iniquity and their sin double, because they have polluted my land with the carcasses of their detestable things, and have filled my inheritance with their abominations." ¹⁹ "LORD, my strength, and my stronghold, and my refuge in the day of affliction, to you shall the nations come from the farthest parts of the earth, and shall say, 'Our fathers have inherited nothing but lies, vanity and things in which there is no profit. ²⁰ Shall a man make to himself gods, which yet are no gods?'" ²¹ "Therefore look, I will cause them to know, this once will I cause them to know my hand and my might; and they shall know that my name is the LORD."

QUESTIONS

QUESTION 1   CTX

"They shall die grievous deaths: they shall not be lamented, neither shall they be buried; they shall be as dung on the surface of the ground...."

Give the context of the above quote:

Who said it, to who, and under what circumstance?

QUESTION 2   CTX

"You shall not take a wife, neither shall you have sons or daughters, in this place."

Give the context of the above quote:

Who said it, to who, and under what circumstance?

QUESTION 3   b

According to Jeremiah chapter 16:

Why did God tell Jeremiah not to mourn or show sympathy for the people of Judah and Jerusalem?

QUESTION 4   CTX

"Both great and small shall die in this land; they shall not be buried, neither shall men lament for them...."

Give the context of the above quote:

Who said it, to who, and under what circumstance?

QUESTION 5   CTX

"Look, I will cause to cease out of this place, before your eyes and in your days, the voice of mirth and the voice of gladness, the voice of the bridegroom and the voice of the bride."

Give the context of the above quote:

Who said it, to who, and under what circumstance?

QUESTION 6   b1

Jeremiah chapter 16:14 says, *"Therefore look, the days come," says the LORD, "that it shall no more be said, 'As the LORD lives, who brought up the sons of Israel out of the land of Egypt.'"*

What would they say instead?

QUESTION 7   b

According to Jeremiah chapter 16:

Why did God say He would double the punishments for the sins of the people of Judah and Jerusalem?

QUESTION 8   c

Jeremiah chapter 16:14–15 says, *"Therefore look, the days come," says the LORD, "that it shall no more be said, 'As the LORD lives, who brought up the sons of Israel out of the land of Egypt; ¹⁵but, 'As the LORD lives, who brought up the sons of Israel from the land of the north, and from all the countries where he had driven them.' I will bring them again into their land that I gave to their fathers."*

Where else in the Bible can the above prophecy be found in similar words?

QUESTION 9   CPC

Jeremiah chapter 16:20–21 says,

"Shall a man make to himself gods, which yet are no gods?"

Complete verse 21.

QUESTION 10   CMB

Read Jeremiah chapter 16:10, preach or write a commentary on the passage with emphasis on salvation.

QUESTION 11   CMB

Read Jeremiah chapter 16:17, preach or write a commentary on the passage with emphasis on salvation.

ANSWERS

ANSWER TO QUESTION 1   CTX

- God
- To Prophet Jeremiah
- When He (God) told Jeremiah not to marry or have children in the land of Judah because Judah's inhabitants would be destroyed (Jeremiah 16:1–4).

ANSWER TO QUESTION 2   CTX

- God
- To Prophet Jeremiah
- When He warned Jeremiah about what would happen to the children that would be born in that land (Jeremiah 16:1–4).

ANSWER TO QUESTION 3   b

Because He had taken away His peace, love and mercy from them (Jeremiah 16:5).

ANSWER TO QUESTION 4   CTX

- God
- To Prophet Jeremiah
- When He (God) told Jeremiah not to mourn or show sympathy for the people of Judah (Jeremiah 16:5–6).

ANSWER TO QUESTION 5   CTX

- God
- To Prophet Jeremiah
- When God was telling Prophet Jeremiah not to go to the feast and parties or eat and drink with the people of Judah (Jeremiah 16:8–9).

ANSWER TO QUESTION 6   b1

They will say, *"As the LORD lives, who brought up the sons of Israel from the land of the north, and from all the countries where he had driven them."* (Jeremiah 16:15.)

ANSWER TO QUESTION 7   b

Because they had defiled the land with the carcasses of detestable things or idols.

Or

They have filled God's inheritance with their abominations or evil deeds (Jeremiah 16:18).

ANSWER TO QUESTION 8   c

Jeremiah 23:7–8.

ANSWER TO QUESTION 9   CPC

"²¹ Therefore look, I will cause them to know, this once will I cause them to know my hand and my might; and they shall know that my name is the LORD." (Jeremiah 16:21.)

HINTS TO QUESTION 10   CMB

- Before Jeremiah delivered God's message of destruction to the people of Judah, God let him know that, after delivering the message, the people would ask him what their faults were. The people made it seem their sins were not grievous enough to warrant such punishment from God. Acknowledging our faults honour God; denying them dishonours Him. We find it easier to complain about the magnitude of the punishments or consequences of our actions, while we fail to recognise that if we had not carried out those actions, the punishments or consequences would never have happened.
- Every disobedience to God is a sin regardless of the magnitude, and all sinners shall be separated from God. Hence, we should not trivialise sins.

HINT TO QUESTION 11   CMB

As far as God was concerned, the Judeans' sins were not hidden. When we live with the consciousness that God sees our every action, it will help us to watch the way we live and not live against the word of God. If we fall into sin in any way, the best option for us at that time is to run back to God and make amends for that mistake and not try to cover it up.

CHAPTER 17

JEREMIAH CHAPTER 17

"The sin of Judah is written with a pen of iron, and with the point of a diamond: it is engraved on the tablet of their heart, and on the horns of your altars; ²while their children remember their altars and their Asherim by the green trees on the high hills. ³My mountain in the field, I will give your substance and all your treasures for a spoil, and your high places, because of sin, throughout all your borders. ⁴You, even of yourself, shall discontinue from your heritage that I gave you; and I will cause you to serve your enemies in the land which you do not know: for you have kindled a fire in my anger which shall burn forever." ⁵Thus says the LORD: "Cursed is the man who trusts in man, and makes flesh his arm, and whose heart departs from the LORD. ⁶For he shall be like the heath in the desert, and shall not see when good comes, but shall inhabit the parched places in the wilderness, a salt land and not inhabited. ⁷Blessed is the man who trusts in the LORD, and whose confidence is in the LORD. ⁸For he shall be as a tree planted by the waters, who spreads out its roots by the river, and shall not fear when heat comes, but its leaf shall be green; and shall not be careful in the year of drought, neither shall cease from yielding fruit. ⁹The heart is deceitful above all things, and it is exceedingly corrupt: who can know it? ¹⁰I, the LORD, search the mind, I try the heart, even to give every man according to his ways, according to the fruit of his doings. ¹¹As the partridge that sits on eggs which she has not laid, so is he who gets riches, and not by right; in the midst of his days they shall leave him, and at his end

he shall be a fool." ¹²"A glorious throne, set on high from the beginning, is the place of our sanctuary. ¹³LORD, the hope of Israel, all who forsake you shall be disappointed. Those who depart from me shall be written in the earth, because they have forsaken the LORD, the spring of living waters. ¹⁴Heal me, O LORD, and I shall be healed; save me, and I shall be saved: for you are my praise. ¹⁵Look, they tell me, 'Where is the word of the LORD? Let it come now.' ¹⁶As for me, I have not hurried from being a shepherd after you; neither have I desired the woeful day; you know: that which came out of my lips was before your face. ¹⁷Do not be a terror to me: you are my refuge in the day of evil. ¹⁸Let them be disappointed who persecute me, but let not me be disappointed; let them be dismayed, but do not let me be dismayed; bring on them the day of disaster, and destroy them with double destruction." ¹⁹Thus said the LORD to me: "Go, and stand in the gate of the children of the people, through which the kings of Judah come in, and by which they go out, and in all the gates of Jerusalem; ²⁰and tell them, 'Hear the word of the LORD, you kings of Judah, and all Judah, and all the inhabitants of Jerusalem, that enter in by these gates: ²¹Thus says the LORD, "Take heed to yourselves, and bear no burden on the Sabbath day, nor bring it in by the gates of Jerusalem; ²²neither carry forth a burden out of your houses on the Sabbath day holy, neither do any work: but make the Sabbath day, as I commanded your fathers. ²³But they did not listen, neither turn their ear, but made their neck stiff, that they might not hear, and might not receive instruction. ²⁴It shall happen, if you diligently listen to me," says the LORD, "to bring in no burden through the gates of this city on the Sabbath day, but to make the Sabbath day holy, to do no work in it; ²⁵then shall there enter in by the gates of this city kings and princes sitting on the throne of David, riding in chariots and on horses, they, and their officials, the men of Judah, and the inhabitants of Jerusalem; and this city shall remain forever. ²⁶They shall come from the cities of Judah, and from the places around Jerusalem, and from the land of Benjamin, and from the lowland, and from *the hill country, and from the Negev, bringing burnt offerings, and sacrifices, and meal offerings, and frankincense, and bringing sacrifices of thanksgiving, to the house of the LORD. ²⁷But if you will not listen to me to make the Sabbath day holy, and not to bear a burden and enter in at the gates of Jerusalem on the Sabbath day; then will I kindle a fire in its gates, and it shall devour the palaces of Jerusalem, and it shall not be quenched.""*

QUESTIONS

QUESTION 1   b1

Jeremiah chapter 17 begins with *"The sin of Judah is written with a pen of iron"*, and verse 2 talks about their children. What did the verse say about the children?

QUESTION 2   b1

According to Jeremiah chapter 17:

What did God say about a person who puts their trust in man?

QUESTION 3   b1

According to Jeremiah chapter 17:

What did God say about a person who puts their trust in Him?

QUESTION 4   b1

Jeremiah chapter 17:8 says, *"For he shall be as a tree planted by the waters, who spreads out its roots by the river, and shall not fear when heat comes, but its leaf shall be green; and shall not be careful in the year of drought, neither shall cease from yielding fruit."*

Where else can a similar quote be found in the Bible?

QUESTION 5   **b**

According to Jeremiah chapter 17:

How was the heart of man described?

QUESTION 6   **b1**

According to Jeremiah chapter 17:

What will happen to those who forsake or abandon the Lord?

QUESTION 7   **b**

Jeremiah chapter 17:19 says, *"Go, and stand in the gate of the children of the people...."*

Who used the gate God told Jeremiah to stand?

QUESTION 8   **b**

According to Jeremiah chapter 17:

What was God's instruction through Prophet Jeremiah to the people of Judah and Jerusalem concerning the Sabbath Day?

QUESTION 9   **b1**

According to Jeremiah chapter 17:

What instruction did God say He gave to the ancestors of the people of Judah and Jerusalem, which they refused to listen to?

QUESTION 10   **b2**

According to Jeremiah chapter 17:

What did God say would happen to the people of Judah and Jerusalem if they did not obey Him by observing the Sabbath?

QUESTION 11   **CMB**

Read Jeremiah chapter 17:5–8, preach or write a commentary on the passage with emphasis on salvation.

QUESTION 12   **CMB**

Read Jeremiah chapter 17:9–10, preach or write a commentary on the passage with emphasis on salvation.

QUESTION 13   **CMB**

Read Jeremiah chapter 17:11, preach or write a commentary on the passage with emphasis on salvation.

QUESTION 14   **CMB**

Read Jeremiah chapter 17:21–23, preach or write a commentary on the passage with emphasis on salvation.

ANSWERS

ANSWER TO QUESTION 1   b1

Their children remember their altars and Asherim by the green trees and under every high hill.

Or

Their children go to worship at their altars and Asherah poles beside the green trees and under every high hill (Jeremiah 17:1–2).

ANSWER TO QUESTION 2   b1

"⁶he shall be like the heath in the desert, and shall not see when good comes, but shall inhabit the parched places in the wilderness, a salt land and not inhabited." (Jeremiah 17:6.)

ANSWER TO QUESTION 3   b1

"⁸For he shall be as a tree planted by the waters, who spreads out its roots by the river, and shall not fear when heat comes, but its leaf shall be green; and shall not be careful in the year of drought, neither shall cease from yielding fruit." (Jeremiah 17:8.)

ANSWER TO QUESTION 4   b1

Psalm 1:3

ANSWER TO QUESTION 5   b

Deceitful and exceedingly or desperately corrupt, wicked or sick (Jeremiah 17:9).

ANSWER TO QUESTION 6   b1

They will be disappointed or ashamed, and they will be written in the dust or earth (Jeremiah 17:13).

ANSWER TO QUESTION 7   b

The kings of Judah (Jeremiah 17:19).

ANSWER TO QUESTION 8   b

They should stop carrying on their trade at Jerusalem's gates on the Sabbath day and do no work on the Sabbath but make it a holy day (Jeremiah 17:21–22).

ANSWER TO QUESTION 9   b1

They should stop carrying on their trade at Jerusalem's gates on the Sabbath day and do no work on the Sabbath but make it a holy day (Jeremiah 17:21–23).

ANSWER TO QUESTION 10   b2

God said He would set fire to their gates, and then the fire would spread to the palaces (citadels or fortresses or streets), and no one would be able to put out the fire (Jeremiah 17:27).

HINTS TO QUESTION 11   CMB

- The verses under consideration speak of two sets of people: on one hand, those that put their trust in man and, on the other hand, those who put their trust in God. Those who belong to the latter category are blessed, for they shall be like a tree planted by the riverside which blooms and remain fruitful regardless of the unfavourable situation they experience. To trust in God means relying on His words. Troubles in life shall not move a person who trusts in God because their hope is in God's word, which never fails.

- In our relationship with fellow humans, a certain degree of trust is needed, but when we trust humans to do the things we should rely on God for, we are bound to fail.

HINT TO QUESTION 12   CMB

The heart of the natural man is desperately corrupt, so everyone needs the transformation of the heart to live in the way God desires.

HINT TO QUESTION 13   CMB

One of the messages God gave through Jeremiah was the vanity of gathering wealth through unrighteous means. When people spend their lives gathering wealth through unwholesome means, they will, in the end, realise the vanity in all their pursuits and how foolish they have been.

HINT TO QUESTION 14   CMB

One of the ways God demonstrated His love for the Judeans was in His constant rebukes for their sins and reminders about His commandments. But the Judeans were stiffnecked. A person who is often rebuked but refuses to obey instructions will face an utter consequence for their rebellion against God. But an open heart to God's instruction is the abode of God's guidance and continual blessings.

CHAPTER 18

JEREMIAH CHAPTER 18

"The word which came to Jeremiah from the LORD, saying, ²"Arise, and go down to the potter's house, and there I will cause you to hear my words." ³Then I went down to the potter's house, and look, he was making a work on the wheels. ⁴When the vessel that he made of the clay was marred in the hand of the potter, he made it again another vessel, as seemed good to the potter to make it. ⁵Then the word of the LORD came to me, saying, ⁶"'House of Israel, can't I do with you as this potter?' says the LORD. 'Look, as the clay in the potter's hand, so are you in my hand, house of Israel.' ⁷At what instant I shall speak concerning a nation, and concerning a kingdom, to pluck up and to break down and to destroy it; ⁸if that nation, concerning which I have spoken, turn from their evil, I will change my mind about the disaster that I thought to do to them. ⁹At what instant I shall speak concerning a nation, and concerning a kingdom, to build and to plant it; ¹⁰if they do that which is evil in my sight, that they not obey my voice, then I will repent of the good, with which I said I would benefit them. ¹¹Now therefore, speak to the men of Judah, and to the inhabitants of Jerusalem, saying, 'Thus says the LORD: Look, I frame evil against you, and devise a device against you: return now everyone from his evil way, and amend your ways and your doings.' ¹²But they say, 'It is in vain; for we will walk after our own devices, and we will do everyone after the stubbornness of his evil heart.'" ¹³Therefore thus says the LORD: "Ask now among the nations, who has heard such things; the virgin of Israel has done a

very horrible thing. *14 Shall the snow of Lebanon fail from the rock of the field? Shall the cold waters that flow down from afar be dried up?* *15 For my people have forgotten me, they have burned incense to false gods; and they have been made to stumble in their ways, in the ancient paths, to walk in byways, in a way not built up;* *16 to make their land an astonishment, and a perpetual hissing; everyone who passes thereby shall be astonished, and shake his head.* *17 I will scatter them as with an east wind before the enemy; I will show them the back, and not the face, in the day of their calamity.*" *18 Then they said, "Come, and let us make plans against Jeremiah; for the law shall not perish from the priest, nor counsel from the wise, nor the word from the prophet. Come, and let us strike him with the tongue, and let us not give heed to any of his words."* *19 "Give heed to me, LORD, and listen to the voice of those who contend with me.* *20 Shall evil be recompensed for good? For they have dug a pit for my soul. Remember how I stood before you to speak good for them, to turn away your wrath from them.* *21 Therefore deliver up their children to the famine, and give them over to the power of the sword; and let their wives become childless, and widows; and let their men be slain of death, and their young men struck of the sword in battle.* *22 Let a cry be heard from their houses, when you shall bring a troop suddenly on them; for they have dug a pit to take me, and hid snares for my feet.* *23 Yet, LORD, you know all their counsel against me to kill me; do not forgive their iniquity, neither blot out their sin from your sight; but let them be overthrown before you; deal you with them in the time of your anger."*

QUESTIONS

QUESTION 1   a

According to Jeremiah chapter 18:

Where did God ask Jeremiah to go so He would speak to him?

QUESTION 2   a

According to Jeremiah chapter 18, when God told Jeremiah to go down to the potter's house:

What was the first thing Jeremiah saw?

QUESTION 3   b

Jeremiah chapter 18:6 says, *"House of Israel, can't I do with you as this potter?..."*

What did the potter do?

QUESTION 4   a

According to Jeremiah chapter 18:

What did God say could make Him change His mind about punishing a nation He had pronounced punishment on?

QUESTION 5   a

According to Jeremiah chapter 18:

What did God say could make Him change His mind about blessing a nation He had promised to bless?

QUESTION 6   b1

According to Jeremiah chapter 18:

What did God say would be the people of Judah's response when Jeremiah warned them to turn from their evil ways and do what was right?

QUESTION 7   CPC

Jeremiah chapter 18:14–15 says,

"Shall the snow of Lebanon fail from the rock of the field? Shall the cold waters that flow down from afar be dried up?"

Complete verse 15.

QUESTION 8 b

According to Jeremiah chapter 18:

What did God say would be the reactions of the people who passed by Judah and Jerusalem when Judah was destroyed?

QUESTION 9 b

Jeremiah chapter 18:18 says, *"Then they said, "Come, and let us make plans against Jeremiah...."*

What plan did the people make against Jeremiah?

QUESTION 10 CTX

"Therefore deliver up their children to the famine, and give them over to the power of the sword...."

Give the context of the above quote:

Who said it, to who, and under what circumstance?

QUESTION 11 CPB

Jeremiah chapter 18:19–20 says,

"Give heed to me, LORD, and listen to the voice of those who contend with me."

Complete verse 20.

QUESTION 12 CMC

Read Jeremiah chapter 18:1–10, preach or write a commentary on the passage with emphasis on salvation.

QUESTION 13 CMB

Read Jeremiah chapter 18:18, preach or write a commentary on the passage with emphasis on salvation.

ANSWERS

ANSWER TO QUESTION 1   **a**

The potter's house (Jeremiah 18:1–2).

ANSWER TO QUESTION 2   **a**

He found the potter working at his wheel (Jeremiah 18:3).

ANSWER TO QUESTION 3   **b**

When the vessel that he made of clay was marred in his hand, he made another vessel, as seemed good to him (Jeremiah 18:4).

ANSWER TO QUESTION 4   **a**

If the nation renounces its evil ways (Jeremiah 18:8).

ANSWER TO QUESTION 5   **a**

If the nation turns to evil and refuses to obey Him (Jeremiah 18:10).

ANSWER TO QUESTION 6   **b1**

They would say Jeremiah's warning is of no use or in vain and that they would walk after their own devices and do after their hearts' stubbornness (Jeremiah 18:12).

ANSWER TO QUESTION 7   **CPC**

"15 For my people have forgotten me, they have burned incense to false gods; and they have been made to stumble in their ways, in the ancient paths, to walk in byways, in a way not built up." (Jeremiah 18:15.)

ANSWER TO QUESTION 8   **b**

They will be astonished and shake their heads in amazement (Jeremiah 18:16).

ANSWER TO QUESTION 9   **b**

To attack him with their tongues or spread rumours about him and not listen to any of his words (Jeremiah 18:18).

122

ANSWER TO QUESTION 10   CTX

- Prophet Jeremiah
- To God
- In Jeremiah's prayer for vengeance when the people of Judah and Jerusalem planned to stop him by attacking him with the tongue or spreading rumours about him (Jeremiah 18:18, 21).

ANSWER TO QUESTION 11   CPB

"20 Shall evil be recompensed for good? For they have dug a pit for my soul. Remember how I stood before you to speak good for them, to turn away your wrath from them." (Jeremiah 18:20.)

HINT TO QUESTION 12   CMC

Children of God are vessels in the hands of God, who is the Potter. As vessels, we ought to be submissive for Him to form us into what He desires. We will incur His wrath when we are rebellious to His workings in our lives rather than being moulded into vessels for honourable usage.

HINT TO QUESTION 13   CMB

Like in the time of Jeremiah, people still have an aversion for the truth and are against those who dissuade them from falsehood because they do not want to forsake their sinful lifestyles, which they find profitable or convenient. True children of God always face opposition ranging from slandering, false accusation and persecution. Believers should be aware of the potential opposition in this world from unbelievers and even supposed believers who are unwilling to hear the truth. Believers should not be distraught when oppositions come their way.

CHAPTER 19

JEREMIAH CHAPTER 19

"Thus said the LORD, "Go, and buy a potter's earthen bottle, and take with you some of the elders of the people, and of the elders of the priests; ²and go forth to the Valley of Ben Hinnom, which is by the entry of the Potsherd Gate, and proclaim there the words that I shall tell you; ³and say, 'Hear the word of the LORD, kings of Judah, and inhabitants of Jerusalem: thus says the LORD of hosts, the God of Israel, "Look, I will bring evil on this place, which whoever hears, his ears shall tingle. ⁴Because they have forsaken me, and have estranged this place, and have burned incense in it to other gods, that they did not know, they and their fathers and the kings of Judah; and have filled this place with the blood of innocents, ⁵and have built the high places of Baal, to burn their sons in the fire for burnt offerings to Baal; which I did not command, nor spoke it, neither came it into my mind: ⁶therefore, look, the days come," says the LORD, "that this place shall no more be called Topheth, nor The Valley of Ben Hinnom, but The valley of Slaughter. ⁷I will make void the counsel of Judah and Jerusalem in this place; and I will cause them to fall by the sword before their enemies, and by the hand of those who seek their life: and their dead bodies will I give to be food for the birds of the sky, and for the animals of the earth. ⁸I will make this city an astonishment, and a hissing; everyone who passes thereby shall be astonished and hiss because of all its plagues. ⁹I will cause them to eat the flesh of their sons and the flesh of their daughters; and they shall eat everyone the flesh of his friend, in the siege and in the distress, with which their enemies, and those who seek their life, shall distress

them.'" [10] Then you shall break the bottle in the sight of the men who go with you, [11] and shall tell them, 'Thus says the LORD of hosts: "Even so will I break this people and this city, as one breaks a potter's vessel, that can't be made whole again; and they shall bury in Topheth, until there is no place to bury. [12] Thus will I do to this place," says the LORD, "and to its inhabitants, even making this city as Topheth: [13] and the houses of Jerusalem, and the houses of the kings of Judah, which are defiled, shall be as the place of Topheth, even all the houses on whose roofs they have burned incense to all the host of heaven, and have poured out drink offerings to other gods."'" [14] Then came Jeremiah from Topheth, where the LORD had sent him to prophesy; and he stood in the court of the LORD's house, and said to all the people: [15] "Thus says the LORD of hosts, the God of Israel, 'Look, I will bring on this city and on all its towns all the evil that I have pronounced against it; because they have made their neck stiff, that they may not hear my words.'"

QUESTIONS

QUESTION 1   a

According to Jeremiah chapter 19:

Who did God say should accompany Jeremiah with the clay pot?

QUESTION 2   CTX

"I will make void the counsel of Judah and Jerusalem...."

Give the context of the above quote:

Who said it, to who, and under what circumstance?

QUESTION 3   CTX

"and they shall eat everyone the flesh of his friend, in the siege and in the distress...."

Give the context of the above quote:

Who said it, to who, and under what circumstance?

QUESTION 4   b1

According to Jeremiah chapter 19:

Which notable landmark is at the Potsherd gate or the gate of the broken pots?

QUESTION 5   a

According to Jeremiah chapter 19:

What cruel act did the people of Judah and Jerusalem do in the pagan shrines they built for Baal in the valley of Ben-Hinnom?

QUESTION 6   a

According to Jeremiah chapter 19:

What did the people of Judah do, which God said never came to His mind, neither did He command nor speak it?

QUESTION 7   b1

According to Jeremiah chapter 19:

What was the message the Lord asked Jeremiah to give to the people of Judah and Jerusalem after Jeremiah had smashed the jar?

QUESTION 8   a

According to Jeremiah chapter 19:

What did God say He would make all the houses in Jerusalem which are defiled, including the palaces, to become like?

QUESTION 9   CTX

"Look, I will bring on this city and on all its towns all the evil that I have pronounced against it; because they have made their neck stiff, that they may not hear my words."

Give the context of the above quote:

Who said it, to who, and under what circumstance?

QUESTION 10   **CMB**

Read Jeremiah chapter 19:5, preach or write a commentary on the passage with emphasis on salvation.

ANSWERS

ANSWER TO QUESTION 1   a

Some of the elders of the people and of the elders of the priests (Jeremiah 19:1).

ANSWER TO QUESTION 2   CTX

- God
- To Prophet Jeremiah
- When God gave him a message to the kings of Judah and the inhabitants or citizens of Jerusalem concerning Ben Hinnom or Topheth (Jeremiah 19:1–7).

ANSWER TO QUESTION 3   CTX

- God
- To Prophet Jeremiah
- When God gave him a message to the kings of Judah and the inhabitants or citizens of Jerusalem concerning Ben Hinnom or Topheth (Jeremiah 19:1–9).

ANSWER TO QUESTION 4   b1

The valley of Ben Hinnom

Or

The valley of the son of Hinnom (Jeremiah 19:2).

ANSWER TO QUESTION 5   a

They burnt their sons as sacrifices to Baal (Jeremiah 19:5).

ANSWER TO QUESTION 6   a

They burnt their sons as sacrifices to Baal (Jeremiah 19:5).

ANSWER TO QUESTION 7   b1

As the jar lies shattered beyond repair, so will God shatter the people of Judah and Jerusalem (Jeremiah 19:10–11).

ANSWER TO QUESTION 8   a

Topheth (Jeremiah 19:13).

ANSWER TO QUESTION 9   CTX

- God, through Prophet Jeremiah
- To the people in the Temple of the Lord
- When Jeremiah gave God's message to the people after he returned from Topheth, where God had sent him (Jeremiah 19:14–15).

HINT TO QUESTION 10   CMB

The people of Judah and Jerusalem burnt their sons as offerings to Baal, a thing God never commanded them to do. One of the worst things that can happen to a person is forsaking God. This can lead a person to do things God never intended for them. Living a perverse lifestyle and engaging in abominable acts are direct consequences of alienating oneself from God.

CHAPTER 20

JEREMIAH CHAPTER 20

"Now Pashhur, the son of Immer the priest, who was chief officer in the house of the LORD, heard Jeremiah prophesying these things. ²Then Pashhur struck Jeremiah the prophet, and put him in the stocks that were in the upper gate of Benjamin, which was in the house of the LORD. ³It happened on the next day, that Pashhur brought forth Jeremiah out of the stocks. Then Jeremiah said to him, "The LORD has not called your name 'Pashhur,' but 'Magor-Missabib. ⁴For thus says the LORD, 'Look, I will make you a terror to yourself, and to all your friends; and they shall fall by the sword of their enemies, and your eyes shall see it; and I will give all Judah into the hand of the king of Babylon, and he shall carry them captive to Babylon, and shall kill them with the sword. ⁵Moreover I will give all the riches of this city, and all its gains, and all the precious things of it, yes, all the treasures of the kings of Judah will I give into the hand of their enemies; and they shall make them a prey, and take them, and carry them to Babylon. ⁶You, Pashhur, and all who dwell in your house shall go into captivity; and you shall come to Babylon, and there you shall die, and there you shall be buried, you, and all your friends, to whom you have prophesied falsely.'" ⁷LORD, you have persuaded me, and I was persuaded. You are stronger than I am, and have prevailed. I have become a laughing-stock all day long; everyone mocks me. ⁸For as often as I speak, I cry out; I cry, "Violence and destruction." because the word of the LORD is made a reproach to me, and a derision, all the day. ⁹If I say, "I will not make mention of him, nor speak any more in his name," then there is in my heart as it were a burning fire shut up in my bones, and

I am weary with forbearing, and I can't contain it. ^{10}*For I have heard the defaming of many, terror on every side. "Denounce, and we will denounce him," say all my familiar friends, those who watch for my fall; "perhaps he will be persuaded, and we shall prevail against him, and we shall take our revenge on him."* ^{11}*But the LORD is with me as an awesome mighty one: therefore my persecutors shall stumble, and they shall not prevail; they shall be utterly disappointed, because they have not dealt wisely, even with an everlasting dishonor which shall never be forgotten.* ^{12}*But, the LORD of hosts, who tests the righteous, who sees the heart and the mind, let me see your vengeance on them; for to you have I revealed my cause.* ^{13}*Sing to the LORD, praise the LORD; for he has delivered the soul of the needy from the hand of evildoers.* ^{14}*Cursed is the day in which I was born: do not let the day in which my mother bore me be blessed.* ^{15}*Cursed is the man who brought news to my father, saying, A boy is born to you; making him very glad.* ^{16}*Let that man be as the cities which the LORD overthrew, and did not repent: and let him hear a cry in the morning, and shouting at noontime;* ^{17}*because he did not kill me from the womb; and so my mother would have been my grave, and her womb always great.* ^{18}*Why came I forth out of the womb to see labor and sorrow, that my days should be consumed with shame?"*

QUESTIONS

QUESTION 1   a

According to Jeremiah chapter 20:

What is the name of the priest who arrested Jeremiah and had him whipped because of his prophecy?

QUESTION 2   a

According to Jeremiah chapter 20:

What was done to Prophet Jeremiah when he was arrested?

QUESTION 3   a

According to Jeremiah chapter 20:

Where was Jeremiah kept when he was arrested?

QUESTION 4   a

According to Jeremiah chapter 20:

When was Jeremiah released after he was arrested?

QUESTION 5   b1

According to Jeremiah chapter 20:

What is the meaning of 'Magor-Missabib,' and under what circumstance was the name given?

QUESTION 6   CTX

"'Look, I will make you a terror to yourself, and to all your friends; and they shall fall by the sword of their enemies....'"

Give the context of the above quote:

Who said it, to who, and under what circumstance?

QUESTION 7   CTX

"I will give all Judah into the hand of the king of Babylon, and he shall carry them captive to Babylon, and shall kill them with the sword."

Give the context of the above quote:

Who said it, to who, and under what circumstance?

QUESTION 8   b1

According to Jeremiah chapter 20:

Mention three things the Lord said to Pashhur after he had released Jeremiah from the stocks.

QUESTION 9   **CTX**

"You are stronger than I am, and have prevailed...."

Give the context of the above quote:

Who said it, to who, and under what circumstance?

QUESTION 10   **CPB**

Jeremiah chapter 20:7–8 says,

"LORD, you have persuaded me, and I was persuaded. You are stronger than I am, and have prevailed. I have become a laughing-stock all day long; everyone mocks me."

Complete verse 8.

QUESTION 11   **CTX**

"There is in my heart as it were a burning fire shut up in my bones...."

Give the context of the above quote:

Who said it, to who, and under what circumstance?

QUESTION 12   **b1**

According to Jeremiah chapter 20:

What did Jeremiah say would happen to him whenever he would not mention the Lord or speak His name?

QUESTION 13   **CTX**

"Sing to the LORD, praise the LORD; for he has delivered the soul of the needy from the hand of evildoers."

Give the context of the above quote:

Who said it, to who, and under what circumstance?

QUESTION 14   **b2**

Jeremiah chapter 20:14 says, *"Cursed is the day in which I was born...."*

Where else can a similar saying be found in the Bible, and under what circumstance was it used?

QUESTION 15 CMB

Read Jeremiah chapter 20:7–9, preach or write a commentary on the passage with emphasis on salvation.

QUESTION 16 CMB

Read Jeremiah chapter 20:14–18, preach or write a commentary on the passage with emphasis on salvation.

ANSWERS

ANSWER TO QUESTION 1 a

Pashhur (Jeremiah 20:1).

ANSWER TO QUESTION 2 a

He was whipped or flogged and put in stocks (Jeremiah 20:2).

ANSWER TO QUESTION 3 a

At the Benjamin's gate of the Lord's temple (Jeremiah 20:2).

ANSWER TO QUESTION 4 a

The next day (Jeremiah 20:3).

ANSWER TO QUESTION 5 b1

- Fear or terror on every side
- It was given to Pashhur by Jeremiah as the name the Lord changed Pashhur's name to after he released Jeremiah from the stocks (Jeremiah 20:3).

ANSWER TO QUESTION 6 CTX

- God, through Prophet Jeremiah
- To Pashhur, (the priest of the Lord's temple)

- After he released Prophet Jeremiah from the stocks (Jeremiah 20:3–4).

ANSWER TO QUESTION 7   CTX

- God, through Prophet Jeremiah
- To Pashhur
- After he released Prophet Jeremiah from the stocks (Jeremiah 20:3–4).

ANSWER TO QUESTION 8   b1

- God said He would send terror upon Pashhur and all his friends, and Pashhur would watch as the swords of the enemy slaughter his friends.
- God would hand the people of Judah over to the king of Babylon, and he would take them captive to Babylon and kill them with the sword.
- He would give Judah's treasures and precious things, as well as the king's treasures, to their enemies, who would carry them to Babylon.
- He said that Pashhur and all his household would be taken captive to Babylon. He and all his friends to whom he prophesied falsely would die and be buried there (Jeremiah 20:4–6).

ANSWER TO QUESTION 9   CTX

- Prophet Jeremiah
- To God
- During his complaint to God after he was released from the stocks (Jeremiah 20:7).

ANSWER TO QUESTION 10   CPB

"⁸For as often as I speak, I cry out; I cry, "Violence and destruction." because the word of the LORD is made a reproach to me, and a derision, all the day." (Jeremiah 20:8.)

ANSWER TO QUESTION 11   CTX

- Prophet Jeremiah
- To God

- During his complaint to God after he was released from the stocks (Jeremiah 20:9).

ANSWER TO QUESTION 12   b1

His heart will feel like a burning fire is shut up in his bones, and he cannot contain it (Jeremiah 20:9).

ANSWER TO QUESTION 13   CTX

- Prophet Jeremiah
- To God
- When he acknowledged God during his complaint after he was released from the stocks (Jeremiah 20:13).

ANSWER TO QUESTION 14   b2

- Job chapter 3
- In Job's first speech during his ordeal.

HINT TO QUESTION 15   CMB

Because of his resolve to serve God and speak the mind of God, Jeremiah became a laughingstock among his people. The way of righteousness has never been popular in any generation because of the depravity of humankind. A person who desires to follow this way, preach it, and hold on to the truth will face many adversities ranging from mockery, persecution and rejection. Hence, every believer should be prepared ahead to face whatever will betide them in the Christian journey.

HINT TO QUESTION 16   CMB

Children of God today should not complain or lament as Jeremiah did in the verses in context, no matter what they pass through. Rather, they should remain steadfast in faith, believing that God has their best interest at heart and that His plans for them are good and not evil.

CHAPTER 21

JEREMIAH CHAPTER 21

"The word which came to Jeremiah from the LORD, when king Zedekiah sent to him Pashhur the son of Malchijah, and Zephaniah the son of Maaseiah, the priest, saying, ²"Please inquire of the LORD for us; for Nebuchadnezzar king of Babylon makes war against us: perhaps the LORD will deal with us according to all his wondrous works, that he may go up from us."³Then Jeremiah said to them, "You shall tell Zedekiah: ⁴'Thus says the LORD, the God of Israel, "Look, I will turn back the weapons of war that are in your hands, with which you fight against the king of Babylon, and against the Chaldeans who besiege you, without the walls; and I will gather them into the midst of this city. ⁵I myself will fight against you with an outstretched hand and with a strong arm, even in anger, and in wrath, and in great indignation. ⁶I will strike the inhabitants of this city, both man and animal: they shall die of a great pestilence. ⁷Afterward," says the LORD, "I will deliver Zedekiah king of Judah, and his servants, and the people, even such as are left in this city from the pestilence, from the sword, and from the famine, into the hand of Nebuchadnezzar king of Babylon, and into the hand of their enemies, and into the hand of those who seek their life: and he shall strike them with the edge of the sword; he shall not spare them, neither have pity, nor have mercy."'⁸To this people you shall say, "Thus says the LORD: 'Look, I set before you the way of life and the way of death. ⁹He who remains in this city shall die by the sword, and by the famine, and by the pestilence; but he who goes out, and passes over to the

Chaldeans who besiege you, he shall live, and his life shall be to him for a prey. ¹⁰*For I have set my face on this city for evil, and not for good,' says the LORD: 'it shall be given into the hand of the king of Babylon, and he shall burn it with fire.'* ¹¹*Touching the house of the king of Judah, hear the word of the LORD:* ¹²*'House of David, thus says the LORD, "Execute justice in the morning, and deliver him who is robbed out of the hand of the oppressor, lest my wrath go forth like fire, and burn so that none can quench it, because of the evil of your doings.* ¹³*Look, I am against you, O inhabitant of the valley, and of the rock of the plain," says the LORD; "you that say, 'Who shall come down against us? Or who shall enter into our habitations?'* ¹⁴*I will punish you according to the fruit of your doings," says the LORD; "and I will kindle a fire in her forest, and it shall devour all that is around her.""*

QUESTIONS

QUESTION 1   b1

According to Jeremiah chapter 21:

Name the people King Zedekiah sent to Prophet Jeremiah to speak to the Lord on his behalf.

QUESTION 2   CTX

"perhaps the LORD will deal with us according to all his wondrous works, that he may go up from us."

Give the context of the above quote:

Who said it, to who, and under what circumstance?

QUESTION 3   CTX

"I will turn back the weapons of war that are in your hands, with which you fight against the king of Babylon...."

Give the context of the above quote:

Who said it, to who, and under what circumstance?

QUESTION 4   b1

According to Jeremiah chapter 21, King Zedekiah sent some people to Prophet Jeremiah:

What message did he give them to the Prophet?

QUESTION 5   CTX

"'Look, I set before you the way of life and the way of death."

Give the context of the above quote:

Who said it, to who, and under what circumstance?

QUESTION 6   a

According to Jeremiah chapter 21:

What did God say was the condition for the Israelites to survive the Babylonian attack?

QUESTION 7   b1

Jeremiah chapter 21:8 says, *"'Look, I set before you the way of life and the way of death."*

What were the way of life and the way of death?

QUESTION 8   CTX

"Execute justice in the morning, and deliver him who is robbed out of the hand of the oppressor...."

Give the context of the above quote:

Who said it, to who, and under what circumstance?

QUESTION 9   CTX

"and I will kindle a fire in her forest, and it shall devour all that is around her."

Give the context of the above quote:

Who said it, to who, and under what circumstance?

QUESTION 10   **CMB**

Read Jeremiah chapter 21:1–2 and 11–14, preach or write a commentary on the passage with emphasis on salvation.

QUESTION 11   **CMB**

Read Jeremiah chapter 21:8–10, preach or write a commentary on the passage with emphasis on salvation.

ANSWERS

ANSWER TO QUESTION 1   b1

- Pashhur (son of Malchijah)
- Zephaniah (son of Maaseiah) (Jeremiah 21:1).

ANSWER TO QUESTION 2   CTX

- King Zedekiah through Pashhur and Zephaniah
- To Prophet Jeremiah
- When King Zedekiah sent Pashhur and Zephaniah to speak to Prophet Jeremiah concerning the invasion of King Nebuchadnezzar in Judah (Jeremiah 21:1–2).

ANSWER TO QUESTION 3   CTX

- God, through Prophet Jeremiah
- To Pashhur (son of Malchijah) and Zephaniah (son of Maaseiah)
- As a response to King Zedekiah, who sent Pashhur (son of Malchijah) and Zephaniah (son of Maaseiah) to speak to Prophet Jeremiah concerning the invasion of King Nebuchadnezzar in Judah (Jeremiah 21:1–3).

ANSWER TO QUESTION 4   b1

King Zedekiah sent the people to ask Prophet Jeremiah to speak to the Lord for them; perhaps the Lord would deal with them according to His wondrous works that would make King Nebuchadnezzar of

Babylon withdraw his armies because he was attacking Judah (Jeremiah 21:2).

ANSWER TO QUESTION 5   CTX

*   God, through Prophet Jeremiah
*   To Pashhur (son of Malchijah) and Zephaniah (son of Maaseiah)
*   As a response to King Zedekiah, who sent Pashhur (son of Malchijah) and Zephaniah (son of Maaseiah) to speak to Prophet Jeremiah concerning the invasion of King Nebuchadnezzar in Judah (Jeremiah 21:8).

ANSWER TO QUESTION 6   a

Coming out to surrender to the king of Babylon (Jeremiah 21:8–9).

ANSWER TO QUESTION 7   b1

*   Those who chose to remain in the city would die
*   Those who surrendered to the king of Babylon would live (Jeremiah 21:9).

ANSWER TO QUESTION 8   CTX

*   God, through Prophet Jeremiah
*   To Pashhur (son of Malchijah) and Zephaniah (son of Maaseiah)
*   As a response to King Zedekiah, who sent Pashhur (son of Malchijah) and Zephaniah (son of Maaseiah) to speak to Prophet Jeremiah concerning the invasion of King Nebuchadnezzar in Judah (Jeremiah 21:11–12).

ANSWER TO QUESTION 9   CTX

*   God, through Prophet Jeremiah
*   To Pashhur (son of Malchijah) and Zephaniah (son of Maaseiah)
*   As a response to King Zedekiah, who sent Pashhur (son of Malchijah) and Zephaniah (son of Maaseiah), to speak to Prophet Jeremiah concerning the invasion of King Nebuchadnezzar in Judah (Jeremiah 21:11–14).

HINTS TO QUESTION 10   CMB

- Just as King Zedekiah inquired of the Lord, intending to alleviate his immediate suffering, many today live in disobedience and only run to God when experiencing the negative effects of their sinful life. They pray to God for relief but are not concerned about doing the right thing.
- As God commanded King Zedekiah to execute justice, God expects everyone to live right.

HINT TO QUESTION 11   CMB

God presented the Judeans with the option to either surrender to the Chaldeans and live or remain in their land and be destroyed. In the dealings of God with humanity, He has always left us with choices. Even while chastising us for going against His words, He does not withdraw our individual choices or decisions to submit or resist His chastening. But as children of God, it is God's expectation of us to submit totally to His chastening because in this alone can one find restoration.

CHAPTER 22

JEREMIAH CHAPTER 22

"Thus said the LORD: "Go down to the house of the king of Judah, and speak there this word, ²Say, 'Hear the word of the LORD, king of Judah, who sits on the throne of David, you, and your servants, and your people who enter in by these gates. ³Thus says the LORD: "Execute justice and righteousness, and deliver him who is robbed out of the hand of the oppressor: and do no wrong, do no violence, to the foreigner, the fatherless, nor the widow; neither shed innocent blood in this place. ⁴For if you do this thing indeed, then shall there enter in by the gates of this house kings sitting on the throne of David, riding in chariots and on horses, he, and his servants, and his people. ⁵But if you will not hear these words, I swear by myself, says the LORD, that this house shall become a desolation." ⁶For thus says the LORD concerning the house of the king of Judah: "You are Gilead to me, the head of Lebanon. Yet surely I will make you a wilderness, cities which are not inhabited. ⁷I will prepare destroyers against you, everyone with his weapons; and they shall cut down your choice cedars, and cast them into the fire. ⁸Many nations shall pass by this city, and they shall say every man to his neighbor, 'Why has the LORD done thus to this great city?' ⁹Then they shall answer, 'Because they forsook the covenant of the LORD their God, and worshiped other gods, and served them.' ¹⁰Do not weep for the dead, neither bemoan him; but weep bitterly for him who goes away; for he shall return no more, nor see his native country." ¹¹For thus says the LORD touching Shallum the son of Josiah, king of Judah, who reigned instead of Josiah his father, and who went forth out of this place: "He shall not return

there any more. ¹² But in the place where they have led him captive, there shall he die, and he shall see this land no more." ¹³ Woe to him who builds his house by unrighteousness, and his rooms by injustice; who uses his neighbor's service without wages, and doesn't give him his hire; ¹⁴ who says, "I will build me a wide house and spacious rooms," and cuts him out windows; and it is ceiling with cedar, and painted with vermilion. ¹⁵ Shall you reign, because you strive to excel in cedar? Did not your father eat and drink, and do justice and righteousness? Then it was well with him. ¹⁶ He judged the cause of the poor and needy; then it was well. Wasn't this to know me?' says the LORD. ¹⁷ "But your eyes and your heart are not but for your covetousness, and for shedding innocent blood, and for oppression, and for violence, to do it. ¹⁸ Therefore thus says the LORD concerning Jehoiakim the son of Josiah, king of Judah: "they shall not lament for him, saying, 'Ah my brother.' or, 'Ah sister.' They shall not lament for him, saying, 'Ah lord.' or, 'Ah his glory.' ¹⁹ He shall be buried with the burial of a donkey, drawn and cast forth beyond the gates of Jerusalem. ²⁰ Go up to Lebanon, and cry; and lift up your voice in Bashan, and cry from Abarim; for all your lovers are destroyed. ²¹ I spoke to you in your prosperity; but you said, 'I will not hear.' This has been your way from your youth, that you did not obey my voice. ²² The wind shall feed all your shepherds, and your lovers shall go into captivity: surely then you will be ashamed and confounded for all your wickedness. ²³ Inhabitant of Lebanon, who makes your nest in the cedars, how greatly to be pitied you will be when pangs come on you, the pain as of a woman in travail. ²⁴ As I live," says the LORD, "though Coniah the son of Jehoiakim king of Judah were the signet on my right hand, yet would I pluck you there; ²⁵ and I will give you into the hand of those who seek your life, and into the hand of them of whom you are afraid, even into the hand of Nebuchadnezzar king of Babylon, and into the hand of the Chaldeans. ²⁶ I will cast you out, and your mother who bore you, into another country, where you were not born; and there you will die. ²⁷ But to the land whereunto their soul longs to return, there shall they not return."

²⁸Is this man Coniah a despised broken vessel? Is he a vessel in which none delights? Why are they cast out, he and his seed, and are cast into the land which they do not know? ²⁹O earth, earth, earth, hear the word of the LORD. ³⁰Thus says the LORD, "Write this man childless, a man who shall not prosper in his days; for no more shall a man of his seed prosper, sitting on the throne of David, and ruling in Judah."

QUESTIONS

QUESTION 1   b

According to Jeremiah chapter 22, when the Lord asked Prophet Jeremiah to speak to the king of Judah:

Who else was the message meant for?

QUESTION 2   b1

According to Jeremiah chapter 22:

Mention three things God said the kings on the throne of David should do to avoid destruction.

QUESTION 3   CPC 2

Jeremiah chapter 22:3–5 says,

"Thus says the LORD: "Execute justice and righteousness, and deliver him who is robbed out of the hand of the oppressor: and do no wrong, do no violence, to the foreigner, the fatherless, nor the widow; neither shed innocent blood in this place."

Complete verses 4 and 5.

QUESTION 4   CPC

Jeremiah chapter 22:6–7 says,

"For thus says the LORD concerning the house of the king of Judah: "You are Gilead to me, the head of Lebanon. Yet surely I will make you a wilderness, cities which are not inhabited."

Complete verse 7.

QUESTION 5   b1

Jeremiah chapter 22:8 says, *"Many nations shall pass by this city, and they shall say every man to his neighbor, 'Why has the LORD done thus to this great city?'"*

What response did the Lord say would be given to the above question?

QUESTION 6   CPC 2

Jeremiah chapter 22:10–12 says,

"Do not weep for the dead, neither bemoan him; but weep bitterly for him who goes away; for he shall return no more, nor see his native country."

Complete verses 11 and 12.

QUESTION 7   c

Jeremiah chapter 22:10 says, *"Do not weep for the dead, neither bemoan him; but weep bitterly for him who goes away; for he shall return no more, nor see his native country."*

Who is the one that goes away in the above passage, how long did he reign, who captured him and who succeeded him?

QUESTION 8   CPB

Jeremiah chapter 22:14–15 says,

"who says, "I will build me a wide house and spacious rooms," and cuts him out windows; and it is ceiling with cedar, and painted with vermilion."

Complete verse 15.

QUESTION 9   b

According to Jeremiah chapter 22:

Why was everything well with Josiah?

QUESTION 10   **b**

According to Jeremiah chapter 22:

What did God say was the meaning of knowing Him?

QUESTION 11   **b**

"He shall be buried with the burial of a donkey, drawn and cast forth beyond the gates of Jerusalem."

Who is the above quote talking about?

QUESTION 12   **b**

"they shall not lament for him, saying, 'Ah my brother. or, Ah sister."

Who is the above quote talking about?

QUESTION 13   **CPB**

Jeremiah chapter 22:20–21 says,

"Go up to Lebanon, and cry; and lift up your voice in Bashan, and cry from Abarim; for all your lovers are destroyed."

Complete verse 21.

QUESTION 14   **b2**

According to Jeremiah chapter 22:

Mention three things God said about Coniah or Jehoiachin.

QUESTION 15   **b1**

What was Jehoiakim's former name, and who changed it to Jehoiakim?

QUESTION 16   **a**

According to Jeremiah chapter 22:

Who was the father of King Coniah or Jehoiachin?

QUESTION 17   **a**

According to Jeremiah chapter 22:

Who did God say He would cast out even if he were the signet on His finger?

QUESTION 18   CPC

Jeremiah chapter 22:29–30 says,

"O earth, earth, earth, hear the word of the LORD."

Complete verse 30.

QUESTION 19   b1

Jeremiah chapter 22 mentions Josiah as one of the kings of Judah:

Who did he succeed as King of Judah?

QUESTION 20   b1

Jeremiah chapter 22 mentions Josiah as one of the kings of Judah:

How long did Josiah reign in Judah?

QUESTION 21   b2

Jeremiah chapter 22 mentions Josiah as one of the kings of Judah:

How did Josiah leave his position as King of Judah? Give a Bible reference for your answer.

QUESTION 22   b1

Jeremiah chapter 22 mentions Josiah as one of the kings of Judah:

Who succeeded Josiah as King of Judah, and how were they related?

QUESTION 23   b1

How long did Shallum or Jehoahaz reign as king in Judah?

QUESTION 24   b1

How did Shallum or Jehoahaz leave his position as king of Judah?

QUESTION 25   b1

Who succeeded Shallum or Jehoahaz as king in Judah, and how were they related?

QUESTION 26   **b1**

Jeremiah chapter 22 mentions Jehoiakim as one of the kings in Judah:

How long did he reign as king in Judah?

QUESTION 27   **b1**

Jeremiah chapter 22 mentions Jehoiakim as one of the kings in Judah:

Who succeeded Jehoiakim as king of Judah, and how were they related?

QUESTION 28   **b1**

Jeremiah chapter 22 mentions Coniah as one of the kings in Judah:

How long did Coniah or Jehoiachin reign as king in Judah?

QUESTION 29   **b1**

Jeremiah chapter 22 mentions Coniah as one of the kings in Judah:

How did Coniah or Jehoiachin leave his position as king of Judah?

QUESTION 30   **b1**

Jeremiah chapter 22 mentions Coniah as one of the kings in Judah:

Who succeeded Coniah or Jehoiachin as king of Judah, and how were they related?

QUESTION 31   **b1**

How did Zedekiah become king of Judah?

QUESTION 32   **b1**

How long did Zedekiah reign as king in Judah?

QUESTION 33   **b1**

How did Zedekiah leave his position as king of Judah?

QUESTION 34   **b1**

Who succeeded King Zedekiah, and how were they related?

QUESTION 35   **b1**

What was Zedekiah's former name, and who changed it to Zedekiah?

QUESTION 36   **b2**

According to the book of Jeremiah:

Mention the five last kings who reigned in Judah before Gedaliah became governor in their order.

QUESTION 37   **CMB**

Read Jeremiah chapter 22:13–16, preach or write a commentary on the passage with emphasis on salvation.

ANSWERS

ANSWER TO QUESTION 1   **b**

The message was also meant for the servants or officials and people who entered through the gate (Jeremiah 22:2).

ANSWER TO QUESTION 2   **b1**

- To execute justice and righteousness
- To deliver those who have been robbed out of the hand of their oppressors
- Do no wrong or violence to foreigners, fatherless or orphans, and widows
- Do not shed innocent blood (Jeremiah 22:2–4).

ANSWER TO QUESTION 3   **CPC 2**

"⁴For if you do this thing indeed, then shall there enter in by the gates of this house kings sitting on the throne of David, riding in chariots and on horses, he, and his servants, and his people. ⁵But if you will not hear these words, I swear by myself, says the LORD, that this house shall become a desolation." (Jeremiah 22:4–5.)

ANSWER TO QUESTION 4   CPC

"⁷I will prepare destroyers against you, everyone with his weapons; and they shall cut down your choice cedars, and cast them into the fire." (Jeremiah 22:7.)

ANSWER TO QUESTION 5   b1

"⁹Because they forsook the covenant of the LORD their God, and worshiped other gods, and served them." (Jeremiah 22:9.)

ANSWER TO QUESTION 6   CPC 2

"¹¹For thus says the LORD touching Shallum the son of Josiah, king of Judah, who reigned instead of Josiah his father, and who went forth out of this place: "He shall not return there any more. ¹²But in the place where they have led him captive, there shall he die, and he shall see this land no more."" (Jeremiah 22:11–12.)

ANSWER TO QUESTION 7   c

- Shallum or Jehoahaz
- 3 months
- Pharoah Necho
- Eliakim or Jehoiakim (Jeremiah 22:11–12, 2 Kings 23:30–35).

ANSWER TO QUESTION 8   CPB

"¹⁵Shall you reign, because you strive to excel in cedar? Did not your father eat and drink, and do justice and righteousness? Then it was well with him." (Jeremiah 22:15.)

ANSWER TO QUESTION 9   b

Because he was just and righteous

Or

Because he judged the cause of the poor and needy

(Jeremiah 22:15–16).

ANSWER TO QUESTION 10   b

Judging the cause of the poor and needy

Or

Giving justice and help to the poor and needy (Jeremiah 22:16).

ANSWER TO QUESTION 11   b

King Jehoiakim (Jeremiah 22:18–19).

ANSWER TO QUESTION 12   b

King Jehoiakim (Jeremiah 22:18–19).

ANSWER TO QUESTION 13   CPB

"²¹I spoke to you in your prosperity; but you said, 'I will not hear.' This has been your way from your youth, that you did not obey my voice." (Jeremiah 22:21.)

ANSWER TO QUESTION 14   b2

- God said He would pluck out Jehoiachin or Coniah, son of Jehoiakim, king of Judah, even if he were the signet on God's right hand
- God would give him into the hands of those who seek his life, and into the hand of King Nebuchadnezzar of Babylon and the Chaldeans whom he feared
- God also said He would cast out Jehoiachin and his mother into another country and there he would die
- He shall not return to his land he longed for (Jeremiah 22:24–27).

ANSWER TO QUESTION 15   b1

- Eliakim
- Pharoah Necho (2 Kings 23:34).

ANSWER TO QUESTION 16   a

Jehoiakim (Jeremiah 22:24).

ANSWER TO QUESTION 17   a

King Coniah or Jehoiachin or Jeconiah (Jeremiah 22:24).

ANSWER TO QUESTION 18   CPC

"*30Thus says the LORD, "Write this man childless, a man who shall not prosper in his days; for no more shall a man of his seed prosper, sitting on the throne of David, and ruling in Judah."* (Jeremiah 22:30.)

ANSWER TO QUESTION 19   b1

He succeeded his father, Amon (2 Kings 21:26).

ANSWER TO QUESTION 20   b1

31 years (2 Kings 22:1).

ANSWER TO QUESTION 21   b2

- He was killed in battle (by Pharaoh Necho)
- 2 Kings 23:29–30

    Or

    He died in Jerusalem after being injured in a battle (by Pharaoh Necho)
    2 Chronicles 35:22–24.

ANSWER TO QUESTION 22   b1

- Shallum or Jehoahaz
- He was his son (2 Kings 23:31).

ANSWER TO QUESTION 23   b1

3 months (2 Kings 23:31).

ANSWER TO QUESTION 24   b1

He was deposed from the throne by Pharaoh Necho (2 Kings 23:33).

ANSWER TO QUESTION 25   b1

- Jehoiakim
- He was his son (2 Kings 23:34).

ANSWER TO QUESTION 26   b1

11 years (2 Kings 23:36).

ANSWER TO QUESTION 27   b1

- Jehoiachin or Coniah or Jeconiah
- He was his son (2 Kings 24:6).

ANSWER TO QUESTION 28   b1

3 months (2 Kings 24:8).

ANSWER TO QUESTION 29   b1

He was exiled to Babylon by King Nebuchadnezzar (2 Kings 24:15).

ANSWER TO QUESTION 30   b1

- Zedekiah or Mattaniah (2 Kings 24:17)
- He was his uncle (2 Kings 24:17).

ANSWER TO QUESTION 31   b1

King Nebuchadnezzar made him king (2 Kings 24:17).

ANSWER TO QUESTION 32   b1

11 years (2 Kings 24:18).

ANSWER TO QUESTION 33   b1

He was arrested by the Babylonian army and brought to Riblah, where he was punished for rebelling against King Nebuchadnezzar (2 Kings 25:6).

ANSWER TO QUESTION 34   b1

- Gedaliah was placed as governor of Judah
- They were not related (for he was not of royal blood) (2 Kings 25:22–23).

ANSWER TO QUESTION 35   b1

- Mattaniah
- King Nebuchadnezzar (2 Kings 24:17).

ANSWER TO QUESTION 36   b2

- Josiah
- Shallum or Jehoahaz
- Jehoiakim
- Coniah or Jehoiachin or Jeconiah
- Zedekiah (Jeremiah chapter 22, Jeremiah 37:1).

HINT TO QUESTION 37   CMB

God spoke concerning Jehoiakim, telling him to look at Josiah, his father, who lived well and maintained justice and righteousness, and it was well with him, saying that is what it is to know Him. God is not against being wealthy, but becoming wealthy by ungodly means. We can become successful in life by following after righteousness. We do not have to exploit others or cheat to become successful.

CHAPTER 23

JEREMIAH CHAPTER 23

"Woe to the shepherds who destroy and scatter the sheep of my pasture." says the LORD. ^{2}*Therefore thus says the LORD, the God of Israel, against the shepherds who feed my people: "You have scattered my flock, and driven them away, and have not visited them; look, I will visit on you the evil of your doings," says the LORD.* ^{3}*"I will gather the remnant of my flock out of all the countries where I have driven them, and will bring them again to their folds; and they shall be fruitful and multiply.* ^{4}*I will set up shepherds over them, who shall feed them; and they shall fear no more, nor be dismayed, neither shall any be lacking," says the LORD.* ^{5}*"Look, the days come," says the LORD, "that I will raise to David a righteous Branch, and he shall reign as king and deal wisely, and shall execute justice and righteousness in the land.* ^{6}*In his days Judah shall be saved, and Israel shall dwell safely; and this is his name by which he shall be called: 'The LORD our righteousness.'* ^{7}*Therefore look, the days come," says the LORD, "that they shall no more say, 'As the LORD lives, who brought up the sons of Israel out of the land of Egypt';* ^{8}*but, 'As the LORD lives, who brought up and who led the seed of the house of Israel out of the north country, and from all the countries where he had driven them.' They shall dwell in their own land."'* ^{9}*Concerning the prophets: My heart within me is broken, all my bones shake; I am like a drunken man, and like a man whom wine has overcome, because of the LORD, and because of his holy words.* ^{10}*For the land is full of adulterers; for because of swearing the land mourns; the pastures of the wilderness are dried up. "Their course*

is evil, and their might is not right; [11] *for both prophet and priest are profane; yes, in my house have I found their wickedness," says the LORD.* [12] *"Therefore their way shall be to them as slippery places in the darkness: they shall be driven on, and fall in it; for I will bring evil on them, even the year of their visitation," says the LORD.* [13] *"I have seen folly in the prophets of Samaria; they prophesied by Baal, and caused my people Israel to err.* [14] *In the prophets of Jerusalem also I have seen a horrible thing: they commit adultery, and walk in lies; and they strengthen the hands of evildoers, so that none does return from his wickedness: they are all of them become to me as Sodom, and its inhabitants as Gomorrah.* [15] *Therefore thus says the LORD of hosts concerning the prophets: 'Look, I will feed them with wormwood, and make them drink the water of gall; for from the prophets of Jerusalem is ungodliness gone forth into all the land.'* [16] *Thus says the LORD of hosts, 'Do not listen to the words of the prophets who prophesy to you: they teach you vanity; they speak a vision of their own heart, and not out of the mouth of the LORD.* [17] *They say continually to those who despise me, "The LORD has said, 'You shall have peace'"; and to everyone who walks in the stubbornness of his own heart they say, "No evil shall come on you."* [18] *For who has stood in the council of the LORD, that he should perceive and hear his word? Who has marked my word, and heard it?* [19] *Look, the storm of the LORD, his wrath, has gone forth. Yes, a whirling storm. It shall burst on the head of the wicked.* [20] *The anger of the LORD shall not return, until he has executed, and until he have performed the intents of his heart: in the latter days you shall understand it perfectly.* [21] *I sent not these prophets, yet they ran: I did not speak to them, yet they prophesied.* [22] *But if they had stood in my council, then had they caused my people to hear my words, and had turned them from their evil way, and from the evil of their doings.* [23] *Am I a God at hand,' says the LORD, 'and not a God afar off?* [24] *Can any hide himself in secret places so that I shall not see him?' says the LORD. 'Do I not fill heaven and earth?' says the LORD.* [25] *'I have heard what the prophets have said, who prophesy lies in my name, saying, "I have dreamed, I have dreamed." ²⁶How long shall this be in the heart of the prophets who prophesy lies, even the prophets of the deceit of their own heart, ²⁷who think to cause my people to forget my name by their dreams which they tell every man to his neighbor, as their fathers forgot my name for Baal. ²⁸The prophet who has a dream, let him tell a dream; and he who has my word, let him speak my word faithfully. What is the straw to the wheat?' says the LORD. ²⁹'Isn't my word like fire?' says the LORD; 'and like a hammer that breaks the rock in pieces? ³⁰Therefore look, I am against the prophets,' says the LORD, 'who steal my words everyone from his neighbor. ³¹Look, I am against the prophets,' says the LORD, 'who use their tongues, and say, "He says." ³²Look, I am against the prophets who prophesy lying dreams,' says the LORD, 'and do tell them, and cause my people to err by their lies, and by their vain boasting: yet I did not send them, nor commanded them; neither do they profit this people at all,' says the LORD. ³³'When this people, or the prophet, or a priest, shall ask you, saying, "What is the burden of the LORD?" Then you shall tell them, "You are the burden, and I will cast you off," says the LORD. ³⁴As for the prophet, and the priest, and the people, who shall say, "The burden of the LORD," I will even punish that man and his house. ³⁵You shall say everyone to his neighbor, and everyone to his brother, "What has the LORD answered?" and, "What has the LORD spoken?" ³⁶You shall mention the burden of the LORD no more: for every man's own word shall be his burden; for you have perverted the words of the living God, of the LORD of hosts our God. ³⁷You shall say to the prophet, "What has the LORD answered you?" and, "What has the LORD spoken?" ³⁸But if you say, "The burden of the LORD"; therefore thus says the LORD: Because you say this word, "The burden of the LORD," and I have sent to you, saying, "You shall not say, 'The burden of the LORD'"; ³⁹therefore, look, I will surely lift you up and I will cast you off, and the city that I gave to you and to your fathers, away from my presence: ⁴⁰and I will bring an everlasting reproach on you, and a perpetual shame, which shall not be forgotten."'*

QUESTIONS

QUESTION 1   b

According to Jeremiah chapter 23:

What did God say the shepherds of His people had done to His people?

QUESTION 2   CPB

Jeremiah chapter 23:3–4 says,

"I will gather the remnant of my flock out of all the countries where I have driven them, and will bring them again to their folds; and they shall be fruitful and multiply."

Complete verse 4.

QUESTION 3   a

Jeremiah chapter 23:5 says, *"Look, the days come,"* says the LORD, *"that I will raise to David a righteous Branch, and he shall reign as king and deal wisely, and shall execute justice and righteousness in the land."*

Who does the righteous Branch refer to?

QUESTION 4   CTX

"Concerning the prophets: My heart within me is broken, all my bones shake; I am like a drunken man, and like a man whom wine has overcome...."

Give the context of the above quote:

Who said it, to who, and under what circumstance?

QUESTION 5   CPC

Jeremiah chapter 23:11–12 says,

"for both prophet and priest are profane; yes, in my house have I found their wickedness," says the LORD.""

Complete verse 12.

QUESTION 6   **CPC**

Jeremiah chapter 23:13–14 says,

"I have seen folly in the prophets of Samaria; they prophesied by Baal, and caused my people Israel to err."

Complete verse 14.

QUESTION 7   **CPC**

Jeremiah chapter 23:16–17 says,

"Thus says the LORD of hosts, 'Do not listen to the words of the prophets who prophesy to you: they teach you vanity; they speak a vision of their own heart, and not out of the mouth of the LORD."

Complete verse 17.

QUESTION 8   **CPB**

Jeremiah chapter 23:21–22 says,

"I sent not these prophets, yet they ran: I did not speak to them, yet they prophesied."

Complete verse 22.

QUESTION 9   **CPB**

Jeremiah chapter 23:23–24 says,

"'Am I a God at hand,' says the LORD, 'and not a God afar off?'"

Complete verse 24.

QUESTION 10   **CPC 2**

Jeremiah chapter 23:25–27 says,

"I have heard what the prophets have said, who prophesy lies in my name, saying, "I have dreamed, I have dreamed.""

Complete verses 26 and 27.

QUESTION 11   **CPB**

Jeremiah chapter 23:28–29 says,

"The prophet who has a dream, let him tell a dream; and he who has my word, let him speak my word faithfully. What is the straw to the wheat?' says the LORD."

Complete verse 29.

QUESTION 12   a

According to Jeremiah chapter 23, when God mentioned the straw and wheat:

What did the straw represent?

QUESTION 13   a

According to Jeremiah chapter 23, when God mentioned the straw and wheat:

What did the wheat represent?

QUESTION 14   b

According to Jeremiah chapter 23:

Mention two things the Lord likened His words to.

QUESTION 15   **CPC 2**

Jeremiah chapter 23:30–32 says,

"Therefore look, I am against the prophets,' says the LORD, 'who steal my words everyone from his neighbor."

Complete verses 31 and 32.

QUESTION 16   b

According to Jeremiah chapter 23:

What response did God say Jeremiah should give to a priest, prophet or person who would ask him what the burden of the Lord was?

QUESTION 17   **b1**

According to Jeremiah chapter 23:

Mention two things the Lord said would happen to anyone who says, 'the burden of the Lord' or 'prophecy from the Lord.'

QUESTION 18   **CMC**

Read Jeremiah chapter 23:1–5, preach or write a commentary on the passage with emphasis on salvation.

QUESTION 19   **CMC**

Read Jeremiah chapter 23:9–10, preach or write a commentary on the passage with emphasis on salvation.

QUESTION 20   **CMC**

Read Jeremiah chapter 23:13–14,16, 25–26, 28–29, preach or write a commentary on the passage with emphasis on salvation.

QUESTION 21   **CMC**

Read Jeremiah chapter 23:21–22, preach or write a commentary on the passage with emphasis on salvation.

QUESTION 22   **CMC**

Read Jeremiah chapter 23:23–24, preach or write a commentary on the passage with emphasis on salvation.

ANSWERS

ANSWER TO QUESTION 1   **b**

They had scattered them, driven them away (and not visited them or cared for them) (Jeremiah 23:2).

ANSWER TO QUESTION 2   **CPB**

"⁴I will set up shepherds over them, who shall feed them; and they shall fear no more, nor be dismayed, neither shall any be lacking," says the LORD." (Jeremiah 23:4.)

ANSWER TO QUESTION 3   a

Jesus Christ (Jeremiah 23:5; Matthew 1:1).

ANSWER TO QUESTION 4   CTX

- Prophet Jeremiah
- To the people of Judah and Jerusalem
- When he heard of the judgement that God passed on the false prophets (Jeremiah 23:9).

ANSWER TO QUESTION 5   CPC

"12"Therefore their way shall be to them as slippery places in the darkness: they shall be driven on, and fall in it; for I will bring evil on them, even the year of their visitation," says the LORD." (Jeremiah 23:12.)

ANSWER TO QUESTION 6   CPC

"14In the prophets of Jerusalem also I have seen a horrible thing: they commit adultery, and walk in lies; and they strengthen the hands of evildoers, so that none does return from his wickedness: they are all of them become to me as Sodom, and its inhabitants as Gomorrah." (Jeremiah 23:14.)

ANSWER TO QUESTION 7   CPC

"17They say continually to those who despise me, "The LORD has said, 'You shall have peace'"; and to everyone who walks in the stubbornness of his own heart they say, "No evil shall come on you."" (Jeremiah 23:17.)

ANSWER TO QUESTION 8   CPB

"22But if they had stood in my council, then had they caused my people to hear my words, and had turned them from their evil way, and from the evil of their doings." (Jeremiah 23:22.)

ANSWER TO QUESTION 9   CPB

"24Can any hide himself in secret places so that I shall not see him?' says the LORD. 'Do I not fill heaven and earth?' says the LORD." (Jeremiah 23:24.)

ANSWER TO QUESTION 10   CPC 2

"²⁶How long shall this be in the heart of the prophets who prophesy lies, even the prophets of the deceit of their own heart, ²⁷who think to cause my people to forget my name by their dreams which they tell every man to his neighbor, as their fathers forgot my name for Baal." (Jeremiah 23:26–27.)

ANSWER TO QUESTION 11   CPB

"²⁹'Isn't my word like fire?' says the LORD; 'and like a hammer that breaks the rock in pieces?" (Jeremiah 23:29.)

ANSWER TO QUESTION 12   a

The dreams the false prophets claimed to have from God (Jeremiah 23:28).

ANSWER TO QUESTION 13   a

God's words (from a true prophet) (Jeremiah 23:28).

ANSWER TO QUESTION 14   b

- Fire
- A hammer that breaks a rock to pieces (Jeremiah 23:29).

ANSWER TO QUESTION 15   CPC 2

"³¹Look, I am against the prophets,' says the LORD, 'who use their tongues, and say, "He says." ³²Look, I am against the prophets who prophesy lying dreams,' says the LORD, 'and do tell them, and cause my people to err by their lies, and by their vain boasting: yet I did not send them, nor commanded them; neither do they profit this people at all,' says the LORD." (Jeremiah 23:31–32.)

ANSWER TO QUESTION 16   b

"You are the burden, and I will cast you off." (Jeremiah 23:33.)

ANSWER TO QUESTION 17   b1

- He will cast them off from His presence, together with the city He gave to them and their fathers
- He would bring an everlasting reproach and a perpetual shame on them which shall not be forgotten (Jeremiah 23:39–40).

HINTS TO QUESTION 18   CMC

- As a loving Shepherd, God is concerned about every aspect of our lives, particularly our spiritual well-being.
- Just like God held the religious leaders of old accountable for misleading His people, today, Christian leaders who are the shepherds of God's people should know that their authority is from God and they are accountable to God.
- Christ is the Great Shepherd all should learn from.

HINT TO QUESTION 19   CMC

Just as Jeremiah lamented over the evil perpetrated by the prophets and people in Judah, a true child of God will always feel bad about sin in the land, and that burden will move such a person to intercede for and preach the gospel of salvation to others.

HINTS TO QUESTION 20   CMC

- The verses under consideration let us understand that false prophets operate in diverse forms; some use divination to prophesy, while others speak lies out of their imaginations but claim they are from God. These tactics of false prophets are still prevalent in our society today. Therefore, we should beware of false prophets and seek righteousness, so we do not fall prey to their schemes.
- The word of God is like fire and a hammer, testing and breaking falsehood (verses 28–29).

HINT TO QUESTION 21   CMC

No one can give what they do not have. For a person to teach the truth, they must know the truth and live by it. For one to know and speak the mind of God, one must spend time in the presence of God. And for one to spend time in the presence of the Lord, one must live holy.

HINT TO QUESTION 22   CMC

There is no distance between God and us. No one should delude themself into thinking they can commit sin and hide from God.

CHAPTER 24

JEREMIAH CHAPTER 24

"The LORD showed me, and look, two baskets of figs set before the LORD's temple, after that Nebuchadnezzar king of Babylon had carried away captive Jeconiah the son of Jehoiakim, king of Judah, and the officials of Judah, with the craftsmen and smiths, from Jerusalem, and had brought them to Babylon. ²One basket had very good figs, like the figs that are first-ripe; and the other basket had very bad figs, which could not be eaten, they were so bad. ³Then the LORD said to me, "What do you see, Jeremiah?" I said, "Figs; the good figs, very good; and the bad, very bad, that can't be eaten, they are so bad." ⁴The word of the LORD came to me, saying, ⁵"Thus says the LORD, the God of Israel: 'Like these good figs, so will I regard the captives of Judah, whom I have sent out of this place into the land of the Chaldeans, for good. ⁶For I will set my eyes on them for good, and I will bring them again to this land: and I will build them, and not pull them down; and I will plant them, and not pluck them up. ⁷I will give them a heart to know me, that I am the LORD: and they shall be my people, and I will be their God; for they shall return to me with their whole heart.' ⁸As the bad figs, which can't be eaten, they are so bad, surely thus says the LORD, 'So will I give up Zedekiah the king of Judah, and his officials, and the remnant of Jerusalem, who remain in this land, and those who dwell in the land of Egypt, ⁹I will even give them up to be tossed back and forth among all the kingdoms of the earth for evil; to be a reproach and a proverb, a taunt and a curse, in all places where I shall drive them. ¹⁰I will send the sword, the famine,

and the pestilence, among them, until they be consumed from off the land that I gave to them and to their fathers.'"

QUESTIONS

QUESTION 1   b

According to Jeremiah chapter 24, after King Nebuchadnezzar had taken captive Jehoiachin, king of Judah, to Babylon:

What was the first vision God gave to Prophet Jeremiah?

QUESTION 2   b1

According to Jeremiah chapter 24:

Mention three sets of people the king of Babylon carried into exile alongside King Jehoiachin of Judah.

QUESTION 3   b1

According to Jeremiah chapter 24:

What do the two baskets of figs in Jeremiah's vision represent?

QUESTION 4   b1

According to Jeremiah chapter 24:

Mention three things God said about the exiles He sent to Babylon.

QUESTION 5   b1

According to Jeremiah chapter 24:

Mention two things God said about those who remained in Jerusalem and those who lived in Egypt.

QUESTION 6   CTX

"I will give them a heart to know me, that I am the LORD...."

Give the context of the above quote:

Who said it, to who, and under what circumstance?

QUESTION 7   **b**

According to Jeremiah chapter 24:

How long did God say He would send sword, famine, and pestilence to the people of Judah?

QUESTION 8   **CMC**

Read Jeremiah chapter 24:1–10, preach or write a commentary on the passage with focus on verses 5–10 and with emphasis on salvation.

ANSWERS

ANSWER TO QUESTION 1   **b**

A vision of two baskets of figs placed in front of the Lord's temple (Jeremiah 24:1).

ANSWER TO QUESTION 2   **b1**

- The officials of Judah
- Craftsmen or skilled workers
- Smiths or Artisans (Jeremiah 24:1).

ANSWER TO QUESTION 3   **b1**

- The first basket represents the exiles sent from Judah to the land of the Babylonians
- The second basket represents King Zedekiah of Judah, his officials, all the people left in Jerusalem, and those who lived in Egypt (Jeremiah 24:4–8).

ANSWER TO QUESTION 4   **b1**

- The Lord said He would set His eyes on them for good
- He would bring them back to their land
- He would build them up and not pull them down
- He would plant them and not pluck them up
- He would give them the heart to know that He is the Lord

- They would be His people, and He would be their God, for they would return to Him with their whole hearts (Jeremiah 24:6–7).

ANSWER TO QUESTION 5   b1

- He would give them up to be tossed back and forth among all the kingdoms of the earth for evil or make them an object of horror. They would be a reproach, a taunt, and a curse in all the places He will drive them.
- He said He would send sword or war, famine, and pestilence or disease until they are consumed from off the land He gave to them and their fathers (Jeremiah 24:8–10).

ANSWER TO QUESTION 6   CTX

- God
- To Prophet Jeremiah
- When He was explaining to him the vision of the good and bad figs

Or

When He was talking about the people He sent to exile in Babylon, those that remained in Jerusalem, and those that went to live in Egypt (Jeremiah 24:7).

ANSWER TO QUESTION 7   b

Until they were consumed from the land which He gave to them and their fathers (Jeremiah 24:10).

HINTS TO QUESTION 8   CMC

- For King Jeconiah, captivity in Babylon may have seemed the worst thing, but it turned out to be for his good. Going through God's refining process is always for our good.
- It is okay to do everything within our power to come out of our undesirable situations, but we should be careful and sensitive to God's leading so that we do not act against His will for us.

CHAPTER 25

JEREMIAH CHAPTER 25

"The word that came to Jeremiah concerning all the people of Judah, in the fourth year of Jehoiakim the son of Josiah, king of Judah (the same was the first year of Nebuchadnezzar king of Babylon), ²which Jeremiah the prophet spoke to all the people of Judah, and to all the inhabitants of Jerusalem, saying: ³"From the thirteenth year of Josiah the son of Amon, king of Judah, even to this day, these twenty-three years, the word of the LORD has come to me, and I have spoken to you, rising up early and speaking; but you have not listened. ⁴The LORD has sent to you all his servants the prophets, rising up early and sending them (but you have not listened, nor inclined your ear to hear) ⁵saying, 'Return now everyone from his evil way, and from the evil of your doings, and dwell in the land that the LORD has given to you and to your fathers, from of old and even forevermore; ⁶and do not go after other gods to serve them or worship them, and do not provoke me to anger with the work of your hands; and I will do you no harm. ⁷Yet you have not listened to me,' says the LORD; 'that you may provoke me to anger with the work of your hands to your own hurt.' ⁸Therefore thus says the LORD of hosts: 'Because you have not heard my words, ⁹behold, I will send and take all the families of the north,' says the LORD, 'and I will send to Nebuchadnezzar the king of Babylon, my servant, and will bring them against this land, and against its inhabitants, and against all these nations around; and I will utterly destroy them, and make them an astonishment, and a hissing, and perpetual desolations.

10Moreover I will take from them the voice of mirth and the voice of gladness, the voice of the bridegroom and the voice of the bride, the sound of the millstones, and the light of the lamp. 11This whole land shall be a desolation, and an astonishment; and these nations shall serve the king of Babylon seventy years. 12It shall happen, when seventy years are accomplished, that I will punish the king of Babylon, and that nation, says the LORD, for their iniquity, and the land of the Chaldeans; and I will make it desolate forever. 13I will bring on that land all my words which I have pronounced against it, even all that is written in this book, which Jeremiah has prophesied against all the nations. 14For many nations and great kings shall make bondservants of them, even of them; and I will recompense them according to their deeds, and according to the work of their hands.'" 15For thus says the LORD, the God of Israel, to me: "Take this cup of the wine of wrath at my hand, and cause all the nations, to whom I send you, to drink it. 16They shall drink, and reel back and forth, and be mad, because of the sword that I will send among them." 17Then took I the cup at the LORD's hand, and made all the nations to drink, to whom the LORD had sent me: 18Jerusalem, and the cities of Judah, and its kings, and its officials, to make them a desolation, an astonishment, a hissing, and a curse, as it is this day; 19Pharaoh king of Egypt, and his servants, and his officials, and all his people; 20and all the mixed people, and all the kings of the land of the Uz, and all the kings of the Philistines, and Ashkelon, and Gaza, and Ekron, and the remnant of Ashdod; 21Edom, and Moab, and the children of Ammon; 22and all the kings of Tyre, and all the kings of Sidon, and the kings of the isle which is beyond the sea; 23Dedan, and Tema, and Buz, and all who have the corners of their beard cut off; 24and all the kings of Arabia, [and all the kings of the mixed people] who dwell in the wilderness; 25and all the kings of Zimri, and all the kings of Elam, and all the kings of the Medes; 26and all the kings of the north, far and near, one with another; and all the kingdoms of the world, which are on the surface of the earth: and the king of Sheshach shall drink after them. 27"You shall tell them, 'Thus says the LORD of hosts, the God of Israel: "Drink, and be drunk, vomit, fall, and rise no more, because of the sword which I will send among you."' [28] It shall be, if they refuse to take the cup at your hand to drink, then you shall tell them, 'Thus says the LORD of hosts: "You shall surely drink. [29] For, look, I begin to work evil at the city which is called by my name; and should you be utterly unpunished? You shall not be unpunished; for I will call for a sword on all the inhabitants of the earth,"' says the LORD of hosts. [30] Therefore prophesy you against them all these words, and tell them, 'The LORD will roar from on high, and utter his voice from his holy habitation; he will mightily roar against his fold; he will give a shout, as those who tread grapes, against all the inhabitants of the earth. [31] A noise shall come even to the end of the earth; for the LORD has a controversy with the nations; he will enter into judgment with all flesh: as for the wicked, he will give them to the sword,' says the LORD. [32] 'Thus says the LORD of hosts, 'Look, evil shall go forth from nation to nation, and a great storm shall be raised up from the uttermost parts of the earth.' [33] The slain of the LORD shall be at that day from one end of the earth even to the other end of the earth: they shall not be lamented, neither gathered, nor buried; they shall be dung on the surface of the ground. [34] Wail, you shepherds, and cry; and wallow in dust, you principal of the flock; for the days of your slaughter and of your dispersions are fully come, and you shall fall like a goodly vessel. [35] The shepherds shall have no way to flee, nor the principal of the flock to escape. [36] A voice of the cry of the shepherds, and the wailing of the principal of the flock. For the LORD lays waste their pasture. [37] The peaceable folds are brought to silence because of the fierce anger of the LORD. [38] He has left his covert, as the lion; for their land has become an astonishment because of the fierceness of the oppression, and because of his fierce anger."

QUESTIONS

QUESTION 1   **b**

According to Jeremiah chapter 25:

Who was the king of Judah when Nebuchadnezzar became king of Babylon, and in what year of his reign did Nebuchadnezzar become king of Babylon?

QUESTION 2   **a**

According to Jeremiah chapter 25:

For how many years had Jeremiah been prophesying in Judah before Nebuchadnezzar became king of Babylon?

QUESTION 3   **Tie**

Jeremiah chapter 25:3 says, *"From the thirteenth year of Josiah the son of Amon, king of Judah, even to this day, these twenty-three years, the word of the LORD has come to me...."*

Mention the kings that ruled during the twenty-three years of Jeremiah's prophesying and how long each of them ruled within that period, which makes up the twenty-three years.

QUESTION 4   **b**

According to Jeremiah chapter 25:

When Jeremiah started prophesying, who was the king in Judah and what year of his reign did Jeremiah start prophesying?

QUESTION 5   **CTX**

"The LORD has sent to you all his servants the prophets, rising up early and sending them (but you have not listened, nor inclined your ear to hear)"

Give the context of the above quote:

Who said it, to who, and under what circumstance?

QUESTION 6 CPC 2

Jeremiah chapter 25:4–6 says,

"The LORD has sent to you all his servants the prophets, rising up early and sending them (but you have not listened, nor inclined your ear to hear)"

Complete verses 5 and 6.

QUESTION 7 CPB

Jeremiah chapter 25:10–11 says,

"Moreover I will take from them the voice of mirth and the voice of gladness, the voice of the bridegroom and the voice of the bride, the sound of the millstones, and the light of the lamp."

Complete verse 11.

QUESTION 8 b2

According to Jeremiah chapter 25:

Mention three things God said would happen to Babylon after seventy years.

QUESTION 9 CTX

"I will bring on that land all my words which I have pronounced against it, even all that is written in this book...."

Give the context of the above quote:

Who said it, to who, and under what circumstance?

QUESTION 10 b1

Jeremiah chapter 25:15 says, *"Take this cup of the wine of wrath at my hand, and cause all the nations, to whom I send you, to drink it."*

What would be the effect of the wine of wrath on the nations that drank from the cup in the above passage?

QUESTION 11   b1

According to Jeremiah chapter 25:

How many towns of the Philistines drank from the cup of the Lord's anger? Mention them.

QUESTION 12   b

Jeremiah chapter 25:20 says, *"and all the mixed people, and all the kings of the land of the Uz...."*

Which notable Bible character lived in the land of Uz?

QUESTION 13   b1

Jeremiah chapter 25:21 says, *"Edom, and Moab, and the children of Ammon...."*

Whose descendants were the people of Edom, Moab, and Ammon?

QUESTION 14   b2

Jeremiah chapter 25:22 says, *"and all the kings of Tyre, and all the kings of Sidon, and the kings of the isle which is beyond the sea."*

What transpired between King Hiram of Tyre and King David and between King Hiram and Solomon?

QUESTION 15   b

Jeremiah chapter 25:26 says, *"and all the kings of the north, far and near, one with another; and all the kingdoms of the world, which are on the surface of the earth: and the king of Sheshach shall drink after them."*

What is another name for Sheshach?

QUESTION 16   CPB

Jeremiah chapter 25:27–28 says,

"You shall tell them, 'Thus says the LORD of hosts, the God of Israel: "Drink, and be drunk, vomit, fall, and rise no more, because of the sword which I will send among you.""'

Complete verse 28.

QUESTION 17   a

According to Jeremiah chapter 25:

How many nations were to drink from the cup of the Lord's anger from the hands of Prophet Jeremiah?

QUESTION 18   b

According to Jeremiah chapter 25:

Which nation was the last to drink from the cup of the Lord's anger from the hands of Jeremiah?

QUESTION 19   CTX

"The LORD will roar from on high, and utter his voice from his holy habitation...."

Give the context of the above quote:

Who said it, to who, and under what circumstance?

QUESTION 20   CPC

Jeremiah chapter 25:32–33 says,

"³²'Thus says the LORD of hosts, 'Look, evil shall go forth from nation to nation, and a great storm shall be raised up from the uttermost parts of the earth.'"

Complete verse 33.

QUESTION 21   b

Jeremiah chapter 25:34 says, *"Wail, you shepherds, and cry; and wallow in dust...."*

Why were the shepherds asked to wail?

QUESTION 22   CPB

Jeremiah chapter 25:37–38 says,

"³⁷The peaceable folds are brought to silence because of the fierce anger of the LORD."

Complete verse 38.

QUESTION 23   **CMB**

Read Jeremiah chapter 25:3–9, preach or write a commentary on the passage with emphasis on salvation.

QUESTION 24   **CMB**

Read Jeremiah chapter 25:8–12, preach or write a commentary on the passage with emphasis on salvation.

ANSWERS

ANSWER TO QUESTION 1   b

- Jehoiakim
- Fourth-year (Jeremiah 25:1).

ANSWER TO QUESTION 2   a

Twenty-three years (Jeremiah 25:1–3).

ANSWER TO QUESTION 3   Tie

Josiah: He ruled for 31 years, and Jeremiah started prophesying during his thirteenth-year rule. From his 13th year to the end of the 31st year of his rule are 18 years and some months (Jeremiah 25:3, 2 Chronicles 34:1).

Jehoahaz: 3 months (2 Kings 23:31).

Jehoiakim: Jeremiah made the above statement in the 4th year of his reign (Jeremiah 25:1).

Therefore, the sum of the years the three kings ruled within this period is approximately 23 years.

ANSWER TO QUESTION 4   b

- King Josiah
- Thirteenth year (Jeremiah 25:3).

ANSWER TO QUESTION 5   CTX

- Prophet Jeremiah
- To the people of Judah and Jerusalem
- When he talked to them about their refusal to hearken to the prophecies he had been giving them for the past 23 years, informing them of the impending captivity (Jeremiah 25:4).

ANSWER TO QUESTION 6   CPC 2

"⁵saying, 'Return now everyone from his evil way, and from the evil of your doings, and dwell in the land that the LORD has given to you and to your fathers, from of old and even forevermore; ⁶and do not go after other gods to serve them or worship them, and do not provoke me to anger with the work of your hands; and I will do you no harm." (Jeremiah 25:5–6.)

ANSWER TO QUESTION 7   CPB

"¹¹This whole land shall be a desolation, and an astonishment; and these nations shall serve the king of Babylon seventy years." (Jeremiah 25:11.)

ANSWER TO QUESTION 8   b2

- God said He would punish the king of Babylon and his people for their iniquities
- He will make Babylon desolate forever
- He will bring upon them all the words written in the book, all the words pronounced by Jeremiah against the nations
- Many nations and great kings shall make bondservants of them
- He will recompense them according to their deeds and the works of their hands (Jeremiah 25:12–14).

ANSWER TO QUESTION 9   CTX

- God, through Prophet Jeremiah
- To the people of Judah and Jerusalem
- When the Lord was telling them about what He would do to Babylon and its people after the seventy years of captivity (Jeremiah 25:13).

ANSWER TO QUESTION 10   b1

They would reel back and forth and be mad because of the sword God would send among them (Jeremiah 25:16).

ANSWER TO QUESTION 11   b1

- Four (4) towns
- The names of the towns are:
  1. Ashkelon
  2. Gaza
  3. Ekron
  4. Ashdod (Jeremiah 25:20).

ANSWER TO QUESTION 12   b

Job (Job 1:1).

ANSWER TO QUESTION 13   b1

The people of Edom were Esau's descendants, Jacob's (Israel's) twin brother (Genesis 25:19–26).

The people of Moab and Ammon were the descendants of Lot (Abraham's nephew), which he had from his two daughters (Genesis 19:30–38).

ANSWER TO QUESTION 14   b2

- King David was a friend to King Hiram of Tyre, who supplied him with cedars, carpenters, and masons he used in building his palace (2 Samuel 5:11)
- After the death of David, the relationship between King Hiram of Tyre and Israel continued with King Solomon. King Hiram of Tyre supplied materials and a workforce for building the temple, while King Solomon supplied him with foodstuff (1 Kings 5:1–18)
- The relationship between King Solomon and King Hiram graduated to a business relationship. Solomon built a fleet of ships while King Hiram sent experienced sailors to sail the ships, so they became business partners (1 Kings 9:26–28).

ANSWER TO QUESTION 15   b

Babylon

ANSWER TO QUESTION 16   CPB

"28 It shall be, if they refuse to take the cup at your hand to drink, then you shall tell them, 'Thus says the LORD of hosts: "You shall surely drink.""'' (Jeremiah 25:28.)

ANSWER TO QUESTION 17   a

All the nations of the world (Jeremiah 25:26).

ANSWER TO QUESTION 18   b

Sheshach or Babylon (Jeremiah 25:26).

ANSWER TO QUESTION 19   CTX

- God, through Prophet Jeremiah
- To the people of Judah and Jerusalem
- When God mentioned the kings and nations He would give the cup of His anger to drink (Jeremiah 25:30).

ANSWER TO QUESTION 20   CPC

"33 The slain of the LORD shall be at that day from one end of the earth even to the other end of the earth: they shall not be lamented, neither gathered, nor buried; they shall be dung on the surface of the ground." (Jeremiah 25:33.)

ANSWER TO QUESTION 21   b

Because the time of their slaughter and dispersions had come (Jeremiah 25:34).

ANSWER TO QUESTION 22   CPB

"38 He has left his covert, as the lion; for their land has become an astonishment because of the fierceness of the oppression, and because of his fierce anger." (Jeremiah 25:38.)

HINTS TO QUESTION 23   CMB

- God, out of love, warns people of their sinful ways, as was the case of the Judeans; when His judgement comes, no one can deny that they are suffering because they spurned God's warnings
- God is still warning us of an impending final judgement at the close of the age and those who disregard this warning will suffer His judgement.

HINT TO QUESTION 24   CMB

God used King Nebuchadnezzar as an instrument to achieve His purpose of disciplining Judah. God can use anyone, and indeed anything, to achieve His purposes. For people who build themselves for honourable practices, God uses them to achieve His honourable purposes. For those who build themselves for dishonourable practices, God uses them for dishonourable purposes, and God rewards both the honourable and the dishonourable instruments accordingly.

CHAPTER 26

JEREMIAH CHAPTER 26

"In the beginning of the reign of Jehoiakim the son of Josiah, king of Judah, came this word from the LORD, saying, ²"Thus says the LORD: Stand in the court of the LORD's house, and speak to all the cities of Judah, which come to worship in the LORD's house, all the words that I command you to speak to them; do not diminish a word. ³It may be they will listen, and turn every man from his evil way; that I may relent of the evil which I purpose to do to them because of the evil of their doings. ⁴You shall tell them, 'Thus says the LORD: If you will not listen to me, to walk in my law, which I have set before you, ⁵to listen to the words of my servants the prophets, whom I send to you, even rising up early and sending them, but you have not listened; ⁶then will I make this house like Shiloh, and will make this city a curse to all the nations of the earth.'" ⁷The priests and the prophets and all the people heard Jeremiah speaking these words in the house of the LORD. ⁸It happened, when Jeremiah had made an end of speaking all that the LORD had commanded him to speak to all the people, that the priests and the prophets and all the people laid hold on him, saying, "You shall surely die. ⁹Why have you prophesied in the name of the LORD, saying, 'This house shall be like Shiloh, and this city shall be desolate, without inhabitant?'" All the people were gathered to Jeremiah in the house of the LORD. ¹⁰When the officials of Judah heard these things, they came up from the king's house to the house of the LORD; and they sat in the entry of the New Gate of the LORD's house. ¹¹Then spoke the priests and the prophets to the officials and to all the people, saying, "This man is

worthy of death; for he has prophesied against this city, as you have heard with your ears." ¹²Then Jeremiah spoke to all the officials and to all the people, saying, "The LORD sent me to prophesy against this house and against this city all the words that you have heard. ¹³Now therefore amend your ways and your doings, and obey the voice of the LORD your God; and the LORD will relent of the disaster that he has pronounced against you. ¹⁴But as for me, look, I am in your hands; do with me as is good and right in your eyes. ¹⁵Only know for certain that, if you put me to death, you will bring innocent blood on yourselves, and on this city, and on its inhabitants; for of a truth the LORD has sent me to you to speak all these words in your ears." ¹⁶Then the officials and all the people said to the priests and to the prophets: "This man is not worthy of death; for he has spoken to us in the name of the LORD our God."

¹⁷Then rose up certain of the elders of the land, and spoke to all the assembly of the people, saying, ¹⁸"Micah the Morashtite prophesied in the days of Hezekiah king of Judah; and he spoke to all the people of Judah, saying, 'Thus says the LORD of hosts: "Zion shall be plowed as a field, and Jerusalem shall become heaps, and the mountain of the house as the high places of a forest."' ¹⁹Did Hezekiah king of Judah and all Judah put him to death? Did he not fear the LORD, and seek the favor of the LORD, and the LORD relented of the disaster which he had pronounced against them? Thus should we commit great evil against our own souls. ²⁰"There was also a man who prophesied in the name of the LORD, Uriah the son of Shemaiah of Kiriath Jearim; and he prophesied against this city and against this land according to all the words of Jeremiah. ²¹And when Jehoiakim the king, with all his mighty men, and all the officials, heard his words, the king sought to put him to death; but when Uriah heard it, he was afraid, and fled, and went into Egypt. ²²And Jehoiakim the king sent men into Egypt, Elnathan the son of Achbor, and certain men with him, into Egypt; ²³and they fetched forth Uriah out of Egypt, and brought him to Jehoiakim the king, who killed him with the sword, and cast his dead body into the graves of the common people." ²⁴But the hand of Ahikam the son of Shaphan was with Jeremiah,

that they should not give him into the hand of the people to put him to death."

QUESTIONS

QUESTION 1   a

Jeremiah chapter 26:2 says, *"Stand in the court of the LORD's house, and speak to all the cities of Judah, which come to worship in the LORD's house...."*

During the reign of which king did the Lord give the above message?

QUESTION 2   b

According to Jeremiah chapter 26:

Why did God send a message of destruction to the people of Judah and Jerusalem?

QUESTION 3   b1

Jeremiah chapter 26:2 says, *"Stand in the court of the LORD's house, and speak to all the cities of Judah, which come to worship in the LORD's house...."*

What was the message Jeremiah was asked to give the people?

QUESTION 4   a

According to Jeremiah chapter 26:

Which place did God say He would make the temple in Jerusalem to be like if the people of Judah refused to listen to Him and walk in His laws?

QUESTION 5   b

According to Jeremiah chapter 26:

Mention the three classes of people that attacked Jeremiah after he had delivered the message the Lord gave him in the court of the Lord's house.

QUESTION 6 b1

According to Jeremiah chapter 26:

What was the people's response after Jeremiah delivered the message God sent him?

QUESTION 7 b

According to Jeremiah chapter 26, when the officials of Judah heard that Jeremiah was mobbed and rushed over to handle the case:

Where did they sit to hear the case?

QUESTION 8 b1

According to Jeremiah chapter 26, when the princes or officials of Judah sat to hear the case brought against Prophet Jeremiah by the priests and the prophets:

What was Jeremiah's defence?

QUESTION 9 b

According to Jeremiah chapter 26, after Jeremiah defended himself before the officials and the people:

What was the officials' verdict?

QUESTION 10 b2

In Jeremiah chapter 26, during the hearing of the case brought against Jeremiah by the priests and the prophets, the elders of the land reminded the people about a prophecy of Micah:

Where else can the prophecy be found in the Bible?

QUESTION 11   **b1**

According to Jeremiah chapter 26:

Who else gave a similar prophecy to that Prophet Jeremiah gave during the reign of King Jehoiakim concerning the destruction of Judah and Jerusalem? Narrate what happened to the person.

QUESTION 12   **a**

According to Jeremiah chapter 26:

Where was Uriah the prophet from?

QUESTION 13   **a**

According to Jeremiah chapter 26:

Who was the father of Uriah, the prophet?

QUESTION 14   **b1**

According to Jeremiah chapter 26:

Who were the people sent to Egypt by King Jehoiakim to capture Uriah?

QUESTION 15   **a**

According to Jeremiah chapter 26:

Who supported Jeremiah during his trial before the council so that he was not handed over to the people to be put to death?

QUESTION 16   **CMC**

Read Jeremiah chapter 26:2–3, preach or write a commentary on the passage with emphasis on salvation.

QUESTION 17   **CMC**

Read Jeremiah chapter 26:16–19, preach or write a commentary on the passage with emphasis on salvation.

ANSWERS

ANSWER TO QUESTION 1   a

King Jehoiakim (Jeremiah 26:1).

ANSWER TO QUESTION 2   b

It may be they will listen and turn from their evil ways, that God may relent from punishing them for their sins (Jeremiah 26:3).

ANSWER TO QUESTION 3   b1

If they will not listen to God and obey His laws, and if they will not listen to His servants, the prophets whom He sent to warn them, then God will destroy the temple as He destroyed Shiloh. And He will make Jerusalem a curse to all the nations of the earth (Jeremiah 26:4–6).

ANSWER TO QUESTION 4   a

Shiloh (Jeremiah 26:6).

ANSWER TO QUESTION 5   b

- The priests
- The prophets
- The congregation or the people or the laymen (Jeremiah 26:8).

ANSWER TO QUESTION 6   b1

They said to him, "you shall surely die," and asked why he prophesied in the name of the Lord that the city and the temple would be desolate (Jeremiah 26:8–9).

ANSWER TO QUESTION 7   b

The entrance of the New Gate of the Lord's house or temple

Or

The New Gate of the temple (Jeremiah 26:10).

ANSWER TO QUESTION 8   b1

- Jeremiah said that the prophecy he gave was from God, and he charged them that if they would change from their evil ways and start obeying God, the Lord would no longer carry out all the evil He had pronounced against them.
- He also said that as for himself, his life was in their hands to do whatever seemed good to them, but if they put him to death, they would bring innocent blood upon themselves, the city and all its inhabitants, for the Lord asked him to speak every word they heard to their hearing (Jeremiah 26:12–15).

ANSWER TO QUESTION 9   b

They said that Jeremiah did not deserve to die, for he spoke in God's name (Jeremiah 26:16).

ANSWER TO QUESTION 10   b2

Micah chapter 3:12.

ANSWER TO QUESTION 11   b1

- Prophet Uriah or Urijah
- When King Jehoiakim heard what Prophet Uriah was prophesying, he sent someone to kill him. But Uriah heard about the plan and escaped in fear to Egypt. The King then sent Elnathan, son of Achbor, to Egypt along with several other men to capture Uriah. When they caught him, they brought him back to King Jehoiakim, who killed Uriah with a sword and had him buried in the grave of common people (Jeremiah 26:20–23).

ANSWER TO QUESTION 12   a

Kiriath Jearim (Jeremiah 26:20).

ANSWER TO QUESTION 13   a

Shemaiah (Jeremiah 26:20).

ANSWER TO QUESTION 14   b1

Elnathan (son of Achbor) and some other men whose names were not mentioned (Jeremiah 26:22–23).

ANSWER TO QUESTION 15   a

Ahikam (son of Shaphan) (Jeremiah 26:24).

HINTS TO QUESTION 16   CMC

- As God required that Jeremiah presents His commands to the people without omitting a word, so God's words are to be declared in full, perhaps sinners will hear and repent, for only the true word of God can save sinners.
- God does not intend that sinners should perish, but they should repent from their sins after hearing His word.

HINT TO QUESTION 17   CMC

Like the elders who stood up for the truth and spoke for Jeremiah, we should speak out and stand up for the truth at all times, not minding who or the number of people against it.

CHAPTER 27

JEREMIAH CHAPTER 27

"In the beginning of the reign of Jehoiakim the son of Josiah, king of Judah, came this word to Jeremiah from the LORD, saying, ²"Thus says the LORD to me: Make bonds and bars, and put them on your neck; ³and send them to the king of Edom, and to the king of Moab, and to the king of the children of Ammon, and to the king of Tyre, and to the king of Sidon, by the hand of the messengers who come to Jerusalem to Zedekiah king of Judah; ⁴and give them a command to their masters, saying, 'Thus says the LORD of hosts, the God of Israel, You shall tell your masters: ⁵"I have made the earth, the men and the animals that are on the surface of the earth, by my great power and by my outstretched arm; and I give it to whom it seems right to me. ⁶Now have I given all these lands into the hand of Nebuchadnezzar the king of Babylon, my servant; and the animals of the field also have I given him to serve him. ⁷All the nations shall serve him, and his son, and his son's son, until the time of his own land come: and then many nations and great kings shall make him their bondservant. ⁸It shall happen, that the nation and the kingdom which will not serve the same Nebuchadnezzar king of Babylon, and that will not put their neck under the yoke of the king of Babylon, that nation will I punish, says the LORD, with the sword, and with the famine, and with the pestilence, until I have consumed them by his hand. ⁹But as for you, do not listen to your prophets, nor to your diviners, nor to your dreams, nor to your soothsayers, nor to your sorcerers, who speak to you, saying, 'You shall not serve the king of Babylon': ¹⁰for they prophesy a lie to you, to remove you far from your land, and

that I should drive you out, and you should perish. *¹¹But the nation that shall bring their neck under the yoke of the king of Babylon, and serve him, that nation will I let remain in their own land, says the LORD; and they shall till it, and dwell in it."""*

¹²I spoke to Zedekiah king of Judah according to all these words, saying, "Bring your necks under the yoke of the king of Babylon, and serve him and his people, and live. ¹³Why will you die, you and your people, by the sword, by the famine, and by the pestilence, as the LORD has spoken concerning the nation that will not serve the king of Babylon? ¹⁴Do not listen to the words of the prophets who speak to you, saying, 'You shall not serve the king of Babylon'; for they prophesy a lie to you. ¹⁵'For I have not sent them,' says the LORD, 'but they prophesy falsely in my name; that I may drive you out, and that you may perish, you, and the prophets who prophesy to you.'" ¹⁶Also I spoke to the priests and to all this people, saying, "Thus says the LORD: 'Do not listen to the words of your prophets who prophesy to you, saying, Look, the vessels of the LORD's house shall now shortly be brought again from Babylon; for they prophesy a lie to you. ¹⁷Do not listen to them; serve the king of Babylon, and live: why should this city become a desolation?' ¹⁸But if they be prophets, and if the word of the LORD be with them, let them now make intercession to the LORD of hosts, that the vessels which are left in the house of the LORD, and in the house of the king of Judah, and at Jerusalem, do not go to Babylon. ¹⁹For thus says the LORD of hosts concerning the pillars, and concerning the sea, and concerning the bases, and concerning the residue of the vessels that are left in this city, ²⁰which Nebuchadnezzar king of Babylon did not take, when he carried away captive Jeconiah the son of Jehoiakim, king of Judah, from Jerusalem to Babylon, and all the nobles of Judah and Jerusalem; ²¹yes, thus says the LORD of hosts, the God of Israel, concerning the vessels that are left in the house of the LORD, and in the house of the king of Judah, and at Jerusalem: ²²'They shall be carried to Babylon, and there shall they be, until the day that I visit them,' says the LORD; 'then will I bring them up, and restore them to this place.'"

QUESTIONS

QUESTION 1   b1

According to Jeremiah chapter 27, when the Lord asked Jeremiah to make bonds and bars or a yoke and fasten it around his neck:

Which five kings did the Lord ask Jeremiah to go and deliver a message to, and through whom was the message sent?

QUESTION 2   a

According to Jeremiah chapter 27:

What did God tell Jeremiah to do before taking a message to the five kings?

QUESTION 3   b1

According to Jeremiah chapter 27:

How many of the nations mentioned in the prophecy about the yoke of King Nebuchadnezzar are related to Israel? Mention them and how each of the nations is related to Israel.

QUESTION 4   a

According to Jeremiah chapter 27:

How did God refer to King Nebuchadnezzar?

QUESTION 5   b

According to Jeremiah chapter 27:

What did God say would happen to the nations who would submit to the king of Babylon, and what would the Lord do to the nations who would refuse to surrender to him?

QUESTION 6   CPB

Jeremiah chapter 27:9–10 says,

"But as for you, do not listen to your prophets, nor to your diviners, nor to your dreams, nor to your soothsayers, nor to your

sorcerers, who speak to you, saying, 'You shall not serve the king of Babylon':"

Complete verse 10.

QUESTION 7   b1

Jeremiah chapter 27:9 says, *"But as for you, do not listen to your prophets, nor to your diviners, nor to your dreams, nor to your soothsayers, nor to your sorcerers, who speak to you, saying, 'You shall not serve the king of Babylon.'"*

Who was God referring to in the above passage?

QUESTION 8   a

Jeremiah chapter 27:13 says, *"Why will you die, you and your people, by the sword, by the famine, and by the pestilence, as the LORD has spoken concerning the nation that will not serve the king of Babylon?"*

Who was the above message given to?

QUESTION 9   b1

According to Jeremiah chapter 27, in Jeremiah's prophecy about the yoke of King Nebuchadnezzar:

What two messages did God send to King Zedekiah of Judah?

QUESTION 10   CTX

"Why will you die, you and your people, by the sword, by the famine, and by the pestilence, as the LORD has spoken concerning the nation that will not serve the king of Babylon?"

Give the context of the above quote:

Who said it, to who, and under what circumstance?

QUESTION 11   CPB

Jeremiah chapter 27:14–15 says,

"Do not listen to the words of the prophets who speak to you, saying, 'You shall not serve the king of Babylon'; for they prophesy a lie to you."

Complete verse 15.

QUESTION 12   b

According to Jeremiah chapter 27:

What false prophecy was given to the priests?

QUESTION 13   b

According to Jeremiah chapter 27, in Jeremiah's prophecy about the yoke of King Nebuchadnezzar:

Mention two messages Jeremiah gave to the priests and the people.

QUESTION 14   b

Jeremiah chapter 27:18 says, *"But if they be prophets, and if the word of the LORD be with them, let them now make intercession to the LORD of hosts...."*

What was to be the subject of the prophet's intercessions?

QUESTION 15   b1

According to Jeremiah chapter 27:

Mention three items King Nebuchadnezzar did not carry from the temple during the reign of King Jehoiachin.

QUESTION 16   b1

According to Jeremiah chapter 27:

What did God say about the vessels left in the house of the Lord and the house of the king of Judah?

QUESTION 17   CMB

Read Jeremiah chapter 27:5–7, preach or write a commentary on the passage with emphasis on salvation.

ANSWERS

ANSWER TO QUESTION 1   b1

- The kings of Edom, Moab, Ammon, Tyre and Sidon
- Through their messengers or ambassadors (Jeremiah 27:1–3).

ANSWER TO QUESTION 2   a

To make bonds and bars or yoke and fasten it around his neck (Jeremiah 27:2).

ANSWER TO QUESTION 3   b1

- Three (3)
- Edom, Moab and Ammon (Jeremiah 27:3)
- Edom is a descent nation of Esau, the older brother of Jacob, who is Israel (Genesis 36:1, Numbers 20:14)
- Moab and Ammon are descent nations from Lot's children. Lot was Abraham's nephew, and Abraham was Israel's grandfather (Genesis 19:36–38, Genesis 12:5).

ANSWER TO QUESTION 4   a

His servant (Jeremiah 27:6).

ANSWER TO QUESTION 5   b

- Those who submit will be allowed to stay in their own country to farm the land
- Those who refuse to submit will have war or sword, famine and disease or pestilence until they are conquered (Jeremiah 27:8–11).

ANSWER TO QUESTION 6   CPB

"10for they prophesy a lie to you, to remove you far from your land, and that I should drive you out, and you should perish." (Jeremiah 27:10.)

ANSWER TO QUESTION 7   b1

The kings of Edom, Tyre, Sidon, Moab and Ammon (Jeremiah 27:3–10).

ANSWER TO QUESTION 8   a

King Zedekiah (Jeremiah 27:12).

ANSWER TO QUESTION 9   b1

- He and his people should bring their necks under the yoke of the king of Babylon to serve him and live
- He should not listen to the prophets who God did not send, who are prophesying falsely in His name in order that Zedekiah and the false prophets will be driven out of the land and perish (Jeremiah 27:12–15).

ANSWER TO QUESTION 10   CTX

- God, through Prophet Jeremiah
- To King Zedekiah
- When Jeremiah gave a message to Zedekiah that he and the people of Judah should bring their necks under the yoke of king Nebuchadnezzar if they wanted to live (Jeremiah 27:12–13).

ANSWER TO QUESTION 11   CPB

"15For I have not sent them,' says the LORD, 'but they prophesy falsely in my name; that I may drive you out, and that you may perish, you, and the prophets who prophesy to you.'" (Jeremiah 27:15.)

ANSWER TO QUESTION 12   b

That the vessels of the Lord's house would shortly be brought back from Babylon (Jeremiah 27:16).

ANSWER TO QUESTION 13   b

- He asked them not to listen to the prophets who claim that soon the gold articles or vessels taken from the Lord's house or Temple will be returned from Babylon; that it is all a lie
- He told them to serve or surrender to the king of Babylon if they wanted to live and asked them why the whole city should be desolate.

- He told them that if the prophets were true prophets, let them pray that the vessels or articles left in the Lord's house or temple, the king's house or palace, and at Jerusalem should not be taken to Babylon
- The Lord said that the pillars and the sea, the bases or the water carts and all the other vessels or articles that were left when king Nebuchadnezzar carried Jeconiah, king of Judah and all the nobles to Babylon, would also be taken to Babylon until the day God visit them, then He would bring them back to their places (Jeremiah 27:16–22).

ANSWER TO QUESTION 14   b

That the vessels left in the Lord's house, the king's house and at Jerusalem would not be carried to Babylon (Jeremiah 27:18).

ANSWER TO QUESTION 15   b1

- The pillars
- The sea or the bronze sea or the bronze basin
- The bases or the water carts
- The residue of the vessels or the rest of the vessels (Jeremiah 27:19).

ANSWER TO QUESTION 16   b1

He said they would be carried off to Babylon, and they shall remain there till He visits them and brings them back to Jerusalem (Jeremiah 27:21–22).

HINT TO QUESTION 17   CMB

God is the supreme ruler of the universe, and everything is under His authority. He gives power to whomever He wills. In the verses under consideration, God declared that He was handing several kingdoms over to King Nebuchadnezzar of Babylon. In His sovereignty, God also set a time that the rulership of Nebuchadnezzar would come to an end; after that, his kingdom would be subjected to other kings.

This teaches us that whatever heights we attain, whatever goal we have accomplished, is subject to God's approval and sovereignty. As such, we should see ourselves as instruments and stewards of whatever God bequeaths to us.

CHAPTER 28

JEREMIAH CHAPTER 28

"It happened the same year, in the beginning of the reign of Zedekiah king of Judah, in the fourth year, in the fifth month, that Hananiah the son of Azzur, the prophet, who was of Gibeon, spoke to me in the house of the LORD, in the presence of the priests and of all the people, saying, ²*"Thus speaks the LORD of hosts, the God of Israel, saying, 'I have broken the yoke of the king of Babylon.* ³*Within two full years will I bring again into this place all the vessels of the LORD's house, that Nebuchadnezzar king of Babylon took away from this place, and carried to Babylon:* ⁴*and I will bring again to this place Jeconiah the son of Jehoiakim, king of Judah, with all the captives of Judah, who went to Babylon,' says the LORD; 'for I will break the yoke of the king of Babylon.'"* ⁵*Then the prophet Jeremiah said to the prophet Hananiah in the presence of the priests, and in the presence of all the people who stood in the house of the LORD,* ⁶*even the prophet Jeremiah said, "Amen: LORD do so; the LORD perform your words which you have prophesied, to bring back the vessels of the LORD's house, and all them of the captivity, from Babylon to this place.* ⁷*Nevertheless hear you now this word that I speak in your ears, and in the ears of all the people:* ⁸*The prophets who have been before me and before you of old prophesied against many countries, and against great kingdoms, of war, and of evil, and of pestilence.* ⁹*The prophet who prophesies of peace, when the word of the prophet shall happen, then shall the prophet be known, that the LORD has truly sent him."* ¹⁰*Then Hananiah the prophet took the bar from off the prophet Jeremiah's neck, and broke it.* ¹¹*Hananiah spoke in the presence of all the people, saying,*

"Thus says the LORD: 'Even so will I break the yoke of Nebuchadnezzar king of Babylon within two full years from off the neck of all the nations.'" The prophet Jeremiah went his way. [12] Then the word of the LORD came to Jeremiah, after that Hananiah the prophet had broken the bar from off the neck of the prophet Jeremiah, saying, [13] "Go, and tell Hananiah, saying, 'Thus says the LORD: You have broken the bars of wood; but you have made in their place bars of iron. [14] For thus says the LORD of hosts, the God of Israel: "I have put a yoke of iron on the neck of all these nations, that they may serve Nebuchadnezzar king of Babylon; and they shall serve him: and I have given him the animals of the field also."'" [15] Then the prophet Jeremiah said to Hananiah the prophet, "Hear now, Hananiah: the LORD has not sent you; but you make this people to trust in a lie. [16] Therefore thus says the LORD, 'Look, I will send you away from off the surface of the earth: this year you shall die, because you have spoken rebellion against the LORD.'" [17] So Hananiah the prophet died the same year in the seventh month."

QUESTIONS

QUESTION 1   b

According to Jeremiah chapter 28:

Who was the king of Judah, and what year of his reign was the symbol of the yoke of the king of Babylon removed from the neck of Jeremiah?

QUESTION 2   b

According to Jeremiah chapter 28:

Where was Prophet Hananiah from, and what was his father's name?

QUESTION 3   a

According to Jeremiah chapter 28:

What was the name of the person that prophesied to Jeremiah in front of the public – priests and people – about the removal of the yoke of the king of Babylon?

QUESTION 4   a

According to Jeremiah chapter 28:

Who was the prophecy of Hananiah directed to?

QUESTION 5   CTX

"I have broken the yoke of the king of Babylon."

Give the context of the above quote:

Who said it, to who, and under what circumstance?

QUESTION 6   CTX

"Amen: LORD do so; the LORD perform your words which you have prophesied...."

Give the context of the above quote:

Who said it, to who, and under what circumstance?

QUESTION 7   CTX

"You have broken the bars of wood; but you have made in their place bars of iron."

Give the context of the above quote:

Who said it, to who, and under what circumstance?

QUESTION 8   b1

According to Jeremiah chapter 28, after Jeremiah told Hananiah that he would die that same year:

How long did it take for Hananiah to die?

QUESTION 9   b1

According to Jeremiah chapter 28:

Mention three things prophet Hananiah said to Jeremiah in his prophecy.

QUESTION 10   b

According to Jeremiah chapter 28, after Hananiah gave the prophecy about the breaking of the yoke of King Nebuchadnezzar:

What was Jeremiah's first statement?

QUESTION 11   a

According to Jeremiah chapter 28:

How did Jeremiah say they would know if the prophecies from a prophet were true?

QUESTION 12   a

According to Jeremiah chapter 28, after Prophet Jeremiah responded to Hananiah's prophecy:

What did Hananiah do next?

QUESTION 13   a

According to Jeremiah chapter 28:

Who removed the symbol of the yoke of the king of Babylon from Jeremiah's neck?

QUESTION 14   b1

According to Jeremiah chapter 28:

What was the prophecy Hananiah gave after breaking off the wooden yoke from Jeremiah's neck?

QUESTION 15   b1

According to Jeremiah chapter 28:

What messages did Jeremiah receive from the Lord for Hananiah after Hananiah had broken the wooden yoke from Jeremiah's neck?

QUESTION 16 **CMB**

Read Jeremiah chapter 28:15–17, preach or write a commentary on
the passage with emphasis on salvation.

ANSWERS

ANSWER TO QUESTION 1 **b**

- Zedekiah
- In the fourth year (Jeremiah 28:1).

ANSWER TO QUESTION 2 **b**

- He was from Gibeon
- Azzur or Azur (Jeremiah 28:1).

ANSWER TO QUESTION 3 **a**

Hananiah (Jeremiah 28:1).

ANSWER TO QUESTION 4 **a**

Prophet Jeremiah (in the presence of the priests and all the people)
(Jeremiah 28:1).

ANSWER TO QUESTION 5 **CTX**

- Hananiah
- To Prophet Jeremiah
- When he was giving a prophecy claiming that the Lord would
  break the wooden yoke of king Nebuchadnezzar from the
  people's necks in two years (Jeremiah 28:1–4).

ANSWER TO QUESTION 6 **CTX**

- Prophet Jeremiah
- To Hananiah
- After Hananiah had given a prophecy claiming that the Lord
  would break off King Nebuchadnezzar's yoke from the people's
  necks in two years (Jeremiah 28:1–6).

ANSWER TO QUESTION 7   CTX

- Prophet Jeremiah
- To Hananiah
- After Hananiah gave a prophecy to Jeremiah in the temple, in the presence of the priests and of all the people, claiming that the Lord would break King Nebuchadnezzar's yoke from the people's necks in two years and demonstrated it by breaking the yoke that was on Jeremiah's neck (Jeremiah 28:1–13).

ANSWER TO QUESTION 8   b1

Two (2) months (Jeremiah 28:1 and 17).

ANSWER TO QUESTION 9   b1

- The Lord has broken the yoke of the king of Babylon
- Within two years, the Lord will bring back all the Temple vessels that King Nebuchadnezzar had carried to Babylon
- The Lord would bring Jeconiah or Jehoiachin, son of Jehoiakim, with all the captives of Judah who went to Babylon (Jeremiah 28:2–4).

ANSWER TO QUESTION 10   b

Jeremiah said: *"Amen: LORD do so; the LORD perform your words which you have prophesied, to bring back the vessels of the LORD's house, and all them of the captivity, from Babylon to this place."* (Jeremiah 28:5–6.)

ANSWER TO QUESTION 11   a

Only when his predictions or prophecies came to pass (Jeremiah 28:9).

ANSWER TO QUESTION 12   a

He took the bar or yoke off Jeremiah's neck and broke it (Jeremiah 28:10).

ANSWER TO QUESTION 13   a

Hananiah (Jeremiah 28:10).

ANSWER TO QUESTION 14   b1

He said that the Lord says, just as the yoke is being broken, that within two years, God will break the yoke of King Nebuchadnezzar of Babylon from off the necks of all the nations (Jeremiah 28:11).

ANSWER TO QUESTION 15   b1

- The first message was that Hananiah had broken the bars of wood or wooden yoke, but he has made in their place bars of iron. God has put an iron yoke on the necks of all the nations that they may serve King Nebuchadnezzar of Babylon and also give him control over the wild animals.
- The second message was that the Lord would send Hananiah off the surface of the earth and that he would die that same year because he preached rebellion against the Lord (Jeremiah 28:12–16).

HINT TO QUESTION 16   CMB

Hananiah spoke falsely in the name of the Lord. Consequently, God declared that he would die that same year, and it came to pass. It is dangerous to say God said a word when He had not spoken it. This action will certainly incur God's judgement if the perpetrator does not repent. The judgement could come immediately or be delayed until the end, depending on God's prerogative.

CHAPTER 29

JEREMIAH CHAPTER 29

"Now these are the words of the letter that Jeremiah the prophet sent from Jerusalem to the residue of the elders of the captivity, and to the priests, to the prophets, and to all the people, whom Nebuchadnezzar had carried away captive from Jerusalem to Babylon, ²(after that Jeconiah the king, the queen mother, the eunuchs, the officials of Judah and Jerusalem, the craftsmen, and the metal workers, had departed from Jerusalem), ³by the hand of Elasah the son of Shaphan, and Gemariah the son of Hilkiah, (whom Zedekiah king of Judah sent to Babylon to Nebuchadnezzar king of Babylon), saying, ⁴"Thus says the LORD of hosts, the God of Israel, to all the captivity, whom I have caused to be carried away captive from Jerusalem to Babylon: ⁵'Build houses, and dwell in them; and plant gardens, and eat their fruit. ⁶Take wives, and father sons and daughters; and take wives for your sons, and give your daughters to husbands, that they may bear sons and daughters; and multiply there, and do not be diminished. ⁷Seek the peace of the city where I have caused you to be carried away captive, and pray to the LORD for it; for in its peace you shall have peace.' ⁸For thus says the LORD of hosts, the God of Israel: 'Do not let your prophets who are in the midst of you, and your diviners, deceive you; neither listen to your dreams which you cause to be dreamed. ⁹For they prophesy falsely to you in my name: I have not sent them,' says the LORD. ¹⁰"For thus says the LORD, 'After seventy years are accomplished for Babylon, I will visit you, and perform my good word toward you, in causing you to return to this place. ¹¹For I know the plans that I have for you,' says the

LORD, 'plans for your welfare, and not for calamity, to give you hope and a future. ¹²You shall call on me, and you shall go and pray to me, and I will listen to you. ¹³You shall seek me, and find me, when you shall search for me with all your heart. ¹⁴I will be found by you,' says the LORD, 'and I will turn again your captivity, and I will gather you from all the nations, and from all the places where I have driven you,' says the LORD; 'and I will bring you again to the place from where I caused you to be carried away captive.' ¹⁵"Because you have said, 'The LORD has raised us up prophets in Babylon'; ¹⁶thus says the LORD concerning the king who sits on the throne of David, and concerning all the people who dwell in this city, your brothers who haven't gone forth with you into captivity; ¹⁷thus says the LORD of hosts; 'Look, I will send on them the sword, the famine, and the pestilence, and will make them like vile figs, that can't be eaten, they are so bad. ¹⁸I will pursue after them with the sword, with the famine, and with the pestilence, and will deliver them to be tossed back and forth among all the kingdoms of the earth, to be an object of horror, and an astonishment, and a hissing, and a reproach, among all the nations where I have driven them; ¹⁹because they have not listened to my words,' says the LORD, 'with which I sent to them my servants the prophets, rising up early and sending them; but you would not hear,' says the LORD. ²⁰'Hear therefore the word of the LORD, all you of the captivity, whom I have sent away from Jerusalem to Babylon.' ²¹"Thus says the LORD of hosts, the God of Israel, concerning Ahiaba the son of Kolaiah, and concerning Zedekiah the son of Maaseiah, who prophesy a lie to you in my name: 'Look, I will deliver them into the hand of Nebuchadnezzar king of Babylon; and he shall kill them before your eyes; ²²and of them shall be taken up a curse by all the captives of Judah who are in Babylon, saying, "The LORD make you like Zedekiah and like Ahiab, whom the king of Babylon roasted in the fire"; ²³because they have worked folly in Israel, and have committed adultery with their neighbors' wives, and have spoken words in my name falsely, which I did not command them; and I am he who knows, and am witness,' says the LORD." ²⁴"Concerning Shemaiah the

Nehelamite you shall speak, saying, ²⁵ *'Thus speaks the LORD of hosts, the God of Israel, saying, "Because you have sent letters in your own name to all the people who are at Jerusalem, and to Zephaniah the son of Maaseiah, the priest, and to all the priests, saying,* ²⁶ *'The LORD has made you priest in the place of Jehoiada the priest, that there may be officers in the house of the LORD, for every man who is mad, and makes himself a prophet, that you should put him in the stocks and in shackles.* ²⁷ *Now therefore, why have you not rebuked Jeremiah of Anathoth, who makes himself a prophet to you,* ²⁸ *because he has sent to us in Babylon, saying, "The captivity is long: build houses, and dwell in them; and plant gardens, and eat their fruit?"'''* ²⁹ *Zephaniah the priest read this letter in the ears of Jeremiah the prophet.* ³⁰ *Then came the word of the LORD to Jeremiah, saying,* ³¹ *"Send to all them of the captivity, saying, 'Thus says the LORD concerning Shemaiah the Nehelamite: "Because Shemaiah has prophesied to you, and I did not send him, and he has caused you to trust in a lie;* ³² *therefore," thus says the LORD, "Look, I will punish Shemaiah the Nehelamite, and his seed; he shall not have a man to dwell among this people, neither shall he see the good that I will do to my people, says the LORD, because he has spoken rebellion against the LORD."'''*

QUESTIONS

QUESTION 1   **b1**

According to Jeremiah chapter 29, Jeremiah wrote and sent a letter to Babylon:

Mention three groups of people he sent the letter to.

QUESTION 2   **b1**

According to Jeremiah chapter 29, Jeremiah wrote and sent a letter to Babylon:

Who did he send the letter through, and why were they going to Babylon?

QUESTION 3   b

According to Jeremiah chapter 29, Jeremiah sent a letter to the Judeans who were exiled in Babylon:

Summarise the letter.

QUESTION 4   b1

According to Jeremiah chapter 29:

Mention four (4) people or groups of people in the last batch who were carried to Babylon before Jeremiah sent a letter to the people of Jerusalem in exile at Babylon.

QUESTION 5   b

Quote Jeremiah chapter 29:11. Begin by stating the Bible version you are quoting from.

QUESTION 6   CTX

"For I know the plans that I have for you"

Give the context of the above quote:

Who said it, to who, and under what circumstance?

QUESTION 7   CPC

Jeremiah chapter 29:13–14 says,

"You shall seek me, and find me, when you shall search for me with all your heart."

Complete verse 14.

QUESTION 8   b1

Jeremiah chapter 29:17 says, *"thus says the LORD of hosts; 'Look, I will send on them the sword, the famine, and the pestilence, and will make them like vile figs, that can't be eaten, they are so bad."*

Which chapter of the book of Jeremiah records Jeremiah's vision of the good and bad figs?

QUESTION 9   **b1**

According to Jeremiah chapter 29:

What were the names of the two prophets who prophesied lies to the exiles in Babylon, and how did Jeremiah say they would be killed?

QUESTION 10   **b1**

According to Jeremiah chapter 29:

What were the two (2) sins committed by the two prophets whom God said He would punish for prophesying lies in His name to the exiles in Babylon?

QUESTION 11   **b**

According to Jeremiah chapter 29:

Who was Zephaniah, and what was his father's name?

QUESTION 12   **b**

According to Jeremiah chapter 29:

Who did Shemaiah say the Lord appointed Zephaniah to replace?

QUESTION 13   **CPB**

Jeremiah chapter 29:26–27 says,

"The LORD has made you priest in the place of Jehoiada the priest, that there may be officers in the house of the LORD, for every man who is mad, and makes himself a prophet, that you should put him in the stocks and in shackles."

Complete verse 27.

QUESTION 14   **b1**

According to Jeremiah chapter 29:

What did God say will happen to Shemaiah?

QUESTION 15   **CMB**

Read Jeremiah chapter 29:4–7, preach or write a commentary on the passage with focus on verse 7 and with emphasis on salvation.

QUESTION 16   **CMB**

Read Jeremiah chapter 29:11–13, preach or write a commentary on the passage with emphasis on salvation.

ANSWERS

ANSWER TO QUESTION 1   b1

He sent the letter to:

- The residue of the elders
- The priests
- The prophets
- And all the (other) people whom Nebuchadnezzar had carried away captive from Jerusalem to Babylon (Jeremiah 29:1).

ANSWER TO QUESTION 2   b1

- He sent the letter through:

Elasah (son of Shaphan) and Gemariah (son of Hilkiah)

- Because King Zedekiah sent them to Babylon, to King Nebuchadnezzar (Jeremiah 29:1–3).

ANSWER TO QUESTION 3   b

He said that the exiles should feel at home and not let themselves be deceived, for they will be in Babylon for seventy years (and the Lord's wrath will fall on the remnants of Judea who did not go to exile) (Jeremiah 29:1–32).

ANSWER TO QUESTION 4   b1

They were:

- King Jeconiah or Jehoiachin
- the queen mother

- the eunuchs
- the princes or officials of Judah and Jerusalem and
- the craftsmen and metal workers or artisans (Jeremiah 29:2).

ANSWER TO QUESTION 5   b

"^{d1}For I know the plans that I have for you,' says the LORD, 'plans for your welfare, and not for calamity, to give you hope and a future." (Jeremiah 29:11.)

ANSWER TO QUESTION 6   CTX

- God, through Prophet Jeremiah
- To the people of Jerusalem in exile in Babylon
- In Jeremiah's letter to them when God assured them that He would bring them back from captivity (Jeremiah 29:11–14).

ANSWER TO QUESTION 7   CPC

"^{d4}I will be found by you,' says the LORD, 'and I will turn again your captivity, and I will gather you from all the nations, and from all the places where I have driven you,' says the LORD; 'and I will bring you again to the place from where I caused you to be carried away captive.'" (Jeremiah 29:14.)

ANSWER TO QUESTION 8   b1

Jeremiah chapter 24.

ANSWER TO QUESTION 9   b1

- Ahiab or Ahab (son of Kolaiah) and Zedekiah (son of Maaseiah)
- They will be roasted or burned to death before the people (Jeremiah 29:21–22).

ANSWER TO QUESTION 10   b1

- They committed adultery with their neighbours' wives
- They lied in God's name, saying things He did not command (Jeremiah 29:23).

ANSWER TO QUESTION 11   b

- He was a priest
- Maaseiah (Jeremiah 29:25).

ANSWER TO QUESTION 12   b

Jehoiada (Jeremiah 29:26).

ANSWER TO QUESTION 13   CPB

"27 Now therefore, why have you not rebuked Jeremiah of Anathoth, who makes himself a prophet to you." (Jeremiah 29:27.)

ANSWER TO QUESTION 14   b1

God would punish him and his seed; he would not have any descendants left among the people, and he would not see the good the Lord would do for His people (Jeremiah 29:32).

HINT TO QUESTION 15   CMB

Contained in the letter sent by Prophet Jeremiah to the people of Jerusalem who were captives in Babylon was an instruction for them to seek the peace of the city and also pray to God for it. Babylon was not their home, but it was God's expectation of them to seek its peace and pray for its prosperity. For a fact, the earth is not the home of believers, for we are sojourners on a journey to our heavenly home. However, as Christians, as long as we are on earth, wherever we find ourselves, we should seek the peace and prosperity of that place by praying and carrying out our civic responsibilities.

HINTS TO QUESTION 16   CMB

- Even when God was punishing Judah for their sins, He still had good plans for them, to give them hope and a future. We should bear in mind that when God disciplines us, it is not for our destruction but to mould our character for His purpose. The plans of God for our lives are good. However, to appropriate them, we have a role to play, and the role is to seek Him with a genuine heart.

- We must learn to trust God in every situation and not go against His word when facing difficult situations. This is the only way to endure until His good plans are manifested.

CHAPTER 30

JEREMIAH CHAPTER 30

"The word that came to Jeremiah from the LORD, saying, ²"Thus speaks the LORD, the God of Israel, saying, 'Write all the words that I have spoken to you in a scroll. ³For, look, the days come, says the LORD, that I will turn again the captivity of my people Israel and Judah,' says the LORD; 'and I will cause them to return to the land that I gave to their fathers, and they shall possess it.'" ⁴These are the words that the LORD spoke concerning Israel and concerning Judah. ⁵For thus says the LORD: "We have heard a voice of trembling, of fear, and not of peace. ⁶Ask now, and see whether a man does travail with child: why do I see every man with his hands on his waist, as a woman in travail, and all faces are turned into paleness? ⁷Alas. for that day is great, so that none is like it: it is even the time of Jacob's trouble; but he shall be saved out of it. ⁸It shall come to pass in that day," says the LORD of hosts, "that I will break his yoke from off your neck, and will burst your bonds; and strangers shall no more make him their bondservant; ⁹but they shall serve the LORD their God, and David their king, whom I will raise up to them. ¹⁰Therefore do not be afraid, O Jacob my servant, says the LORD; neither be dismayed, Israel: for, look, I will save you from afar, and your seed from the land of their captivity; and Jacob shall return, and shall be quiet and at ease, and none shall make him afraid. ¹¹For I am with you, says the LORD, to save you: for I will make a full end of all the nations where I have scattered you, but I will not make a full end of you; but I will correct you in measure, and will in no

way leave you unpunished." ¹²For thus says the LORD, "Your hurt is incurable, and your wound grievous. ¹³There is none to plead your cause, that you may be bound up: you have no healing medicines. ¹⁴All your lovers have forgotten you; they do not seek you: for I have wounded you with the wound of an enemy, with the chastisement of a cruel one, for the greatness of your iniquity, because your sins were increased. ¹⁵Why do you cry for your hurt? Your pain is incurable: for the greatness of your iniquity, because your sins were increased, I have done these things to you. ¹⁶Therefore all those who devour you shall be devoured; and all your adversaries, everyone of them, shall go into captivity; and those who plunder you shall be plundered, and all who prey on you I will make a prey. ¹⁷For I will restore health to you, and I will heal you of your wounds," says the LORD; "because they have called you an outcast, saying, 'It is Zion, whom no man seeks after.'" ¹⁸Thus says the LORD: "Look, I will turn again the captivity of Jacob's tents, and have compassion on his dwelling places; and the city shall be built on its own hill, and the palace shall be inhabited in its own way. ¹⁹Out of them shall proceed thanksgiving and the voice of those who make merry: and I will multiply them, and they shall not be few; I will also glorify them, and they shall not be small. ²⁰Their children also shall be as before, and their congregation shall be established before me; and I will punish all who oppress them. ²¹Their prince shall be of themselves, and their ruler shall proceed from their midst; and I will cause him to draw near, and he shall approach to me: for who is he who has had boldness to approach to me? says the LORD. ²²You shall be my people, and I will be your God. ²³Look, the storm of the LORD, his wrath, has gone forth, a sweeping storm: it shall burst on the head of the wicked. ²⁴The fierce anger of the LORD will not return, until he has executed, and until he has performed the intentions of his heart. In the latter days you will understand it."

QUESTIONS

QUESTION 1   CPC

Jeremiah chapter 30:2–3 says,

"Thus speaks the LORD, the God of Israel, saying, 'Write all the words that I have spoken to you in a scroll.'"

Complete verse 3.

QUESTION 2   CPC

Jeremiah chapter 30:5–6 says,

"For thus says the LORD: "We have heard a voice of trembling, of fear, and not of peace."

Complete verse 6.

QUESTION 3   CPB

Jeremiah chapter 30:8–9 says,

"It shall come to pass in that day," says the LORD of hosts, "that I will break his yoke from off your neck, and will burst your bonds; and strangers shall no more make him their bondservant;"

Complete verse 9.

QUESTION 4   b

According to Jeremiah chapter 30:

Mention two personalities God said His people would serve when He delivers them.

QUESTION 5   b

In Jeremiah chapter 30:11, God said He would destroy the nations in which He scattered Israel, but He would not destroy the Israelites:

What did He say He would do to Israel instead?

QUESTION 6 CPB

Jeremiah chapter 30:12–13 says,

"For thus says the LORD, "Your hurt is incurable, and your wound grievous."

Complete verse 13.

QUESTION 7 b

In Jeremiah chapter 30, God said He had wounded Israel cruelly, as though He were their enemy.

Why?

QUESTION 8 b

"For I will restore health to you, and I will heal you of your wounds," says the LORD…."

Who is the above passage referring to, and who initially wounded them?

QUESTION 9 b1

According to Jeremiah chapter 30, what did God say would happen to the following people:

1. Those who devour His people?
2. The adversaries of His people?
3. Those who plunder His people?
4. Those who prey upon His people?

QUESTION 10 CPB

Jeremiah chapter 30:18–19 says,

"Thus says the LORD: "Look, I will turn again the captivity of Jacob's tents, and have compassion on his dwelling places; and the city shall be built on its own hill, and the palace shall be inhabited in its own way."

Complete verse 19.

QUESTION 11   CPB

Jeremiah chapter 30:20–21 says,

"Their children also shall be as before, and their congregation shall be established before me; and I will punish all who oppress them."

Complete verse 21.

QUESTION 12   b

Jeremiah chapter 30:23 says, *"Look, the storm of the LORD, his wrath, has gone forth, a sweeping storm...."*

What shall the storm do?

QUESTION 13   CMC

Read Jeremiah chapter 30:10–11, preach or write a commentary on the passage with emphasis on salvation.

ANSWERS

ANSWER TO QUESTION 1   CPC

"³For, look, the days come, says the LORD, that I will turn again the captivity of my people Israel and Judah,' says the LORD; 'and I will cause them to return to the land that I gave to their fathers, and they shall possess it.'" (Jeremiah 30:3.)

ANSWER TO QUESTION 2   CPC

"⁶Ask now, and see whether a man does travail with child: why do I see every man with his hands on his waist, as a woman in travail, and all faces are turned into paleness?" (Jeremiah 30:6.)

ANSWER TO QUESTION 3   CPB

"⁹but they shall serve the LORD their God, and David their king, whom I will raise up to them." (Jeremiah 30:9.)

ANSWER TO QUESTION 4   b

- The Lord their God
- David their king or the King God will raise from David's lineage (Jeremiah 30:9).

ANSWER TO QUESTION 5   b

He would correct or discipline them in due measure (He will not let them go unpunished) (Jeremiah 30:11).

ANSWER TO QUESTION 6   CPB

"13 There is none to plead your cause, that you may be bound up: you have no healing medicines." (Jeremiah 30:13.)

ANSWER TO QUESTION 7   b

Because their iniquities were great, and their sins were increased (Jeremiah 30:14).

ANSWER TO QUESTION 8   b

- Israel (Israel and Judah as a nation)
- God (Jeremiah 30:14, 15 and 17).

ANSWER TO QUESTION 9   b1

- They will be devoured
- They will be sent to exile or captivity
- They will be plundered
- They will be made prey (Jeremiah 30:16).

ANSWER TO QUESTION 10   CPB

"19 Out of them shall proceed thanksgiving and the voice of those who make merry: and I will multiply them, and they shall not be few; I will also glorify them, and they shall not be small." (Jeremiah 30:19.)

ANSWER TO QUESTION 11   CPB

"21 Their prince shall be of themselves, and their ruler shall proceed from their midst; and I will cause him to draw near, and he shall

approach to me: for who is he who has had boldness to approach to me? says the LORD." (Jeremiah 30:21.)

ANSWER TO QUESTION 12   b

It shall burst or fall with pain on the head of the wicked (Jeremiah 30:23).

HINT TO QUESTION 13   CMC

Although Israel had been dispersed into different nations due to their sins, God promised to restore and bless them. When we submit to God's discipline, obeying His every instruction, He will restore and bless us in the end. However, if we refuse to obey His instructions, we will sever our relationship with Him and risk facing His wrath.

CHAPTER 31

"At that time," says the LORD, "will I be the God of all the families of Israel, and they shall be my people." ²Thus says the LORD, "The people who were left of the sword found favor in the wilderness; even Israel, when I went to cause him to rest. ³The LORD appeared of old to me, saying, 'Yes, I have loved you with an everlasting love: therefore with loving kindness have I drawn you. ⁴Again will I build you, and you shall be built, O virgin of Israel: again you shall be adorned with your tambourines, and shall go forth in the dances of those who make merry. ⁵Again you shall plant vineyards on the mountains of Samaria; the planters shall plant, and shall enjoy its fruit. ⁶For there shall be a day, that the watchmen on the hills of Ephraim shall cry, "Arise, and let us go up to Zion to the LORD our God."'" ⁷For thus says the LORD, "Sing with gladness for Jacob, and shout for the chief of the nations: publish, praise, and say, 'For the LORD has saved your people, the remnant of Israel.' ⁸'Look, I will bring them from the north country, and gather them from the uttermost parts of the earth, along with the blind and the lame, the woman with child and her who travails with child together: a great company shall they return here. ⁹They shall come with weeping; and with petitions will I lead them: I will cause them to walk by rivers of waters, in a straight way in which they shall not stumble; for I am a father to Israel, and Ephraim is my firstborn.'" ¹⁰Hear the word of the LORD, you nations, and declare it in the islands afar off; and say, "He who scattered Israel will gather him, and keep him, as shepherd does his flock." ¹¹For the LORD has ransomed Jacob, and

redeemed him from the hand of him who was stronger than he. ¹²They shall come and sing in the height of Zion, and they shall be radient over the goodness of the LORD, to the grain, and to the new wine, and to the oil, and to the young of the flock and of the herd: and their soul shall be as a watered garden; and they shall not sorrow any more at all. ¹³"Then shall the virgin rejoice in the dance, and the young men and the old together; for I will turn their mourning into joy, and will comfort them, and make them rejoice from their sorrow. ¹⁴I will satiate the soul of the priests with fatness, and my people shall be satisfied with my goodness," says the LORD. ¹⁵Thus says the LORD: "A voice is heard in Ramah, lamentation and weeping and great bitterness, Rachel weeping for her children; she refuses to be comforted for her children, because they are no more. ¹⁶Thus says the LORD: "Refrain your voice from weeping, and your eyes from tears; for your work shall be rewarded," says the LORD; "and they shall come again from the land of the enemy. ¹⁷There is hope for your latter end," says the LORD; "and your children shall come again to their own border. ¹⁸I have surely heard Ephraim bemoaning himself thus, 'You have chastised me, and I was chastised, as an untrained calf: turn me, and I shall be turned; for you are the LORD my God. ¹⁹Surely after that I was turned, I repented; and after that I was instructed, I struck on my thigh: I was ashamed, yes, even confounded, because I bore the reproach of my youth.' ²⁰Is Ephraim my dear son? Is he a darling child? For as often as I speak against him, I do earnestly remember him still: therefore my heart yearns for him; I will surely have mercy on him," says the LORD. ²¹"Set up road signs, make guideposts; set your heart toward the highway, even the way by which you went: turn again, virgin of Israel, turn again to these your cities. ²²How long will you go here and there, you backsliding daughter? For the LORD has created a new thing in the earth: a woman shall encompass a man." ²³Thus says the LORD of hosts, the God of Israel, "Yet again shall they use this speech in the land of Judah and in its cities, when I shall bring again their captivity: 'The LORD bless you, habitation of righteousness, mountain of holiness.' ²⁴Judah and all its cities shall dwell in it together, the *farmers, and those who go about with flocks. ²⁵For I have satisfied the weary soul, and I have filled every sorrowful soul." ²⁶On this I awakened, and saw; and my sleep was sweet to me. ²⁷"Look, the days come, " says the LORD, "that I will sow the house of Israel and the house of Judah with the seed of man, and with the seed of animal. ²⁸It shall happen that, like as I have watched over them to pluck up and to break down and to overthrow and to destroy and to afflict, so will I watch over them to build and to plant," says the LORD. ²⁹"In those days they shall say no more, 'The fathers have eaten sour grapes, and the children's teeth are set on edge.' ³⁰But everyone shall die for his own iniquity: every man who eats the sour grapes, his teeth shall be set on edge. ³¹Look, the days come," says the LORD, "when I will make a new covenant with the house of Israel, and with the house of Judah: ³²not according to the covenant that I made with their fathers in the day that I took them by the hand to bring them out of the land of Egypt; which my covenant they broke, and I disregarded them," says the LORD. ³³"But this is the covenant that I will make with the house of Israel after those days," says the LORD: "I will put my law in their minds, and write it on their hearts; and I will be their God, and they shall be my people: ³⁴and they shall teach no more every man his neighbor, and every man his brother, saying, 'Know the LORD'; for they shall all know me, from their least to their greatest, for I will forgive their iniquity, and their sins I will remember no more." ³⁵Thus says the LORD, who gives the sun for a light by day, and the ordinances of the moon and of the stars for a light by night, who stirs up the sea, so that its waves roar; the LORD of hosts is his name: ³⁶"If these ordinances depart from before me," says the LORD, "then the descendants of Israel also shall cease from being a nation before me forever." ³⁷Thus says the LORD: "If heaven above can be measured, and the foundations of the earth searched out beneath, then will I also cast off all the descendants of Israel for all that they have done," says the LORD. ³⁸"Look, the days come," says the LORD, "that the city shall be built to the LORD from the tower of Hananel to the Corner Gate. ³⁹The measuring line shall go out further straight onward to the hill*

*Gareb, and shall turn about to Goah. *⁴⁰*The whole valley of the dead bodies and of the ashes, and all the fields to the brook Kidron, to the corner of the Horse Gate toward the east, shall be holy to the LORD; it shall not be plucked up, nor thrown down any more forever.* "

QUESTIONS

QUESTION 1   **b1**

Jeremiah chapter 31:1 says, *""At that time," says the LORD, "will I be the God of all the families of Israel, and they shall be my people.""*

What time is the above scripture talking about?

QUESTION 2   **a**

According to Jeremiah chapter 31:

How did God describe the love He had for the people of Israel and Judah?

QUESTION 3   **b**

According to Jeremiah chapter 31:

Where did God say the people of Israel and Judah would once again plant their vines or vineyards?

QUESTION 4   **b**

According to Jeremiah chapter 31:

From where did God say He would bring back the remnants of Israel?

QUESTION 5   **c**

In Jeremiah chapter 31:7–8, when the Lord promised to bring the people of Israel back from exile, the Lord added: *"the blind and the lame, the woman with child and her who travails with child together: a great company shall they return here.* "

Narrate how the above quote came to pass.

QUESTION 6 b2

Jeremiah chapter 31:9 says, *"for I am a father to Israel, and Ephraim is my firstborn."*

How did Ephraim, a grandchild, become the firstborn?

QUESTION 7 CPA

Jeremiah chapter 31:10–11 says,

"Hear the word of the LORD, you nations, and declare it in the islands afar off; and say, "He who scattered Israel will gather him, and keep him, as shepherd does his flock.""

Complete verse 11.

QUESTION 8 c

Jeremiah chapter 31:15 says, *"A voice is heard in Ramah, lamentation and weeping and great bitterness, Rachel weeping for her children; she refuses to be comforted for her children, because they are no more."*

Where can this quote be found in the New Testament? Narrate the events that led to it.

QUESTION 9 CPA

Jeremiah chapter 31:16–17 says,

"Thus says the LORD: "Refrain your voice from weeping, and your eyes from tears; for your work shall be rewarded," says the LORD; "and they shall come again from the land of the enemy.""

Complete verse 17.

QUESTION 10 CPC

Jeremiah chapter 31:18–19 says,

CHAPTER 31

"I have surely heard Ephraim bemoaning himself thus, 'You have chastised me, and I was chastised, as an untrained calf: turn me, and I shall be turned; for you are the LORD my God.'"

Complete verse 19.

QUESTION 11   c

According to Jeremiah chapter 31:

What did God say about sour grapes, and where else can a similar saying be found in the Bible?

QUESTION 12   a

Jeremiah chapter 31:34 says, *"and they shall teach no more every man his neighbor, and every man his brother, saying, 'Know the LORD'...."*

Why did God say they would not need to teach the people to know Him?

QUESTION 13   CPB

Jeremiah chapter 31:35–36 says,

"Thus says the LORD, who gives the sun for a light by day, and the ordinances of the moon and of the stars for a light by night, who stirs up the sea, so that its waves roar; the LORD of hosts is his name:"

Complete verse 36.

QUESTION 14   CMB

Read Jeremiah chapter 31:18–20, preach or write a commentary on the passage with emphasis on salvation.

QUESTION 15   CMB

Read Jeremiah chapter 31:29–30, preach or write a commentary on the passage with emphasis on salvation.

QUESTION 16   CMB

Read Jeremiah chapter 31:33–34, preach or write a commentary on the passage with emphasis on salvation.

227

ANSWERS

ANSWER TO QUESTION 1   b1

The time when the Lord will bring back the people of Israel (Israel and Judah as one) home from their captivity and restore their fortunes (Jeremiah 30:18).

ANSWER TO QUESTION 2   a

An everlasting love (Jeremiah 31:3).

ANSWER TO QUESTION 3   b

On the mountains or hills of Samaria (Jeremiah 31:5).

ANSWER TO QUESTION 4   b

From the North country and the uttermost part of the Earth (Jeremiah 31:8).

ANSWER TO QUESTION 5   c

King Cyrus of Persia gave a proclamation in writing to all the kingdoms of the earth that every Jew, wherever they were, could go back to Jerusalem to rebuild the temple.

He commanded that the Jews be given every needed assistance for their return and provisions for the temple.

This implied that the Jews would go back in peace with the blind, the lame, the pregnant women and expectant mothers. No one would be left behind in Babylon or any other nation except it is of their own accord (Ezra 1:1–4).

ANSWER TO QUESTION 6   b2

Ephraim was Joseph's second son and Jacob's (Israel's) grandson. At the time Jacob was about to die, Joseph had taken his two sons to Jacob for blessing, where Jacob adopted Joseph's two sons, Manasseh, the firstborn and Ephraim, the second, as his. On that occasion, Jacob, through divine inspiration, gave Ephraim the firstborn blessings instead of Manasseh. Ephraim and his brother Manasseh thus were enlisted among the twelve tribes of Israel. When Jacob was about to bless his children in Genesis chapter 49, he cursed Reuben, his first son, for sleeping with his concubine. 1 Chronicles 5:1–2 lets us know that Reuben lost his position as a result of his immoral act, and that position was given to the sons of Joseph. Having gotten the firstborn blessing, Ephraim took the place of Israel's firstborn, whom God referred to as His firstborn.

ANSWER TO QUESTION 7   CPA

"11For the LORD has ransomed Jacob, and redeemed him from the hand of him who was stronger than he." (Jeremiah 31:11.)

ANSWER TO QUESTION 8   c

- Matthew 2:18
- It was quoted as a fulfilment of Jeremiah's prophecy when King Herod massacred every male child, two years old and below, in Bethlehem and its vicinity, at the news of Jesus' birth. (When the wise men following the stars informed Herod of the new King's birth, Herod tried to deceptively get more information from them so that he could kill the newborn king, but an angel appeared to the wise men and instructed them not to return to Herod. They went back through another route at the angel's instruction. When Herod realised that he had been outsmarted, he ordered the killing of every male child, two years old and below, in line with the period the wise men told him they saw the star. But before Herod's massacre of the children, an angel had appeared to Joseph, instructing him to take Mary, his wife and the baby to Egypt to escape the sword of Herod.)

ANSWER TO QUESTION 9   CPA

"17There is hope for your latter end," says the LORD; "and your children shall come again to their own border." (Jeremiah 31:17.)

ANSWER TO QUESTION 10   CPC

"19Surely after that I was turned, I repented; and after that I was instructed, I struck on my thigh: I was ashamed, yes, even

confounded, because I bore the reproach of my youth." (Jeremiah 31:19.)

ANSWER TO QUESTION 11   c

- God said parents would no longer eat sour grapes while their children's teeth are set on edge or irritated. Rather, anyone who eats sour grapes will bear the consequences themself (Jeremiah 31:29–30).
- Ezekiel 18:2.

ANSWER TO QUESTION 12   a

Because everyone shall know Him (Jeremiah 31:34).

ANSWER TO QUESTION 13   CPB

36 "If these ordinances depart from before me," says the LORD, "then the descendants of Israel also shall cease from being a nation before me forever."" (Jeremiah 31:36.)

HINT TO QUESTION 14   CMB

Ephraim was chastised due to his sins, yet God still loved him and would not cast him away. God showed him mercy as a loving Father to a dear child. God's love for His children is everlasting, but this would not cause Him to turn a blind eye to our sins. God will discipline us out of love when we go astray; if we turn to Him in repentance, He will restore us.

HINT TO QUESTION 15   CMB

Here, God announced the end of the era where He visited the parents' sins on their children and the birth of the era where everyone would bear the consequences of their sins. Some believers wrongly believe that they suffer for the sins of their parents, hinging their belief on scriptures like Exodus 20:5–6, which places the sins of the fathers on their children, even to the fourth generation, without being aware that God later nullified generational transfer of punishment for sins as seen in the verses under consideration. Believers have been liberated from every ancestral curse by virtue of being born again. We should be

CHAPTER 31

well-versed in the word of God so that we may know the parts of God's word that have been fulfilled and the parts that are still applicable to us today.

HINT TO QUESTION 16   CMB

God promised to make a new covenant with His people. A covenant that will ensure that His laws are written in His people's hearts. We live in the era of the fulfilment of that promise. The old covenant was sealed with the blood of animals, while the new covenant was sealed with the blood of Christ. The new covenant is accompanied by the gift of the Holy Spirit, which teaches us to know the Lord and convicts us of sin. The enduring relationship we have now is through Christ and His finished work.

CHAPTER 32

JEREMIAH CHAPTER 32

"The word that came to Jeremiah from the LORD in the tenth year of Zedekiah king of Judah, which was the eighteenth year of Nebuchadnezzar. ²Now at that time the king of Babylon's army was besieging Jerusalem; and Jeremiah the prophet was shut up in the court of the guard, which was in the king of Judah's house. ³For Zedekiah king of Judah had shut him up, saying, "Why do you prophesy, and say, 'Thus says the LORD, "Look, I will give this city into the hand of the king of Babylon, and he shall take it; ⁴and Zedekiah king of Judah shall not escape out of the hand of the Chaldeans, but shall surely be delivered into the hand of the king of Babylon, and shall speak with him mouth to mouth, and his eyes shall see his eyes; ⁵and he shall bring Zedekiah to Babylon, and he shall be there until I visit him," says the LORD: "though you fight with the Chaldeans, you shall not prosper?"'" ⁶Jeremiah said, "The word of the LORD came to me, saying, ⁷'Look, Hanamel the son of Shallum your uncle shall come to you, saying, "Buy my field that is in Anathoth; for the right of redemption is yours to buy it."' ⁸So Hanamel my uncle's son came to me in the court of the guard according to the word of the LORD, and said to me, "Please buy my field that is in Anathoth, which is in the land of Benjamin; for the right of inheritance is yours, and the redemption is yours; buy it for yourself.' Then I knew that this was the word of the LORD. ⁹I bought the field that was in Anathoth of Hanamel my uncle's son, and weighed him the money, even seventeen shekels of silver. ¹⁰I subscribed the deed, and sealed it, and called witnesses, and weighed him the money in the balances. ¹¹So I took the deed of the

purchase, both that which was sealed, containing the terms and conditions, and that which was open; ¹² and I delivered the deed of the purchase to Baruch the son of Neriah, the son of Mahseiah, in the presence of Hanamel my uncle's son, and in the presence of the witnesses who subscribed the deed of the purchase, before all the Jews who sat in the court of the guard. ¹³ I commanded Baruch before them, saying, ¹⁴'Thus says the LORD of hosts, the God of Israel: "Take these deeds, this deed of the purchase which is sealed, and this deed which is open, and put them in an earthen vessel; that they may continue many days."' ¹⁵ For thus says the LORD of hosts, the God of Israel: 'Houses and fields and vineyards shall yet again be bought in this land.' ¹⁶ Now after I had delivered the deed of the purchase to Baruch the son of Neriah, I prayed to the LORD, saying, ¹⁷'Ah, Lord GOD. Look, you have made the heavens and the earth by your great power and by your outstretched arm; there is nothing too hard for you, ¹⁸ who show loving kindness to thousands, and recompense the iniquity of the fathers into the bosom of their children after them; the Great, the Mighty God, the LORD of hosts is his name; ¹⁹ great in counsel, and mighty in work; whose eyes are open on all the ways of the sons of men, to give everyone according to his ways, and according to the fruit of his doings: ²⁰ who performed signs and wonders in the land of Egypt, even to this day, both in Israel and among other men; and made yourself a name, as in this day; ²¹ and brought forth your people Israel out of the land of Egypt with signs, and with wonders, and with a strong hand, and with an outstretched arm, and with great terror; ²² and gave them this land, which you swore to their fathers to give them, a land flowing with milk and honey; ²³ and they came in, and possessed it, but they did not obey your voice, neither walked in your law; they have done nothing of all that you commanded them to do: therefore you have caused all this evil to come on them. ²⁴ Look, the mounds, they have come to the city to take it; and the city is given into the hand of the Chaldeans who fight against it, because of the sword, and of the famine, and of the pestilence; and what you have spoken has happened; and, look, you see it. ²⁵ You have said to me, Lord GOD, "Buy the field for money, and call witnesses"; whereas the city is given into the hand of the Chaldeans.'" ²⁶ Then came the word of the LORD to Jeremiah, saying, ²⁷ "Look, I am the LORD, the God of all flesh: is there anything too difficult for me? ²⁸ Therefore thus says the LORD: 'Look, I will give this city into the hand of the Chaldeans, and into the hand of Nebuchadnezzar king of Babylon, and he shall take it: ²⁹ and the Chaldeans, who fight against this city, shall come and set this city on fire, and burn it, with the houses, on whose roofs they have offered incense to Baal, and poured out drink offerings to other gods, to provoke me to anger. ³⁰ For the sons of Israel and the children of Judah have done only that which was evil in my sight from their youth; for the sons of Israel have only provoked me to anger with the work of their hands, says the LORD. ³¹ For this city has been to me a provocation of my anger and of my wrath from the day that they built it even to this day; that I should remove it from before my face, ³² because of all the evil of the sons of Israel and of the children of Judah, which they have done to provoke me to anger, they, their kings, their officials, their priests, and their prophets, and the men of Judah, and the inhabitants of Jerusalem. ³³ They have turned to me the back, and not the face: and though I taught them, rising up early and teaching them, yet they have not listened to receive instruction. ³⁴ But they set their abominations in the house which is called by my name, to defile it. ³⁵ They built the high places of Baal, which are in the Valley of Ben Hinnom, to cause their sons and their daughters to pass through fire to Moloch; which I did not command them, neither did it come into my mind, that they should do this abomination, to cause Judah to sin.' ³⁶ "Now therefore thus says the LORD, the God of Israel, concerning this city, about which you say, 'It is given into the hand of the king of Babylon by the sword, and by the famine, and by the pestilence': ³⁷ 'Look, I will gather them out of all the countries, where I have driven them in my anger, and in my wrath, and in great indignation; and I will bring them again to this place, and I will cause them to dwell safely: ³⁸ and they shall be my people, and I will be their God: ³⁹ and I will give them one heart and one way, that they may fear me forever, for their good, and of their children *after them: ⁴⁰and I will make an everlasting covenant with them, that I will not turn away from following them, to do them good; and I will put my fear in their hearts, that they may not depart from me. ⁴¹Yes, I will rejoice over them to do them good, and I will plant them in this land assuredly with my whole heart and with my whole soul.' ⁴²"For thus says the LORD: 'Just as I have brought all this great disaster on this people, so will I bring on them all the good that I have promised them. ⁴³Fields shall be bought in this land, about which you say, "It is desolate, without man or animal; it is given into the hand of the Chaldeans." ⁴⁴Men shall buy fields for money, and subscribe the deeds, and seal them, and call witnesses, in the land of Benjamin, and in the places about Jerusalem, and in the cities of Judah, and in the cities of the hill country, and in the cities of the lowland, and in the cities of the Negev: for I will cause their captivity to return,' says the LORD."*

QUESTIONS

QUESTION 1   a

According to Jeremiah chapter 32, while King Zedekiah was in the tenth year of his reign:

What year was King Nebuchadnezzar of Babylon on the throne?

QUESTION 2   b1

According to Jeremiah chapter 32:

Why did king Zedekiah put Jeremiah in prison, and where was the prison?

QUESTION 3   a

According to Jeremiah chapter 32, while Jerusalem was under siege by the Babylonians:

Where was Prophet Jeremiah?

QUESTION 4   **b**

According to Jeremiah chapter 32, the Lord told Jeremiah that his cousin was coming to meet him to sell his land:

Why did the Lord ask Jeremiah to buy the land?

QUESTION 5   **a**

According to Jeremiah chapter 32:

What was the name of the person whom Jeremiah bought land from?

QUESTION 6   **b1**

According to Jeremiah chapter 32:

Why would Jeremiah's cousin go to meet Jeremiah in prison to buy his land?

QUESTION 7   **b**

According to Jeremiah chapter 32:

Who was Shallum?

QUESTION 8   **a**

According to Jeremiah chapter 32:

Who was Hanamel?

QUESTION 9   **a**

According to Jeremiah chapter 32:

Mention one asset Jeremiah owned.

QUESTION 10   **a**

According to Jeremiah chapter 32:

How much did Jeremiah purchase the land he acquired?

QUESTION 11   **b**

According to Jeremiah chapter 32:

What part did Baruch play in the purchase of land by Jeremiah?

QUESTION 12   **b1**

According to Jeremiah chapter 32:

Mention the people present when Jeremiah handed over the deeds of the land he purchased to Baruch.

QUESTION 13   **a**

According to Jeremiah chapter 32:

Who was Neriah?

QUESTION 14   **a**

According to Jeremiah chapter 32:

Who was Mahseiah?

QUESTION 15   **b**

According to Jeremiah chapter 32:

What are the names of the witnesses who signed the deeds of the asset Jeremiah bought?

QUESTION 16   **a**

According to Jeremiah chapter 32, Jeremiah bought a field from his cousin:

Where was the transaction carried out?

QUESTION 17   **b1**

According to Jeremiah chapter 32:

What was God's instruction given to Baruch through Prophet Jeremiah concerning the deeds of the asset Jeremiah purchased?

QUESTION 18   **b2**

According to Jeremiah chapter 32, Jeremiah prayed to God after he bought a field from his cousin:

State four components of his prayer.

QUESTION 19   **b**

Jeremiah chapter 32:35 says, *"which I did not command them, neither did it come into my mind, that they should do this abomination, to cause Judah to sin.'"*

Which abomination is the above passage talking of?

QUESTION 20   **CPB 2**

Jeremiah chapter 32:37–39 says,

"Look, I will gather them out of all the countries, where I have driven them in my anger, and in my wrath, and in great indignation; and I will bring them again to this place, and I will cause them to dwell safely:"

Complete verses 38 and 39.

QUESTION 21   **CMB**

Read Jeremiah chapter 32:3–5, preach or write a commentary on the passage with emphasis on salvation.

QUESTION 22   **CMB**

Read Jeremiah chapter 32:10–12, preach or write a commentary on the passage with emphasis on salvation.

QUESTION 23   **CMB**

Read Jeremiah chapter 32:17, 27, preach or write a commentary on the passage with emphasis on salvation.

QUESTION 24   **CMB**

Read Jeremiah chapter 32:35–39, preach or write a commentary on the passage with focus on verse 39 and with emphasis on salvation.

CHAPTER 32

ANSWERS

ANSWER TO QUESTION 1   a

Eighteenth year (Jeremiah 32:1).

ANSWER TO QUESTION 2   b1

- Because he prophesied against King Zedekiah and the city

Or

Because he prophesied that the Lord would hand the city into the hands of the king of Babylon, and King Zedekiah would not escape but would be captured by the Babylonians and brought to meet king Nebuchadnezzar one on one, then he would be taken to Babylon where God would deal with him there. And if Zedekiah fought against the Babylonians, he would not succeed (Jeremiah 32:2–5).

- The prison was in the courtyard of the guard (Jeremiah 32:2).

ANSWER TO QUESTION 3   a

He was in prison (Jeremiah 32:2).

ANSWER TO QUESTION 4   b

To show that the exiles would someday return to the land and again own property in the land of Judah and Jerusalem and buy and sell houses, vineyards and fields (Jeremiah 32:6–15).

ANSWER TO QUESTION 5   a

Hanamel (Jeremiah 32:7).

ANSWER TO QUESTION 6   b1

By right, Jeremiah was the person to buy the land from his cousin, except if he turned the offer down, then the land could be sold to another person (Jeremiah 32:7).

ANSWER TO QUESTION 7   b

He was the father of Hanamel and uncle to Jeremiah (Jeremiah 32:7).

ANSWER TO QUESTION 8   a

Jeremiah's cousin or the son of Shallum or the person Jeremiah bought a field from (Jeremiah 32:7–8).

ANSWER TO QUESTION 9   a

A field (at Anathoth) (Jeremiah 32:9).

ANSWER TO QUESTION 10   a

Seventeen pieces or shekels of silver (Jeremiah 32:9).

ANSWER TO QUESTION 11   b

He kept the purchase deed or agreement (Jeremiah 32:12).

ANSWER TO QUESTION 12   b1

- Hanamel, his cousin
- The witnesses who signed the deed
- The Jews in the courtyard of the guard (Jeremiah 32:12).

ANSWER TO QUESTION 13   a

He was the father of Baruch (Jeremiah 32:12).

ANSWER TO QUESTION 14   a

He was the grandfather of Baruch (Jeremiah 32:12).

ANSWER TO QUESTION 15   b

Their names were not mentioned (Jeremiah 32:12).

ANSWER TO QUESTION 16   a

At the court of the guard or court of the prison (Jeremiah 32:12).

ANSWER TO QUESTION 17   b1

The instruction was that Baruch should take both the sealed deed and the unsealed copy and put them into an earthen vessel so that they would be preserved for a long time (Jeremiah 32:14).

ANSWER TO QUESTION 18   b2

- He worshipped and adored God for His might, love and faithfulness
- He recounted God's goodness and mercies to Israel
- He recounted Israel's unfaithfulness and stated God's justice in bringing disaster upon them
- Finally, he mentioned that God had commanded him to purchase the land even when the city was under siege (Jeremiah 32:17–25).

ANSWER TO QUESTION 19   b

The people of Judah's act of sacrificing their sons and daughters to Moloch or Molech (Jeremiah 32:35).

ANSWER TO QUESTION 20   CPB 2

"³⁸and they shall be my people, and I will be their God: ³⁹and I will give them one heart and one way, that they may fear me forever, for their good, and of their children after them." (Jeremiah 32:38–39.)

HINT TO QUESTION 21   CMB

Zedekiah's attitude in imprisoning Jeremiah represents the attitude of many people today who are rebellious against God. Such people would go to any extent to make sure that those who preach the truth of God's word are silenced. True believers should not succumb to pressure to preach a diluted version of God's message to gain the acceptance of people and give up on proclaiming God's message. For friendship with the world is enmity with God.

HINT TO QUESTION 22   CMB

Jeremiah formalised and documented the transaction of the field he purchased from Hanamel in the presence of witnesses. He also handed the deed of purchase to Baruch for safekeeping. We can draw a lesson from Jeremiah's actions. It is wise to formalise and document transactions of any sort and keep the documents safe. It is also important to have people witness the sealing of such transactions.

HINT TO QUESTION 23   CMB

The verses under consideration speak of the omnipotent nature of God; nothing is too difficult or impossible for Him to do. In this world, we could experience difficulties and insurmountable issues that could weigh us down, but our consolation and joy are that there is nothing difficult for our God.

HINT TO QUESTION 24   CMB

God said He would bring the Israelites to fear Him for their good and the good of their descendants. This shows that serving God and living according to the word of God is for our good. The things we stand to suffer as a result of choosing the way of the world outweigh the fleeting pleasures the world promises.

CHAPTER 33

JEREMIAH CHAPTER 33

"Moreover the word of the LORD came to Jeremiah the second time, while he was yet shut up in the court of the guard, saying, ² "Thus says the LORD who made the earth, the LORD who forms it to establish it; the LORD is his name: ³ 'Call to me, and I will answer you, and will show you great and hidden things, which you do not know.' ⁴ For thus says the LORD, the God of Israel, concerning the houses of this city, and concerning the houses of the kings of Judah, which are broken down to make a defense against the mounds and against the sword; ⁵ while men come to fight with the Chaldeans, and to fill them with the dead bodies of men, whom I have killed in my anger and in my wrath, and for all whose wickedness I have hidden my face from this city: ⁶ 'Look, I will bring it health and healing, and I will heal them; and I will reveal to them abundance of peace and truth. ⁷ I will cause the captivity of Judah and the captivity of Israel to return, and will build them, as at the first. ⁸ I will cleanse them from all their iniquity, by which they have sinned against me; and I will pardon all their iniquities, by which they have sinned against me, and by which they have transgressed against me. ⁹ This city shall be to me for a name of joy, for a praise and for a glory, before all the nations of the earth, which shall hear all the good that I do to them, and shall fear and tremble for all the good and for all the peace that I procure to it.' ¹⁰ "Thus says the LORD: 'Yet again there shall be heard in this place, about which you say, "It is waste, without man and without animal," even in the cities of Judah, and in the streets of Jerusalem, that are desolate, without man and without inhabitant and

without animal, [11] *the voice of joy and the voice of gladness, the voice of the bridegroom and the voice of the bride, the voice of those who say, "Give thanks to the LORD of hosts, for the LORD is good, for his loving kindness endures forever; who bring thanksgiving into the house of the LORD." For I will cause the captivity of the land to return as at the first,' says the LORD.* [12] *Thus says the LORD of hosts: 'Yet again shall there be in this place, which is waste, without man and without animal, and in all its cities, a habitation of shepherds causing their flocks to lie down.* [13] *In the cities of the hill country, in the cities of the lowland, and in the cities of the Negev, and in the land of Benjamin, and in the places about Jerusalem, and in the cities of Judah, shall the flocks again pass under the hands of him who numbers them,' says the LORD.* [14] *'Look, the days come,' says the LORD, 'that I will perform that good word which I have spoken concerning the house of Israel and concerning the house of Judah.* [15] *In those days, and at that time, will I cause a Branch of righteousness to grow up to David; and he shall execute justice and righteousness in the land.* [16] *In those days shall Judah be saved, and Jerusalem shall dwell safely; and this is the name by which she shall be called: "The LORD our righteousness."* [17] *For thus says the LORD: "David shall never want a man to sit on the throne of the house of Israel;* [18] *neither shall the priests the Levites want a man before me to offer burnt offerings, and to burn meal offerings, and to do sacrifice continually."'"* [19] *The word of the LORD came to Jeremiah, saying,* [20] *"Thus says the LORD: 'If you can break my covenant of the day, and my covenant of the night, so that there shall not be day and night in their season;* [21] *then may also my covenant be broken with David my servant, that he shall not have a son to reign on his throne; and with the Levites the priests, my ministers.* [22] *As the host of heaven can't be numbered, neither the sand of the sea measured; so will I multiply the seed of David my servant, and the Levites who minister to me.'"* [23] *The word of the LORD came to Jeremiah, saying,* [24] *"Do not consider what this people has spoken, saying, 'The two families which the LORD chose, he has cast them off?' Thus do they despise my people, that they should be no more a* *nation before them. ²⁵Thus says the LORD: 'If my covenant of day and night fails, if I have not appointed the ordinances of heaven and earth; ²⁶then will I also cast away the seed of Jacob, and of David my servant, so that I will not take of his seed to be rulers over the seed of Abraham, Isaac, and Jacob: for I will cause their captivity to return, and will have mercy on them.'"*

QUESTIONS

QUESTION 1   b1

Jeremiah chapter 33:1 says, *"Moreover the word of the LORD came to Jeremiah the second time, while he was yet shut up in the court of the guard...."*

What was the first message Jeremiah received from the LORD while he was yet shut up in the court of the guard?

QUESTION 2   CPA

Jeremiah chapter 33:2–3 says,

"Thus says the LORD who made the earth, the LORD who forms it to establish it; the LORD is his name:"

Complete verse 3.

QUESTION 3   CPC

Jeremiah chapter 33:8–9 says,

"I will cleanse them from all their iniquity, by which they have sinned against me; and I will pardon all their iniquities, by which they have sinned against me, and by which they have transgressed against me."

Complete verse 9.

QUESTION 4   b1

According to Jeremiah chapter 33:

Mention three sets of people whom God said their voices would be heard once again in desolate Jerusalem.

QUESTION 5   b1

Jeremiah chapter 33:10 says, *"Thus says the LORD: 'Yet again there shall be heard in this place, about which you say, "It is waste…."*

What shall be heard?

QUESTION 6   b1

According to Jeremiah chapter 33:

Mention three (3) places God said that the shepherds will once again count their flocks.

QUESTION 7   b

According to Jeremiah chapter 33:

What was the first thing God said about the descendant of David?

QUESTION 8   a

Jeremiah chapter 33:16 says, *"In those days shall Judah be saved, and Jerusalem shall dwell safely; and this is the name by which she shall be called…."*

What name shall Jerusalem be called?

QUESTION 9   c

Jeremiah chapter 33:17 says, *"For thus says the LORD: "David shall never want a man to sit on the throne of the house of Israel."*

When did God first make this promise to David, and where can it be found in the Bible?

QUESTION 10   CPB

Jeremiah chapter 33:17–18 says,

"For thus says the LORD: "David shall never want a man to sit on the throne of the house of Israel."""

Complete verse 18.

QUESTION 11   **b1**

According to Jeremiah chapter 33:

What did God say to Jeremiah to affirm His determination to fulfil the covenant which He made to King David?

QUESTION 12   **b**

Jeremiah chapter 33:23–24 says, *"The word of the LORD came to Jeremiah, saying, ²⁴"Do not consider what this people has spoken...."*

What did the people say?

QUESTION 13   **b1**

According to Jeremiah chapter 33:

What did God say to affirm to Jeremiah, His promise of not abandoning Israel and Judah?

QUESTION 14   **CMB**

Read Jeremiah chapter 33:1–3, preach or write a commentary on the passage with emphasis on salvation.

QUESTION 15   **CMB**

Read Jeremiah chapter 33:17–23, preach or write a commentary on the passage with emphasis on salvation.

ANSWERS

ANSWER TO QUESTION 1   **b1**

The Lord told him that Hanamel (his cousin, the son of Shallum, his uncle) would approach him, requesting that he buys his field, and he should buy it (Jeremiah 32:7).

ANSWER TO QUESTION 2   CPA

"³Call to me, and I will answer you, and will show you great and hidden things, which you do not know.'" (Jeremiah 33:3.)

ANSWER TO QUESTION 3   CPC

"⁹This city shall be to me for a name of joy, for a praise and for a glory, before all the nations of the earth, which shall hear all the good that I do to them, and shall fear and tremble for all the good and for all the peace that I procure to it." (Jeremiah 33:9.)

ANSWER TO QUESTION 4   b1

- The bridegroom
- The bride
- Those who say: *"Give thanks to the LORD of hosts for the LORD is good, for his loving kindness endures forever; who bring thanksgiving into the house of the LORD...."* (Jeremiah 33:11.)

ANSWER TO QUESTION 5   b1

- The voice of joy and gladness
- The voice of the bridegroom
- The voice of the bride
- The voice of those who say, *"Give thanks to the LORD of hosts for the LORD is good, for his loving kindness endures forever; who bring thanksgiving into the house of the LORD."* (Jeremiah 33:11.)

ANSWER TO QUESTION 6   b1

- Cities of the hill country or cities of the mountains
- Cities of the lowland or foothills
- Cities of the Negev or South
- The land of Benjamin
- The places around Jerusalem
- The cities of Judah (Jeremiah 33:13).

ANSWER TO QUESTION 7   b

He will cause a Branch of righteousness to grow up to David, and he shall execute justice and righteousness in the land (Jeremiah 33:15).

ANSWER TO QUESTION 8   a

The LORD our righteousness (Jeremiah 33:16).

ANSWER TO QUESTION 9   c

- It was when David told Nathan of his plans to build a temple for God that God sent Nathan to tell David of the things He would do for him. The verse in the question is one of the promises.
- 2 Samuel 7:1–17.

ANSWER TO QUESTION 10   CPB

"18 neither shall the priests the Levites want a man before me to offer burnt offerings, and to burn meal offerings, and to do sacrifice continually." (Jeremiah 33:18.)

ANSWER TO QUESTION 11   b1

God said if one can break His covenant of the day and night so that day and night cease to exist, only then will His covenant with David be broken (Jeremiah 33:20–21).

ANSWER TO QUESTION 12   b

They said that the Lord had cast off or rejected the two families (Judah and Israel) which He chose (Jeremiah 33:24).

ANSWER TO QUESTION 13   b1

God said that His promise of not rejecting His people is as sure as His laws that govern the night, day, heaven and earth (Jeremiah 33:25).

HINT TO QUESTION 14   CMB

When Jeremiah was imprisoned in the court of the guard, God spoke to him, encouraging him to call on God. God assured him of an answer and a revelation of hidden things. This is an encouragement to us that we should call on God at all times and in all situations. Children of God who call upon the name of the Lord get a response, even if the response may not be as expected. We should rest on the understanding that God's ways are better and higher than ours.

HINT TO QUESTION 15   CMB

In the verses under consideration, God reiterated His covenant of raising an everlasting King from David's lineage (Psalm 89:3–4) and having an enduring priesthood. He fulfilled this promise in the person of Jesus Christ. God is faithful in keeping His promises. We should always trust God that He will do what He says.

CHAPTER 34

JEREMIAH CHAPTER 34

"The word which came to Jeremiah from the LORD, when Nebuchadnezzar king of Babylon, and all his army, and all the kingdoms of the earth that were under his dominion, and all the peoples, were fighting against Jerusalem, and against all the cities of it, saying: ²*"Thus says the LORD, the God of Israel, 'Go, and speak to Zedekiah king of Judah, and tell him, "Thus says the LORD, 'Look, I will give this city into the hand of the king of Babylon, and he shall burn it with fire:* ³*and you shall not escape out of his hand, but shall surely be taken, and delivered into his hand; and your eyes shall see the eyes of the king of Babylon, and he shall speak with you mouth to mouth, and you shall go to Babylon.'* ⁴*Yet hear the word of the LORD, O Zedekiah king of Judah: thus says the LORD concerning you, 'You shall not die by the sword;* ⁵*you shall die in peace; and with the burnings of your fathers, the former kings who were before you, so shall they make a burning for you; and they shall lament you, saying, "Ah Lord." for I have spoken the word,' says the LORD.'"'"* ⁶*Then Jeremiah the prophet spoke all these words to Zedekiah king of Judah in Jerusalem,* ⁷*when the king of Babylon's army was fighting against Jerusalem, and against all the cities of Judah that were left, against Lachish and against Azekah; for these alone remained of the cities of Judah as fortified cities.* ⁸*The word that came to Jeremiah from the LORD, after that the king Zedekiah had made a covenant with all the people who were at Jerusalem, to proclaim liberty to them;* ⁹*that every man should let his male servant, and every man his female servant, who is a Hebrew or a Hebrewess, go free; that none*

should make bondservants of them, of a Jew his brother. *¹⁰And all the officials and all the people obeyed, who had entered into the covenant, that everyone should let his male servant, and everyone his female servant, go free, that none should make bondservants of them any more; they obeyed, and let them go: ¹¹but afterwards they turned, and caused the servants and the handmaids, whom they had let go free, to return, and brought them into subjection for servants and for handmaids. ¹²Therefore the word of the LORD came to Jeremiah from the LORD, saying, ¹³"Thus says the LORD, the God of Israel: 'I made a covenant with your fathers in the day that I brought them forth out of the land of Egypt, out of the house of bondage, saying, ¹⁴"At the end of seven years you shall let go every man his brother who is a Hebrew, who has been sold to you, and has served you six years, you shall let him go free from you": but your fathers did not listen to me, neither inclined their ear. ¹⁵You had now turned, and had done that which is right in my eyes, in proclaiming liberty every man to his neighbor; and you had made a covenant before me in the house which is called by my name: ¹⁶but you turned and profaned my name, and caused every man his servant, and every man his handmaid, whom you had let go free at their pleasure, to return; and you brought them into subjection, to be to you for servants and for handmaids. ¹⁷Therefore thus says the LORD: "You have not listened to me, to proclaim liberty, every man to his brother, and every man to his neighbor: look, I proclaim to you a liberty, says the LORD, to the sword, to the pestilence, and to the famine; and I will make you to be tossed back and forth among all the kingdoms of the earth. ¹⁸I will give the men who have transgressed my covenant, who have not performed the words of the covenant which they made before me, when they cut the calf in two and passed between its parts; ¹⁹the officials of Judah, and the officials of Jerusalem, the eunuchs, and the priests, and all the people of the land, who passed between the parts of the calf; ²⁰I will even give them into the hand of their enemies, and into the hand of those who seek their life; and their dead bodies shall be for food to the birds of the sky, and to the animals of the earth.* ²¹*And Zedekiah king of Judah and his officials will I give into the hand of their enemies, and into the hand of those who seek their life, and into the hand of the king of Babylon's army, who have gone away from you.* ²²*Look, I will command, says the LORD, and cause them to return to this city; and they shall fight against it, and take it, and burn it with fire: and I will make the cities of Judah a desolation, without inhabitant."""*

QUESTIONS

QUESTION 1   a

According to Jeremiah chapter 34:

Which armies did King Nebuchadnezzar deploy to fight against Jerusalem?

QUESTION 2   CTX

"and you shall not escape out of his hand, but shall surely be taken, and delivered into his hand; and your eyes shall see the eyes of the king of Babylon...."

Give the context of the above quote:

Who said it, to who, and under what circumstance?

QUESTION 3   a

According to Jeremiah chapter 34:

How did God say King Zedekiah would die?

QUESTION 4   b

According to Jeremiah chapter 34:

What two things did God say the people would do for Zedekiah when he died?

QUESTION 5   b

According to Jeremiah chapter 34:

What were the last three fortified cities in Judah to be captured by King Nebuchadnezzar?

QUESTION 6   b

According to Jeremiah chapter 34:

What covenant did king Zedekiah make with the people?

QUESTION 7   a

According to Jeremiah chapter 34:

What did the people of Judah do after they had freed their Hebrew slaves?

QUESTION 8   CTX

"At the end of seven years you shall let go every man his brother who is a Hebrew, who has been sold to you...."

Give the context of the above quote:

Who said it, to who, and under what circumstance?

QUESTION 9   b1

According to Jeremiah chapter 34, the Lord says the people of Judah entered into a covenant with Him to free their Hebrew slaves:

Mention the place where they entered into the covenant with God and how they solemnised the covenant.

QUESTION 10   c

Jeremiah chapter 34:13–14 says, *"Thus says the LORD, the God of Israel: 'I made a covenant with your fathers in the day that I brought them forth out of the land of Egypt, out of the house of bondage, saying, ¹⁴"At the end of seven years you shall let go every man his brother who is a Hebrew, who has been sold to you, and has served you six years, you shall let him go free from you": but your fathers did not listen to me, neither inclined their ear."*

Mention a passage in the Bible where God initially gave the above command to the Israelites.

QUESTION 11   CPC

Jeremiah chapter 34:15–16 says,

"You had now turned, and had done that which is right in my eyes, in proclaiming liberty every man to his neighbor; and you had made a covenant before me in the house which is called by my name."

Complete verse 16.

QUESTION 12   b

Jeremiah chapter 34:17 says, *"look, I proclaim to you a liberty, says the LORD, to the sword, to the pestilence, and to the famine."*

Why did God proclaim liberty to the sword, pestilence and famine upon the people of Judah?

QUESTION 13   CPC 2

Jeremiah chapter 34:18–20 says,

"¹⁸I will give the men who have transgressed my covenant, who have not performed the words of the covenant which they made before me, when they cut the calf in two and passed between its parts."

Complete verses 19 and 20.

QUESTION 14   c

Jeremiah chapter 34:18 says, *"I will give the men who have transgressed my covenant, who have not performed the words of the covenant which they made before me, when they cut the calf in two and passed between its parts."*

Where else in the Bible was a similar ritual of cutting animals into two and passing through them done, and what circumstance or event led to the ritual?

QUESTION 15   CMC

Read Jeremiah chapter 34:8–11, 17–18, and preach or write a commentary on the passage with emphasis on salvation.

ANSWERS

ANSWER TO QUESTION 1   a

The armies of all the kingdoms of the earth which he ruled (Jeremiah 34:1).

ANSWER TO QUESTION 2   CTX

- God, through Prophet Jeremiah
- To King Zedekiah
- When the king of Babylon and all the armies from the kingdoms he ruled besieged Jerusalem and the other towns of Judah (Jeremiah 34:1–3).

ANSWER TO QUESTION 3   a

He said King Zedekiah would die peacefully and not by sword or in war (Jeremiah 34:4–5).

ANSWER TO QUESTION 4   b

- The people will make burnings for him.
- They would lament (mourn and cry) for him (Jeremiah 34:5).

ANSWER TO QUESTION 5   b

Lachish, Jerusalem and Azekah (Jeremiah 34:7).

ANSWER TO QUESTION 6   b

He entered into a covenant with the people to free their Hebrew slaves (Jeremiah 34:8–9).

ANSWER TO QUESTION 7   a

They changed their minds and took back their slaves (Jeremiah 34:11).

ANSWER TO QUESTION 8   CTX

- God, through Prophet Jeremiah
- To the people of Judah and Jerusalem
- When they took back their Hebrew slaves after they had freed them as they had agreed with King Zedekiah. (God was displeased and stated the command He gave to their ancestors and their subsequent disobedience) (Jeremiah 34:13–15).

ANSWER TO QUESTION 9   b1

- The Temple (Jeremiah 34:15).
- They cut the calf into two and passed between its parts (Jeremiah 34:18).

ANSWER TO QUESTION 10   c

Exodus 21:2 or Deuteronomy 15:12.

ANSWER TO QUESTION 11   CPC

"¹⁶but you turned and profaned my name, and caused every man his servant, and every man his handmaid, whom you had let go free at their pleasure, to return; and you brought them into subjection, to be to you for servants and for handmaids." (Jeremiah 34:16.)

ANSWER TO QUESTION 12   b

Because they went back on the oath they made before the Lord by taking back their Hebrew slaves, which they had set free (Jeremiah 34:16–17).

ANSWER TO QUESTION 13   CPC 2

"¹⁹the officials of Judah, and the officials of Jerusalem, the eunuchs, and the priests, and all the people of the land, who passed between

the parts of the calf; ²⁰I will even give them into the hand of their enemies, and into the hand of those who seek their life; and their dead bodies shall be for food to the birds of the sky, and to the animals of the earth." (Jeremiah 34:19–20.)

ANSWER TO QUESTION 14   c

- Genesis 15:9–21
- When the Lord promised to give Abraham the whole land of Canaan, and Abraham cut a heifer, a ram, and a goat into two, and he placed them on both sides (but he did not cut the turtledove and pigeon, which God also asked him to bring). But in this case, a smoking furnace and a flaming torch passed between the sacrifice.

HINT TO QUESTION 15   CMC

The people of Judah obeyed God initially to free their Hebrew slaves but turned back to enslave them. Today, many abide by God's instructions, but when they consider the inconveniences that their obedience to God may pose, the things they would have to give up or the challenges encountered, they could turn back to their lives of sin, forgetting their initial promise to obey God.

CHAPTER 35

JEREMIAH CHAPTER 35

"The word which came to Jeremiah from the LORD in the days of Jehoiakim the son of Josiah, king of Judah, saying, ²*"Go to the house of the Rechabites, and speak to them, and bring them into the house of the LORD, into one of the rooms, and give them wine to drink."* ³*Then I took Jaazaniah the son of Jeremiah, the son of Habazziniah, and his brothers, and all his sons, and the whole house of the Rechabites.* ⁴*And I brought them into the house of the LORD, into the room of the sons of Hananiah son of Gedaliah, the man of God, which was by the room of the officials, which was above the room of Maaseiah the son of Shallum, the keeper of the threshold.* ⁵*I set before the sons of the house of the Rechabites bowls full of wine, and cups; and I said to them, "Drink wine."* ⁶*But they said, "We will drink no wine; for Jonadab the son of Rechab, our father, commanded us, saying, 'You shall drink no wine, neither you, nor your sons, forever:* ⁷*neither shall you build house, nor sow seed, nor plant vineyard, nor have any; but all your days you shall dwell in tents; that you may live many days in the land in which you live.'* ⁸*We have obeyed the voice of Jonadab the son of Rechab, our father, in all that he commanded us, to drink no wine all our days, we, our wives, our sons, or our daughters;* ⁹*nor to build houses for us to dwell in; neither have we vineyard, nor field, nor seed:* ¹⁰*but we have lived in tents, and have obeyed, and done according to all that Jonadab our father commanded us.* ¹¹*But it happened, when Nebuchadnezzar king of Babylon came up into the land, that we said, 'Come, and let us go to Jerusalem for fear of*

*the army of the Chaldeans, and for fear of the army of the Syrians';
so we dwell at Jerusalem." ¹²Then came the word of the LORD to
Jeremiah, saying, ¹³"Thus says the LORD of hosts, the God of
Israel: 'Go, and tell the men of Judah and the inhabitants of
Jerusalem, "Will you not receive instruction to listen to my words?"
says the LORD. ¹⁴"The words of Jonadab the son of Rechab, that
he commanded his sons, not to drink wine, are performed; and to
this day they drink none, for they obey their father's commandment:
but I have spoken to you, rising up early and speaking; and you
have not listened to me. ¹⁵I have sent also to you all my servants
the prophets, rising up early and sending them, saying, 'Return
now every man from his evil way, and amend your doings, and do
not go after other gods to serve them, and you shall dwell in the
land which I have given to you and to your fathers': but you have
not inclined your ear, nor listened to me. ¹⁶Because the sons of
Jonadab the son of Rechab have performed the commandment of
their father which he commanded them, but this people has not
listened to me; ¹⁷therefore thus says the LORD, the God of hosts,
the God of Israel: 'Look, I will bring on Judah and on all the
inhabitants of Jerusalem all the disaster that I have pronounced
against them; because I have spoken to them, but they have not
listened; and I have called to them, but they have not answered.'"'"
¹⁸Jeremiah said to the house of the Rechabites, "Thus says the
LORD of hosts, the God of Israel: 'Because you have obeyed the
commandment of Jonadab your father, and kept all his precepts,
and done according to all that he commanded you'; ¹⁹therefore
thus says the LORD of hosts, the God of Israel: 'Jonadab the son of
Rechab shall not want a man to stand before me forever.'"*

QUESTIONS

QUESTION 1   a

According to Jeremiah chapter 35:

Who was king in Judah when God sent Jeremiah to the Rechabites?

QUESTION 2   a

According to Jeremiah chapter 35:

What instruction did God give Jeremiah concerning the Rechabites?

QUESTION 3   b1

According to Jeremiah chapter 35, when Jeremiah went to meet the Rechabites:

What was the name of the Rechabite mentioned? Who were his father and grandfather?

QUESTION 4   b1

According to Jeremiah chapter 35:

Describe the location of the temple chamber where Jeremiah took the Rechabites when God sent him to them.

QUESTION 5   b1

According to Jeremiah chapter 35:

How did Jeremiah describe Gedaliah, also known as Igdaliah, when he mentioned him? What was Gedaliah's son's name, and why did Jeremiah mention them?

QUESTION 6   b

According to Jeremiah chapter 35:

What was the Rechabites' response when Prophet Jeremiah offered them wine, and what was the reason for their response?

QUESTION 7   b1

According to Jeremiah chapter 35:

Mention four (4) commands that Jonadab (Jehonadab) gave to his descendants.

QUESTION 8   b

According to Jeremiah chapter 35:

What did Jonadab (Jehonadab) say would be his descendants' reward if they obeyed his instructions?

QUESTION 9   b

According to Jeremiah chapter 35:

How did the Rechabites come to be in Jerusalem?

QUESTION 10   CTX

"Come, and let us go to Jerusalem for fear of the army of the Chaldeans...."

Give the context of the above quote:

Who said it, to who, and under what circumstance?

QUESTION 11   b

According to Jeremiah chapter 35:

What comparison did God make between the Rechabites and the people of Judah and Jerusalem?

QUESTION 12   b

According to Jeremiah chapter 35:

What did God say He would do to the people of Judah and Jerusalem for not obeying His commands?

QUESTION 13   b

According to Jeremiah chapter 35:

How did God reward the Rechabites for their obedience to their father's instruction?

QUESTION 14   CMB

Read Jeremiah chapter 35:14–16, preach or write a commentary on the passage with emphasis on salvation.

ANSWERS

ANSWER TO QUESTION 1   a

Jehoiakim (Jeremiah 35:1–2).

ANSWER TO QUESTION 2   a

God told Jeremiah to invite the Rechabites to the temple, take them into one of the rooms or chambers and give them wine to drink (Jeremiah 35:2).

ANSWER TO QUESTION 3   b1

- Jaazaniah
- Jeremiah was his father
- Habazziniah was his grandfather (Jeremiah 35:3).

ANSWER TO QUESTION 4   b1

The chamber was by the room of the officials or princes and above the room of Maaseiah, son of Shallum, the keeper of the threshold (Jeremiah 35:4).

ANSWER TO QUESTION 5   b1

- Jeremiah described him as a man of God
- His son's name was Hananiah or Hanan
- Jeremiah mentioned them because he brought the Rechabites into their family's temple chamber (Jeremiah 35:4).

ANSWER TO QUESTION 6   b

- They said they would not drink
- Because their father or ancestor Jonadab or Jehonadab, son of Rechab commanded them not to drink wine (Jeremiah 35:6).

ANSWER TO QUESTION 7   b1

- They must not drink wine
- They must not sow seed
- They must never plant or have vineyards

- They must not build houses but always live in tents (Jeremiah 35:6–7).

ANSWER TO QUESTION 8   b

They will live long in the land where they lived (Jeremiah 35:7).

ANSWER TO QUESTION 9   b

When king Nebuchadnezzar invaded their land, they fled to Jerusalem for fear of the army of the Chaldeans and Syrians (Jeremiah 35:11).

ANSWER TO QUESTION 10   CTX

- The Rechabites
- To Prophet Jeremiah
- When they were explaining to Jeremiah how they came to be in Jerusalem (after Jeremiah had given them wine to drink and they refused) (Jeremiah 35:11).

ANSWER TO QUESTION 11   b

The Rechabites were obedient to their father or ancestor Jonadab (who told them not to drink wine), while the people of Judah and Jerusalem were disobedient to God's instructions (Jeremiah 35:13–15).

ANSWER TO QUESTION 12   b

God said He would bring upon Judah and Jerusalem all the disasters He had pronounced against them (Jeremiah 35:17).

ANSWER TO QUESTION 13   b

God declared that Jonadab (the son of Rechab) would always have a man that would stand before Him or serve Him (Jeremiah 35:19).

HINT TO QUESTION 14   CMB

If the Rechabites could be careful to keep their earthly father's words or commandments, a mere mortal who could not tell what tomorrow would be, we should be more careful in keeping the word of God, our true Father who is all-knowing, for His instructions are for our good.

CHAPTER 36

JEREMIAH CHAPTER 36

"It happened in the fourth year of Jehoiakim the son of Josiah, king of Judah, that this word came to Jeremiah from the LORD, saying, ²"Take a scroll, and write on it all the words that I have spoken to you against Israel, and against Judah, and against all the nations, from the day I spoke to you, from the days of Josiah, even to this day. ³It may be that the house of Judah will hear all the evil which I purpose to do to them; that they may return every man from his evil way; that I may forgive their iniquity and their sin."
⁴Then Jeremiah called Baruch the son of Neriah; and Baruch wrote from the mouth of Jeremiah all the words of the LORD, which he had spoken to him, on a scroll. ⁵Jeremiah commanded Baruch, saying, "I am shut up; I can't go into the house of the LORD: ⁶therefore you go, and read from the scroll, which you have written from my mouth, the words of the LORD in the ears of the people in the LORD's house on the fast day; and also you shall read them in the ears of all Judah who come out of their cities. ⁷It may be they will present their petition before the LORD, and will return everyone from his evil way; for great is the anger and the wrath that the LORD has pronounced against this people."
⁸Baruch the son of Neriah did according to all that Jeremiah the prophet commanded him, reading from the scroll the words of the LORD in the LORD's house. ⁹Now it happened in the fifth year of Jehoiakim the son of Josiah, king of Judah, in the ninth month, that all the people in Jerusalem, and all the people who came from the cities of Judah to Jerusalem, proclaimed a fast before the LORD. ¹⁰Then Baruch read from the scroll the words of Jeremiah

in the house of the LORD, in the room of Gemariah the son of Shaphan, the scribe, in the upper court, at the entry of the New Gate of the LORD's house, in the ears of all the people. ¹¹ *When Micaiah the son of Gemariah, the son of Shaphan, had heard from the scroll all the words of the LORD,* ¹²*he went down into the king's house, into the scribe's room: and look, all the officials were sitting there, Elishama the scribe, and Delaiah the son of Shemaiah, and Elnathan the son of Achbor, and Gemariah the son of Shaphan, and Zedekiah the son of Hananiah, and all the officials.* ¹³*Then Micaiah declared to them all the words that he had heard, when Baruch read the scroll in the hearing of the people.* ¹⁴*Therefore all the officials sent Jehudi the son of Nethaniah, the son of Shelemiah, the son of Cushi, to Baruch, saying, "Take in your hand the scroll in which you have read in the ears of the people, and come." So Baruch the son of Neriah took the scroll in his hand, and came to them.* ¹⁵*They said to him, "Sit down now, and read it in our ears." So Baruch read it in their ears.* ¹⁶*Now it happened, when they had heard all the words, they turned in fear one toward another, and said to Baruch, "We will surely tell the king of all these words."* ¹⁷*They asked Baruch, saying, "Tell us now, How did you write all these words at his mouth?"* ¹⁸*Then Baruch answered them, "He pronounced all these words to me with his mouth, and I wrote them with ink on the scroll."* ¹⁹*Then the officials said to Baruch, "Go, hide, you and Jeremiah; and let no man know where you are."* ²⁰*They went in to the king into the court; but they had put the scroll in the room of Elishama the scribe; and they told all the words in the ears of the king.* ²¹*So the king sent Jehudi to get the scroll; and he took it out of the room of Elishama the scribe. Jehudi read it in the ears of the king, and in the ears of all the officials who stood beside the king.* ²²*Now the king was sitting in the winter house in the ninth month: and there was a fire in the brazier burning before him.* ²³*It happened, when Jehudi had read three or four columns, that the king cut it with a knife, and cast it into the fire that was in the brazier, until all the scroll was consumed in the fire that was in the brazier.* ²⁴*They were not afraid, nor tore their garments, neither the king, nor any of his* servants who heard all these words. ²⁵Moreover Elnathan and Delaiah and Gemariah had made intercession to the king that he would not burn the scroll; but he would not hear them. ²⁶The king commanded Jerahmeel the king's son, and Seraiah the son of Azriel, and Shelemiah the son of Abdeel, to take Baruch the scribe and Jeremiah the prophet; but the LORD hid them. ²⁷Then the word of the LORD came to Jeremiah, after that the king had burned the scroll, and the words which Baruch wrote at the mouth of Jeremiah, saying, ²⁸"Take again another scroll, and write on it all the former words that were in the first scroll, which Jehoiakim the king of Judah has burned. ²⁹Concerning Jehoiakim king of Judah you shall say, 'Thus says the LORD: "You have burned this scroll, saying, 'Why have you written in it, saying, "The king of Babylon shall certainly come and destroy this land, and shall cause to cease from there man and animal?"'" ³⁰Therefore thus says the LORD concerning Jehoiakim king of Judah: "He shall have none to sit on the throne of David; and his dead body shall be cast out in the day to the heat, and in the night to the frost. ³¹I will punish him and his seed and his servants for their iniquity; and I will bring on them, and on the inhabitants of Jerusalem, and on the men of Judah, all the evil that I have pronounced against them, but they did not listen."'" ³²Then Jeremiah took another scroll, and gave it to Baruch the scribe, the son of Neriah, who wrote on it at the instruction of Jeremiah all the words of the scroll which Jehoiakim king of Judah had burned in the fire; and there were added besides to them many like words."

QUESTIONS

QUESTION 1   b1

According to Jeremiah chapter 36, when God first told Jeremiah to take a scroll:

What did He ask him to write on it, and for what purpose?

QUESTION 2   CTX

"I am shut up; I can't go into the house of the LORD."

Give the context of the above quote:

Who said it, to who, and under what circumstance?

QUESTION 3   b

According to Jeremiah chapter 36, when God asked Jeremiah to pick up a scroll and write down His messages:

How did Jeremiah carry out the instruction?

QUESTION 4   CTX

"Take in your hand the scroll in which you have read in the ears of the people, and come...."

Give the context of the above quote:

Who said it, to who, and under what circumstance?

QUESTION 5   b

According to Jeremiah chapter 36, God asked Jeremiah to write down His messages on a scroll for the people:

Who took the message to the people in the temple and why?

QUESTION 6   a

According to Jeremiah chapter 36, Jeremiah instructed that the message of God written on the scroll be delivered on a particular day:

What day was that?

QUESTION 7   b

According to Jeremiah chapter 36:

During which month of the year was the message of the Lord written on a scroll and delivered to the people in the temple?

QUESTION 8   **b1**

According to Jeremiah chapter 36:

Who was the King in Judah when God asked Jeremiah to write His messages on a scroll for the people, and what year of his reign did this happen?

QUESTION 9   **a**

According to Jeremiah chapter 36, when the message of the Lord was read in the temple:

Which towns or cities did the people in the temple come from?

QUESTION 10   **b1**

According to Jeremiah chapter 36:

In whose room did Baruch stand to deliver God's message to the people in the temple? Describe the location of the room.

QUESTION 11   **b**

According to Jeremiah chapter 36:

Who were Micaiah's father and grandfather?

QUESTION 12   **b1**

According to Jeremiah chapter 36:

Mention the names of three officials Micaiah met in the scribe's chamber or secretary's room of the palace.

QUESTION 13   **b**

According to Jeremiah chapter 36:

What did Micaiah do when he heard the message Baruch read in the temple?

QUESTION 14   **a**

According to Jeremiah chapter 36, when Micaiah told the officials that were meeting in the scribe's chambers of the palace about the message he heard in the temple:

What did they do?

QUESTION 15   **CTX**

"Go, hide, you and Jeremiah; and let no man know where you are."

Give the context of the above quote:

Who said it, to who, and under what circumstance?

QUESTION 16   **b**

According to Jeremiah chapter 36, when the scroll of Jeremiah and Baruch was taken to the king's court:

Where was it kept before the king sent for it to be read to him?

QUESTION 17   **a**

According to Jeremiah chapter 36:

Who read the scroll of Jeremiah and Baruch to King Jehoiakim?

QUESTION 18   **b**

According to Jeremiah chapter 36, when the king was informed about the message which was read in the temple:

What were the things he did in response?

QUESTION 19   **a**

Jeremiah chapter 36:25 says that some temple officials made intercession to the king:

What was the intercession for?

QUESTION 20   **a**

According to Jeremiah chapter 36:

What is the name of King Jehoiakim's son mentioned among those the king sent to take Baruch and Jeremiah?

QUESTION 21   **b1**

According to Jeremiah chapter 36:

How many people did King Jehoiakim send to take or arrest Jeremiah and his secretary? Mention them.

QUESTION 22   **a**

According to Jeremiah chapter 36, after King Jehoiakim had burned the first scroll in which God's message was written:

What was God's message to Jeremiah?

QUESTION 23   **b**

According to Jeremiah chapter 36, in God's second message to Jeremiah:

What did God say was the reason King Jehoiakim burned the first scroll?

QUESTION 24   **b1**

According to Jeremiah chapter 36:

Mention three things God said would happen to King Jehoiakim for burning the first scroll.

QUESTION 25   **b**

According to Jeremiah chapter 36, after King Jehoiakim had burned the first scroll, God asked Prophet Jeremiah to rewrite the scroll:

How did Jeremiah carry out this instruction?

QUESTION 26   **CMC**

Read Jeremiah chapter 36:1–6, preach or write a commentary on the passage with emphasis on salvation.

QUESTION 27   **CMC**

Read Jeremiah chapter 36:9, preach or write a commentary on the passage with emphasis on salvation.

ANSWERS

ANSWER TO QUESTION 1   b1

- To write down all God's words against Israel, Judah and all the nations God has spoken against since the days of King Josiah up to the time Jeremiah received the instruction.
- Perhaps the people of Judah would hear His words about the terrible things He was about to bring on them and would repent (Jeremiah 36:1–3).

ANSWER TO QUESTION 2   CTX

- Prophet Jeremiah
- To Baruch
- When Jeremiah asked Baruch to take the scroll he had written and read it to those in the temple of the Lord (Jeremiah 36:1–6).

ANSWER TO QUESTION 3   b

Jeremiah dictated the messages to Baruch, who wrote down the words on the scroll (Jeremiah 36:4).

ANSWER TO QUESTION 4   CTX

- The temple officials at the scribe's chambers of the king's house
- To Baruch through Jehudi
- When Micaiah told the temple officials the message Baruch read in the temple, they sent Jehudi to go and tell Baruch to come with the scroll and read to them (Jeremiah 36:4–14).

ANSWER TO QUESTION 5   b

- Baruch
- Because Jeremiah was shut up, or he was in prison or because Jeremiah sent him (Jeremiah 36:5).

ANSWER TO QUESTION 6   a

The day of fasting (Jeremiah 36:6).

ANSWER TO QUESTION 7   b

The ninth month (Jeremiah 36:9).

ANSWER TO QUESTION 8   b1

- King Jehoiakim
- In the fifth year of his reign (Jeremiah 36:9).

ANSWER TO QUESTION 9   a

All the towns and cities of Judah (Jeremiah 36:9).

ANSWER TO QUESTION 10   b1

- In the temple room of Gemariah (son of Shaphan, the secretary)
- In the upper court, at the entry of the new gate of the Lord's house (Jeremiah 36:10).

ANSWER TO QUESTION 11   b

- Gemariah was his father
- Shaphan was his grandfather (Jeremiah 36:11).

ANSWER TO QUESTION 12   b1

- Elishama (the scribe)
- Delaiah (son of Shemaiah)
- Elnathan (son of Achbor)
- Gemariah (son of Shaphan)
- Zedekiah (son of Hananiah) (Jeremiah 36:12).

ANSWER TO QUESTION 13   b

He went to where the administrative officials were gathered and informed them of the words Baruch was reading from the scrolls (Jeremiah 36:12–13).

ANSWER TO QUESTION 14   a

They sent for Baruch to come and read to them (Jeremiah 36:14).

273

ANSWER TO QUESTION 15   CTX

- The temple officials at the scribe's chambers of the kings' house
- To Baruch
- When Baruch read to them the message of God from Jeremiah, which he had read in the temple (Jeremiah 36:19).

ANSWER TO QUESTION 16   b

The room of Elishama the scribe (Jeremiah 36:20–21)

ANSWER TO QUESTION 17   a

Jehudi (Jeremiah 36:21).

ANSWER TO QUESTION 18   b

He sent for the scroll, and as it was read to him, he tore and burned it (Jeremiah 36:21–23).

ANSWER TO QUESTION 19   a

For the king not to burn the scroll which Baruch read in the temple (Jeremiah 36:25).

ANSWER TO QUESTION 20   a

Jerahmeel (Jeremiah 36:26).

ANSWER TO QUESTION 21   b1

- Three (3) persons
- Jerahmeel (the king's son)

Seraiah (the son of Azriel)

Shelemiah (the son of Abdeel) (Jeremiah 36:26).

ANSWER TO QUESTION 22   a

To get another scroll and rewrite everything that was on the first scroll (Jeremiah 36:27–28).

ANSWER TO QUESTION 23   b

Because it was written in the scroll that the king of Babylon would destroy the land and they will be no men or animals in it (Jeremiah 36:29).

ANSWER TO QUESTION 24   b1

- Jehoiakim would have no one to sit on the throne of David
- His dead body shall be cast out in the day to the heat and in the night to the frost
- God would punish King Jehoiakim, his seed and his servants for their iniquities and the whole of Jerusalem and Judah for their sins by bringing on them all that He had pronounced against them (Jeremiah 36:30–31).

ANSWER TO QUESTION 25   b

Jeremiah dictated the message to Baruch, who wrote down the words on the scroll (Jeremiah 36:32).

HINT TO QUESTION 26   CMC

As Jeremiah worked with Baruch to ensure God's words reached the people of Judah even when he was restricted from entering the temple, we should learn from him to employ different avenues of preaching the gospel. There is no room for an excuse.

HINT TO QUESTION 27   CMC

The people of Judah proclaimed a fast before the Lord while they were still living in disobedience to Him. Their fast was not in repentance of their sins. Religious practices are no substitute for obedience to God. Obedience is better than sacrifice. Many believers are more interested in the outward display of piety than obeying the word of God, having the form of godliness but denying the power that could make them godly (2 Timothy 3:5).

CHAPTER 37

JEREMIAH CHAPTER 37

"Zedekiah the son of Josiah reigned as king, instead of Coniah the son of Jehoiakim, whom Nebuchadnezzar king of Babylon made king in the land of Judah. ²But neither he, nor his servants, nor the people of the land, listened to the words of the LORD, which he spoke by the prophet Jeremiah. ³Zedekiah the king sent Jehucal the son of Shelemiah, and Zephaniah the son of Maaseiah, the priest, to the prophet Jeremiah, saying, "Pray now to the LORD our God for us." ⁴Now Jeremiah came in and went out among the people; for they had not put him into prison. ⁵Pharaoh's army had come forth out of Egypt; and when the Chaldeans who were besieging Jerusalem heard news of them, they broke up from Jerusalem. ⁶Then came the word of the LORD to the prophet Jeremiah, saying, ⁷"Thus says the LORD, the God of Israel, 'You shall tell the king of Judah, who sent you to me to inquire of me: "Look, Pharaoh's army, which has come forth to help you, shall return to Egypt into their own land. ⁸The Chaldeans shall come again, and fight against this city; and they shall take it, and burn it with fire." ⁹Thus says the LORD, "Do not deceive yourselves, saying, 'The Chaldeans shall surely depart from us'; for they shall not depart. ¹⁰For though you had struck the whole army of the Chaldeans who fight against you, and there remained but wounded men among them, yes would they rise up every man in his tent, and burn this city with fire."'" ¹¹It happened that, when the army of the Chaldeans was broken up from Jerusalem for fear of Pharaoh's army, ¹²then Jeremiah went forth out of Jerusalem to go into the land of Benjamin, to receive his portion there, in the midst of the

people. ¹³*When he was in the Benjamin Gate, a captain of the guard was there, whose name was Irijah, the son of Shelemiah, the son of Hananiah; and he laid hold on Jeremiah the prophet, saying, "You are falling away to the Chaldeans."* ¹⁴*Then Jeremiah said, "It is false; I am not falling away to the Chaldeans." But he did not listen to him; so Irijah laid hold on Jeremiah, and brought him to the officials.* ¹⁵*And the officials were angry with Jeremiah, and struck him, and put him in prison in the house of Jonathan the scribe; for they had made that the prison.* ¹⁶*When Jeremiah had come into the dungeon house, and into the cells, and Jeremiah had remained there many days;* ¹⁷*Then Zedekiah the king sent, and fetched him: and the king asked him secretly in his house, and said, "Is there any word from the LORD?" Jeremiah said, "There is." He said also, "You shall be delivered into the hand of the king of Babylon."* ¹⁸*Moreover Jeremiah said to king Zedekiah, "Wherein have I sinned against you, or against your servants, or against this people, that you have put me in prison?* ¹⁹*Where now are your prophets who prophesied to you, saying, The king of Babylon shall not come against you, nor against this land?* ²⁰*Now please hear, my lord the king: please let my petition be presented before you, that you not cause me to return to the house of Jonathan the scribe, lest I die there."* ²¹*Then Zedekiah the king commanded, and they committed Jeremiah into the court of the guard; and they gave him daily a loaf of bread out of the bakers' street, until all the bread in the city was spent. Thus Jeremiah remained in the court of the guard."*

QUESTIONS

QUESTION 1   b1

According to Jeremiah chapter 37:

Who did Zedekiah succeed as the king of Judah, and how did he become king?

QUESTION 2   **b1**

According to Jeremiah chapter 37, when Jeremiah had not yet been put in prison:

What were the names of the people King Zedekiah sent to Prophet Jeremiah, and what was his request from the prophet?

QUESTION 3   **a**

According to Jeremiah chapter 37:

What was the king of Egypt's mission in Judah?

QUESTION 4   **c**

Jeremiah chapter 37:7–8 says, *"Thus says the LORD, the God of Israel, 'You shall tell the king of Judah, who sent you to me to inquire of me: "Look, Pharaoh's army, which has come forth to help you, shall return to Egypt into their own land. [8] The Chaldeans shall come again, and fight against this city; and they shall take it, and burn it with fire."'"*

Who else prophesied about this incident, and where can it be found in the Bible?

QUESTION 5   **CTX**

"Do not deceive yourselves, saying, 'The Chaldeans shall surely depart from us'; for they shall not depart."

Give the context of the above quote:

Who said it, to who, and under what circumstance?

QUESTION 6   **b**

According to Jeremiah chapter 37:

What did God say would happen even if the people of Judah were to destroy the entire Chaldean or Babylonian armies, leaving only wounded men?

QUESTION 7   **b1**

According to Jeremiah chapter 37, when the Chaldeans or Babylonians began to withdraw from attacking Jerusalem because of the Egyptians who were approaching:

What did Jeremiah do, and what happened to him?

QUESTION 8   **a**

According to Jeremiah chapter 37:

What was the name of the captain of the guard that arrested Jeremiah?

QUESTION 9   **a**

According to Jeremiah chapter 37, when Jeremiah was falsely accused and imprisoned:

Where was he imprisoned?

QUESTION 10   **a**

According to Jeremiah chapter 37:

Whose house was turned into a prison?

QUESTION 11   **a**

According to Jeremiah chapter 37:

What did the officials do to Jeremiah before throwing him into prison?

QUESTION 12   **b1**

According to Jeremiah chapter 37:

Narrate how Jeremiah left the prison house of Jonathan, the secretary to the court of the guard or palace prison.

QUESTION 13   **b1**

According to Jeremiah chapter 37, King Zedekiah secretly consulted Jeremiah in his house:

What did Zedekiah inquire from Jeremiah, and what was Jeremiah's response?

QUESTION 14   **CTX**

"Wherein have I sinned against you, or against your servants, or against this people...."

Give the context of the above quote:

Who said it, to who, and under what circumstance?

QUESTION 15   **b1**

According to Jeremiah chapter 37:

What did Prophet Jeremiah ask King Zedekiah about his prophets?

QUESTION 16   **a**

According to Jeremiah chapter 37:

What did Prophet Jeremiah say would happen if he was sent back to the prison where he was?

QUESTION 17   **b1**

According to Jeremiah chapter 37:

What was Jeremiah's request to King Zedekiah when he was falsely accused of defecting to the Chaldeans or Babylonians and imprisoned, and what did King Zedekiah do?

QUESTION 18   **a**

According to Jeremiah chapter 37:

With what did King Zedekiah order Jeremiah to be fed daily when he was moved to the court of the guard or palace prison, and for how long?

QUESTION 19   **CMB**

Read Jeremiah chapter 37:6–9, 16–17, preach or write a commentary on the passage with emphasis on salvation.

ANSWERS

ANSWER TO QUESTION 1   b1

- Coniah or Jehoiachin or Jeconiah
- Nebuchadnezzar made him king of Judah (Jeremiah 37:1).

ANSWER TO QUESTION 2   b1

- Jehucal (son of Shelemiah) and Zephaniah the priest (son of Maaseiah)
- That Jeremiah should please pray to God for them (Jeremiah 37:3).

ANSWER TO QUESTION 3   a

To ally with Judah and defend them against the Chaldeans or Babylonians (Jeremiah 37:5–7).

ANSWER TO QUESTION 4   c

- Prophet Ezekiel
- Ezekiel 17:1–24 (the whole chapter) or Ezekiel 17:17.

ANSWER TO QUESTION 5   CTX

- God, through Prophet Jeremiah
- To King Zedekiah through his messengers
- When King Zedekiah sent messengers to ask Jeremiah if he had any message from God (Jeremiah 37:9).

ANSWER TO QUESTION 6   b

The wounded men would still rise from their tents and burn down the entire city to the ground with fire (Jeremiah 37:10).

ANSWER TO QUESTION 7   b1

- He set out on a journey to the land of Benjamin to claim his share of the property among his relatives.
- On his way, Irijah, a captain of the guard, arrested Jeremiah, accusing him of defecting to the Chaldeans or Babylonians, but

as Jeremiah protested, Irijah would not listen, so he brought Jeremiah to the officials who had Jeremiah flogged and imprisoned (Jeremiah 37:11–16).

ANSWER TO QUESTION 8   a

Irijah (Jeremiah 37:13).

ANSWER TO QUESTION 9   a

In the house of Jonathan (the scribe or Secretary) (Jeremiah 37:15).

ANSWER TO QUESTION 10   a

The house of Jonathan (the scribe or secretary) (Jeremiah 37:15).

ANSWER TO QUESTION 11   a

They struck or flogged him (Jeremiah 37:15).

ANSWER TO QUESTION 12   b1

It was when Jeremiah was in the prison house of Jonathan, the secretary, that king Zedekiah secretly sent for him to be brought to the palace so that he could inquire from him the message from the Lord. After responding to the king's inquiry, Jeremiah requested that the king not send him back to the dungeon in Jonathan's house. That was when the king commanded that Jeremiah should be kept in the court of the guard or palace prison (Jeremiah 37:16–21).

ANSWER TO QUESTION 13   b1

- He inquired to know if there were any messages from God
- The response from Jeremiah was that he would be delivered into the hands of the king of Babylon (Jeremiah 37:17).

ANSWER TO QUESTION 14   CTX

- Prophet Jeremiah
- To King Zedekiah
- While he was in prison (in Jonathan's house), the king secretly sent for him to inquire if he had any message from God. After Jeremiah responded to the king, he asked the question quoted above (Jeremiah 37:17–18).

ANSWER TO QUESTION 15   b1

He asked Zedekiah the whereabouts of his prophets, who had prophesied that the king of Babylon would not attack him or the land (Jeremiah 37:19).

ANSWER TO QUESTION 16   a

He said he would die there (Jeremiah 37:20).

ANSWER TO QUESTION 17   b1

- He requested that King Zedekiah should not send him back to the dungeon
- King Zedekiah transferred Jeremiah to the court of the guard or palace prison (and ordered that he be given a loaf of bread every day as long as bread was available in the city) (Jeremiah 37:20–21).

ANSWER TO QUESTION 18   a

- A loaf of bread
- Until there was no more bread left in Jerusalem (Jeremiah 37:21).

HINTS TO QUESTION 19   CMB

- Zedekiah inquired of the Lord from Jeremiah twice in this chapter. But not once did he take the words of the Lord from Jeremiah seriously because he only wanted to hear a positive message different from what Jeremiah told him. We should not go to God with a preconceived notion of what we want to hear from God but with a willing heart to accept what God has to tell us.
- In this dispensation, we have the written word of God, which we can use as a guide; therefore, we should be disposed to obey it. While reading God's word, we should be cautious to accept the truth of God's word and not try to twist it to suit our motives or desires.

CHAPTER 38

JEREMIAH CHAPTER 38

"Shephatiah the son of Mattan, and Gedaliah the son of Pashhur, and Jucal the son of Shelemiah, and Pashhur the son of Malchijah, heard the words that Jeremiah spoke to all the people, saying, ²"Thus says the LORD, 'He who remains in this city shall die by the sword, by the famine, and by the pestilence; but he who goes forth to the Chaldeans shall live, and his life shall be to him for a prey, and he shall live.' ³Thus says the LORD, 'This city shall surely be given into the hand of the army of the king of Babylon, and he shall take it.'" ⁴Then the officials said to the king, "Please let this man be put to death; because he weakens the hands of the men of war who remain in this city, and the hands of all the people, in speaking such words to them: for this man doesn't seek the welfare of this people, but the hurt." ⁵Zedekiah the king said, "Look, he is in your hand; for the king is not he who can do anything against you." ⁶Then took they Jeremiah, and cast him into the dungeon of Malchiah the king's son, that was in the court of the guard: and they let down Jeremiah with cords. In the dungeon there was no water, but mire; and Jeremiah sank in the mire. ⁷Now when Ebedmelech the Ethiopian, a eunuch, who was in the king's house, heard that they had put Jeremiah in the dungeon (the king then sitting in the Benjamin Gate), ⁸Ebedmelech went forth out of the king's house, and spoke to the king, saying, ⁹ "My lord the king, these men have done evil in all that they have done to Jeremiah the prophet, whom they have cast into the dungeon; and he is likely to die in the place where he is, because of the famine; for there is no more bread in the city." ¹⁰Then the king commanded Ebedmelech the Ethiopian, saying, "Take from here thirty men with you, and take up Jeremiah the prophet out of the dungeon, before he dies." *¹¹*So Ebedmelech took the men with him, and went into the house of the king under the treasury, and took there rags and worn-out garments, and let them down by cords into the dungeon to Jeremiah. *¹²*Ebedmelech the Ethiopian said to Jeremiah, "Put now these rags and worn-out garments under your armpits under the cords." Jeremiah did so. *¹³*So they drew up Jeremiah with the cords, and took him up out of the dungeon: and Jeremiah remained in the court of the guard. *¹⁴*Then Zedekiah the king sent, and took Jeremiah the prophet to him into the third entry that is in the house of the LORD: and the king said to Jeremiah, "I will ask you something. Hide nothing from me." *¹⁵*Then Jeremiah said to Zedekiah, "If I declare it to you, will you not surely put me to death? And if I give you counsel, you will not listen to me." *¹⁶*So Zedekiah the king swore secretly to Jeremiah, saying, "As the LORD lives, who made us this soul, I will not put you to death, neither will I give you into the hand of these men who seek your life." *¹⁷*Then Jeremiah said to Zedekiah, "Thus says the LORD, the God of hosts, the God of Israel: 'If you will go forth to the king of Babylon's officiers, then your soul shall live, and this city shall not be burned with fire; and you shall live, and your house. *¹⁸*But if you will not go forth to the king of Babylon's officiers, then shall this city be given into the hand of the Chaldeans, and they shall burn it with fire, and you shall not escape out of their hand.'" *¹⁹*Zedekiah the king said to Jeremiah, "I am afraid of the Jews who are fallen away to the Chaldeans, lest they deliver me into their hand, and they mock me." *²⁰*But Jeremiah said, "They shall not deliver you. Obey, I beg you, the voice of the LORD, in that which I speak to you: so it shall be well with you, and your soul shall live. *²¹*But if you refuse to go forth, this is the word that the LORD has shown me: *²²*behold, all the women who are left in the king of Judah's house shall be brought forth to the king of Babylon's officers, and those women shall say, 'Your familiar friends have set you on, and have prevailed over you. Your feet are sunk in the mire, they have turned away back.'

²³ They shall bring out all your wives and your children to the Chaldeans; and you shall not escape out of their hand, but shall be taken by the hand of the king of Babylon: and you shall cause this city to be burned with fire." ²⁴ Then Zedekiah said to Jeremiah, "Let no man know of these words, and you shall not die. ²⁵ But if the officials hear that I have talked with you, and they come to you, and tell you, 'Declare to us now what you have said to the king; do not hide it from us, and we will not put you to death; also what the king said to you': ²⁶ then you shall tell them, 'I presented my petition before the king, that he would not cause me to return to Jonathan's house, to die there.'" ²⁷ Then all the officials came to Jeremiah, and asked him; and he told them according to all these words that the king had commanded. So they left off speaking with him; for the matter was not perceived. ²⁸ So Jeremiah stayed in the court of the guard until the day that Jerusalem was taken."

QUESTIONS

QUESTION 1   b2

According to Jeremiah chapter 38:

Name the four men who told King Zedekiah that Jeremiah must die and what was their reason?

QUESTION 2   b

According to Jeremiah chapter 38, when some of the king's officials went to King Zedekiah, requesting that Jeremiah be put to death:

What was the king's response?

QUESTION 3   b

According to Jeremiah chapter 38, when King Zedekiah gave permission for Jeremiah to be dealt with:

What did the officials do to Jeremiah?

QUESTION 4   **b**

According to Jeremiah chapter 38, Jeremiah was put into a dungeon or cistern:

Who did the dungeon or cistern belong to?

QUESTION 5   **a**

According to Jeremiah chapter 38:

What was in the dungeon or cistern that Jeremiah was put into?

QUESTION 6   **b**

According to Jeremiah chapter 38:

What is the name of the person who spoke in favour of Jeremiah to the king when he heard that Jeremiah was put in a dungeon or cistern and what was his nationality?

QUESTION 7   **a**

According to Jeremiah chapter 38:

Where was King Zedekiah when one of his officials spoke to him about Jeremiah while Jeremiah was in the dungeon or cistern?

QUESTION 8   **b**

According to Jeremiah chapter 38, when King Zedekiah was told that Jeremiah would soon die of hunger in the dungeon or cistern:

What was the king's response?

QUESTION 9   **a**

According to Jeremiah chapter 38:

How many men did the king release to go and rescue Jeremiah while he was in the dungeon or cistern?

QUESTION 10   **b**

According to Jeremiah chapter 38:

What materials were used to pull Jeremiah out of the dungeon or cistern, and where were they gotten?

QUESTION 11   b

According to Jeremiah chapter 38, after Jeremiah was rescued by the palace official from the dungeon or cistern:

Where was Jeremiah taken to?

QUESTION 12   a

According to Jeremiah chapter 38, after Jeremiah was removed from the dungeon or cistern, King Zedekiah asked for a meeting with Jeremiah:

Where was the meeting held?

QUESTION 13   CTX

"If I declare it to you, will you not surely put me to death? And if I give you counsel, you will not listen to me."

Give the context of the above quote:

Who said it, to who, and under what circumstance?

QUESTION 14   b

According to Jeremiah chapter 38:

What did King Zedekiah swear secretly to Jeremiah?

QUESTION 15   b

According to Jeremiah chapter 38:

What was king Zedekiah's fear of surrendering to the king of Babylon?

QUESTION 16   b1

According to Jeremiah chapter 38:

What did Prophet Jeremiah say would happen to the women who would be left in the palace if King Zedekiah would not surrender to the king of Babylon, and what would the women say to the king?

QUESTION 17   **CTX**

"Let no man know of these words, and you shall not die."

Give the context of the above quote:

Who said it, to who, and under what circumstance?

QUESTION 18   **b**

According to Jeremiah chapter 38:

What did King Zedekiah ask Prophet Jeremiah to tell any official who might ask him about their private conversation?

QUESTION 19   **b**

According to Jeremiah chapter 38:

Who went to Jeremiah to find out the details of Jeremiah's conversation with King Zedekiah, and what did they do when Jeremiah gave them an answer?

QUESTION 20   **b**

According to Jeremiah chapter 38:

How long did Prophet Jeremiah remain in the court of the guard or palace prison?

QUESTION 21   **CMB**

Read Jeremiah chapter 38:7–13, preach or write a commentary on the passage with emphasis on salvation.

ANSWERS

ANSWER TO QUESTION 1   **b2**

- The four men are:
  1. Shephatiah (son of Mattan)
  2. Gedaliah (son of Pashhur)

3. Jucal or Jehucal (son of Shelemiah)
4. Pashhur (son of Malchijah)
- Their reason was that Jeremiah was discouraging the few fighting men and the people left in the city by the things he was saying; that everyone who stayed in Jerusalem would die by famine, sword or pestilence and that the Babylonians would certainly capture the city of Jerusalem (Jeremiah 38:1–4).

ANSWER TO QUESTION 2   b

The king told them that Jeremiah was in their hands and they should do to him as they liked (Jeremiah 38:5).

ANSWER TO QUESTION 3   b

They took him and cast him by a rope into a dungeon or cistern (Jeremiah 38:6).

ANSWER TO QUESTION 4   b

It belonged to Malchiah or Malchijah (the king's son or a member of the royal family, son of Hammelech) (Jeremiah 38:6).

ANSWER TO QUESTION 5   a

Mire or mud (Jeremiah 38:6).

ANSWER TO QUESTION 6   b

- Ebedmelech
- He was an Ethiopian (Jeremiah 38:7).

ANSWER TO QUESTION 7   a

He was at the Benjamin Gate (Jeremiah 38:7).

ANSWER TO QUESTION 8   b

He ordered that Jeremiah be brought out of the dungeon or cistern before he died (Jeremiah 38:10).

ANSWER TO QUESTION 9   a

Thirty (30) men (Jeremiah 38:10).

ANSWER TO QUESTION 10   b

- Rags, worn-out garments and cords or ropes
- They were gotten from a room under the treasury in the palace (Jeremiah 38:11–12).

ANSWER TO QUESTION 11   b

He was taken to the court of the guard or the court of the prison (Jeremiah 38:13).

ANSWER TO QUESTION 12   a

At the third entry of the Lord's house (Jeremiah 38:14).

ANSWER TO QUESTION 13   CTX

- Prophet Jeremiah
- To King Zedekiah
- When King Zedekiah sent for Jeremiah to inquire from him the message of the Lord after Jeremiah was brought out of the dungeon or cistern (Jeremiah 38:14).

ANSWER TO QUESTION 14   b

That he would not kill Jeremiah or hand him over to the men who wanted him dead if Jeremiah told him the message from the Lord (Jeremiah 38:15–16).

ANSWER TO QUESTION 15   b

He was afraid he would be handed over to the Jews who had gone there before to be mocked or mistreated (Jeremiah 38:19).

ANSWER TO QUESTION 16   b1

- The women would be brought out and given to the Babylonian officers.
- *"Your familiar friends have set you on, and have prevailed over you. Your feet are sunk in the mire, they have turned away back."* (Jeremiah 38:22.)

ANSWER TO QUESTION 17   CTX

- King Zedekiah
- To Prophet Jeremiah
- When Jeremiah told him the message from the Lord during their meeting after Jeremiah was pulled from the dungeon or cistern (Jeremiah 38:24).

ANSWER TO QUESTION 18   b

He asked Jeremiah to tell them that he was begging the king not to send him back to the prison in Jonathan's house (Jeremiah 38:25–26).

ANSWER TO QUESTION 19   b

- The king's officials
- They left him alone (Jeremiah 38:27).

ANSWER TO QUESTION 20   b

Until the day Jerusalem was taken or captured (Jeremiah 38:28).

HINT TO QUESTION 21   CMB

When Ebedmelech heard about the suffering of Jeremiah, he approached the king and spoke on Jeremiah's behalf. Through his intervention, Jeremiah was rescued from the dungeon. Ebedmelech's action is worthy of emulation. James 4:17 says, *"To him therefore who knows to do good, and does not do it, to him it is sin."* As believers, when one is in a situation where we can help, we should have compassion and help or rescue the person.

CHAPTER 39

JEREMIAH CHAPTER 39

"It happened when Jerusalem was taken, (in the ninth year of Zedekiah king of Judah, in the tenth month, came Nebuchadnezzar king of Babylon and all his army against Jerusalem, and besieged it; ²in the eleventh year of Zedekiah, in the fourth month, the ninth day of the month, a breach was made in the city). ³Then all the officials of the king of Babylon came in, and sat in the middle gate, Nergal Sharezer the Samgar, Nebo Sarsekim the Rabsaris, Nergal Sharezer the Rabmag, with all the rest of the officers of the king of Babylon. ⁴It happened that, when Zedekiah the king of Judah and all the men of war saw them, then they fled, and went forth out of the city by night, by the way of the king's garden, through the gate between the two walls; and he went out toward the Arabah. ⁵But the army of the Chaldeans pursued after them, and overtook Zedekiah in the plains of Jericho: and when they had taken him, they brought him up to Nebuchadnezzar king of Babylon to Riblah in the land of Hamath; and he gave judgment on him. ⁶Then the king of Babylon killed the sons of Zedekiah in Riblah before his eyes: also the king of Babylon killed all the nobles of Judah. ⁷Moreover he put out Zedekiah's eyes, and bound him in fetters, to carry him to Babylon. ⁸The Chaldeans burned the king's house, and the houses of the people, with fire, and broke down the walls of Jerusalem. ⁹Then Nebuzaradan the captain of the guard carried away captive into Babylon the residue of the people who remained in the city, the deserters also who fell away to him, and the residue of the people who remained. ¹⁰But Nebuzaradan the captain of the guard left of the poor of the people, who had

nothing, in the land of Judah, and gave them vineyards and fields at the same time. ¹¹Now Nebuchadnezzar king of Babylon commanded Nebuzaradan the captain of the guard concerning Jeremiah, saying, ¹²"Take him, and look well to him, and do him no harm; but do to him even as he shall tell you."¹³So Nebuzaradan the captain of the guard sent, and Nebushazban, Rabsaris, and Nergal Sharezer, Rabmag, and all the chief officers of the king of Babylon; ¹⁴they sent, and took Jeremiah out of the court of the guard, and committed him to Gedaliah the son of Ahikam, the son of Shaphan, that he should carry him home: so he lived among the people. ¹⁵Now the word of the LORD came to Jeremiah, while he was shut up in the court of the guard, saying, ¹⁶"Go, and speak to Ebedmelech the Ethiopian, saying, 'Thus says the LORD of hosts, the God of Israel: "Look, I will bring my words on this city for disaster, and not for prosperity; and they shall be fulfilled before you in that day. ¹⁷But I will deliver you in that day, says the LORD; and you shall not be given into the hand of the men of whom you are afraid. ¹⁸For I will surely save you, and you shall not fall by the sword, but your life will be given to you as a reward; because you have put your trust in me,'" says the LORD."

QUESTIONS

QUESTION 1   b1

According to Jeremiah chapter 39:

In which month of what year of King Zedekiah's reign did the King of Babylon besiege Jerusalem, and when did the King of Babylon finally overtake Jerusalem?

QUESTION 2   b

According to Jeremiah chapter 39, when the Babylonians broke through the walls of Jerusalem:

What did the Babylonian officials do first?

QUESTION 3   b

According to Jeremiah chapter 39:

What did King Zedekiah and his soldiers do when they saw that the Babylonian armies had broken into their city?

QUESTION 4   a

According to Jeremiah chapter 39:

Where was King Nebuchadnezzar when his soldiers brought King Zedekiah to him?

QUESTION 5   b

According to Jeremiah chapter 39:

Mention the last thing King Zedekiah saw before he was taken to Babylon.

QUESTION 6   b1

In Jeremiah chapter 39, the Lord sent a message of blessing to Ebedmelech, telling him that He would rescue him from those he feared the most and that he would not fall by the sword, but He would preserve him:

Who was Ebedmelech, where was he from, and what did he do that made God pronounce a blessing on him?

QUESTION 7   b

According to Jeremiah chapter 39, when the Babylonians invaded Jerusalem, they took away King Zedekiah and everybody in the land as exiles to Babylon but left behind some people:

What class of people did they leave behind, and what did they give to them?

QUESTION 8   CTX

"Take him, and look well to him, and do him no harm; but do to him even as he shall tell you."

Give the context of the above quote:

Who said it, to who, and under what circumstance?

QUESTION 9   a

According to Jeremiah chapter 39, when King Nebuchadnezzar sent the order for Jeremiah to be released from prison:

Who did King Nebuchadnezzar's officials appoint to look after Jeremiah?

QUESTION 10   CMB

Read Jeremiah chapter 39:15–18, preach or write a commentary on the passage with emphasis on salvation.

ANSWERS

ANSWER TO QUESTION 1   b1

- Jerusalem was besieged in the tenth month of the ninth year of King Zedekiah's reign
- The King of Babylon finally overtook Jerusalem on the ninth day of the fourth month in the eleventh year of King Zedekiah's reign (Jeremiah 39:1–2).

ANSWER TO QUESTION 2   b

They went in and sat at the middle gate (Jeremiah 39:3).

ANSWER TO QUESTION 3   b

They fled and went out of the city by night. (Though the Babylonians caught up with King Zedekiah in the plains of Jericho) (Jeremiah 39:4–5).

ANSWER TO QUESTION 4   a

At Riblah (in Hamath) (Jeremiah 39:5).

ANSWER TO QUESTION 5   b

The killing of his sons and the nobles (or princes or officials) of Judah (Jeremiah 39:6–7).

ANSWER TO QUESTION 6   b1

- He was a eunuch in the king's palace
- Ethiopia
- He saved Jeremiah's life when Jeremiah was put in the dungeon or cistern by going to king Zedekiah to speak in favour of Jeremiah (and the king gave thirty of his men to go with him and rescue Jeremiah from the dungeon) (Jeremiah 38:7–13).

ANSWER TO QUESTION 7   b

- The poor of the people
- Vineyards and fields (Jeremiah 39:10).

ANSWER TO QUESTION 8   CTX

- King Nebuchadnezzar
- To Nebuzaradan, the captain of the guards
- When the king gave orders that Jeremiah should be removed from the court of the guard and taken care of (Jeremiah 39:12).

ANSWER TO QUESTION 9   a

Gedaliah (son of Ahikam and grandson of Shaphan) (Jeremiah 39:14).

HINT TO QUESTION 10   CMB

Ebedmelech, a non-Israelite who lived and served as the king's official, found favour in God's sight because of his good gesture to Jeremiah, a Prophet of God. God promised to save him from the impending destruction of Jerusalem, where the King would be captured and all his officials killed. God is impartial; race, gender or status are not determinants when it comes to His recompensing individuals for their deeds. No act of goodness goes unnoticed or unrewarded by God. Our rewards may not come immediately or in the way we expect, but He will reward all who have been kind to others in due time and season.

CHAPTER 40

JEREMIAH CHAPTER 40

"The word which came to Jeremiah from the LORD, after that Nebuzaradan the captain of the guard had let him go from Ramah, when he had taken him being bound in chains among all the captives of Jerusalem and Judah, who were carried away captive to Babylon. ²The captain of the guard took Jeremiah, and said to him, "The LORD your God pronounced this evil on this place; ³and the LORD has brought it, and done according as he spoke: because you have sinned against the LORD, and have not obeyed his voice, therefore this thing has come on you. ⁴Now, look, I release you this day from the chains which are on your hand. If it seems good to you to come with me into Babylon, come, and I will take care of you; but if it seems bad to you to come with me into Babylon, do not: look, all the land is before you; where it seems good and right to you to go, there go." ⁵Now while he had not yet gone back, "Go back then," he said, "to Gedaliah the son of Ahikam, the son of Shaphan, whom the king of Babylon has made governor over the cities of Judah, and dwell with him among the people; or go wherever it seems right to you to go." So the captain of the guard gave him food and a present, and let him go. ⁶Then went Jeremiah to Gedaliah the son of Ahikam to Mizpah, and lived with him among the people who were left in the land. ⁷Now when all the captains of the forces who were in the fields, even they and their men, heard that the king of Babylon had made Gedaliah the son of Ahikam governor in the land, and had committed to him men, and women, and children, and of the poorest of the land, of those who were not carried away captive to Babylon; ⁸then they

came to Gedaliah to Mizpah, Ishmael the son of Nethaniah, and Johanan and Jonathan the sons of Kareah, and Seraiah the son of Tanhumeth, and the sons of Ephai the Netophathite, and Jezaniah the son of the Maacathite, they and their men. ^{9}Gedaliah the son of Ahikam the son of Shaphan swore to them and to their men, saying, "Do not be afraid to serve the Chaldeans: dwell in the land, and serve the king of Babylon, and it shall be well with you. ^{10}As for me, look, I will dwell at Mizpah, to stand before the Chaldeans who shall come to us: but you, gather wine and summer fruits and oil, and put them in your vessels, and dwell in your cities that you have taken." ^{11}Likewise when all the Jews who were in Moab, and among the children of Ammon, and in Edom, and who were in all the countries, heard that the king of Babylon had left a remnant of Judah, and that he had set over them Gedaliah the son of Ahikam, the son of Shaphan; ^{12}then all the Jews returned out of all places where they were driven, and came to the land of Judah, to Gedaliah, to Mizpah, and gathered wine and summer fruits very much. ^{13}Moreover Johanan the son of Kareah, and all the captains of the forces who were in the fields, came to Gedaliah to Mizpah, ^{14}and said to him, "Do you know that Baalis the king of the children of Ammon has sent Ishmael the son of Nethaniah to take your life?" But Gedaliah the son of Ahikam did not believe them. ^{15}Then Johanan the son of Kareah spoke to Gedaliah in Mizpah secretly, saying, "Please let me go, and I will kill Ishmael the son of Nethaniah, and no man shall know it: why should he take your life, that all the Jews who are gathered to you should be scattered, and the remnant of Judah perish?" ^{16}But Gedaliah the son of Ahikam said to Johanan the son of Kareah, "You shall not do this thing; for you speak falsely of Ishmael."

QUESTIONS

QUESTION 1 a

According to Jeremiah Chapter 40:

Where did Nebuzaradan find Jeremiah chained among the captives?

QUESTION 2   CTX

"The LORD your God pronounced this evil on this place."

Give the context of the above quote:

Who said it, to who, and under what circumstance?

QUESTION 3   b2

According to Jeremiah chapter 40:

List the four options Nebuzaradan gave Jeremiah after he had released him from chains. Which option did Jeremiah choose?

QUESTION 4   b

According to Jeremiah chapter 40, when Nebuzaradan released Jeremiah from chains and gave him options concerning where he should live:

What did Nebuzaradan give to him after Jeremiah made his choice?

QUESTION 5   b

According to Jeremiah chapter 40, when Nebuzaradan sent off Jeremiah:

Where and who did Jeremiah go to?

QUESTION 6   b1

According to Jeremiah chapter 40:

Name three Judean army leaders who went with Ishmael to visit Gedaliah in Mizpah.

QUESTION 7   b1

According to Jeremiah chapter 40, when the captains of the forces came to visit Gedaliah:

What did Gedaliah ask them to do?

QUESTION 8   **b**

According to Jeremiah chapter 40, when the captains of the forces came to visit Gedaliah:

What did Gedaliah tell them he was going to do?

QUESTION 9   **b1**

According to Jeremiah chapter 40:

Mention three nations some of the Judeans that escaped during the invasion of Judah went to and why did they later return to Judah.

QUESTION 10   **b**

According to Jeremiah chapter 40, when the people of Judah came back from the countries they fled to when Nebuchadnezzar invaded Judah:

Where did they stop first, and for what reason?

QUESTION 11   **b**

According to Jeremiah chapter 40:

When the people of Judah who fled to other countries during the attack of king Nebuchadnezzar returned to Judah:

What did they do after meeting with the Governor?

QUESTION 12   **b**

According to Jeremiah chapter 40:

Who was sent to kill Gedaliah, and who sent him?

QUESTION 13   **b**

According to Jeremiah chapter 40:

Who told Gedaliah about the plot to kill him?

QUESTION 14   b1

In Jeremiah chapter 40, someone volunteered to kill another person for Gedaliah:

Who volunteered, and who did he volunteer to kill?

ANSWERS

ANSWER TO QUESTION 1   a

At Ramah (Jeremiah 40:1).

ANSWER TO QUESTION 2   CTX

- Nebuzaradan (the captain of the guard of the king of Babylon)
- To Prophet Jeremiah
- When he found Jeremiah in chains among the other captives in Ramah going on exile to Babylon and freed him (Jeremiah 40:2).

ANSWER TO QUESTION 3   b2

- The options were:
  1. To go to Babylon with him
  2. To remain in the land, that the whole land is at his disposal
  3. He should go back to Gedaliah, son of Ahikam, whom King Nebuchadnezzar had appointed governor over the land of Judah, and live among the people
  4. To go wherever he wanted
- Jeremiah's choice:

He chose the option of going back to Gedaliah (Jeremiah 40:4–6).

ANSWER TO QUESTION 4   b

- Food or victuals or provisions
  and
- A present or money or reward (Jeremiah 40:5).

ANSWER TO QUESTION 5   b

He went to Mizpah to stay with Gedaliah (Jeremiah 40:6).

ANSWER TO QUESTION 6   b1

1. Johanan (son of Kareah)
2. Jonathan (son of Kareah)
3. Seraiah (son of Tanhumeth)
4. Jezaniah (son of the Maacathite) (Jeremiah 40:8).

ANSWER TO QUESTION 7   b1

To serve the king of Babylon, gather wine and summer fruits and oil, put them in their vessels, and dwell in the cities that they had taken (Jeremiah 40:10).

ANSWER TO QUESTION 8   b

He would dwell in Mizpah and stand before the Chaldeans or Babylonians that would come to them (Jeremiah 40:10).

ANSWER TO QUESTION 9   b1

- Moab, Ammon, and Edom.
- They returned to Judah because they heard that the king of Babylon had left some people in Judah and had made Gedaliah the governor (Jeremiah 40:11).

ANSWER TO QUESTION 10   b

- Mizpah
- To meet with Gedaliah (Jeremiah 40:12).

ANSWER TO QUESTION 11   b

They gathered a large quantity of wine and summer fruits (Jeremiah 40:12).

ANSWER TO QUESTION 12   b

- Ishmael (son of Nethaniah)
- Baalis (king of Ammon) (Jeremiah 40:13–14).

ANSWER TO QUESTION 13   b

Johanan and all the captains of the forces (who were in the fields) (Jeremiah 40:13).

ANSWER TO QUESTION 14   b1

- Johanan (son of Kareah)
- Ishmael (son of Nethaniah) (Jeremiah 40:13–16).

CHAPTER 41

JEREMIAH CHAPTER 41

"Now it happened in the seventh month, that Ishmael the son of Nethaniah, the son of Elishama, of the royal family and one of the chief officers of the king, and ten men with him, came to Gedaliah the son of Ahikam to Mizpah; and there they ate bread together in Mizpah. [2] *Then arose Ishmael the son of Nethaniah, and the ten men who were with him, and struck Gedaliah the son of Ahikam the son of Shaphan with the sword, and killed him, whom the king of Babylon had made governor over the land.* [3] *Ishmael also killed all the Jews who were with him, with Gedaliah, at Mizpah, and the Chaldeans who were found there, the men of war.* [4] *It happened the second day after he had killed Gedaliah, and no man knew it,* [5] *that there came men from Shechem, from Shiloh, and from Samaria, even eighty men, having their beards shaved and their clothes torn, and having cut themselves, with meal offerings and frankincense in their hand, to bring them to the house of the LORD.* [6] *Ishmael the son of Nethaniah went forth from Mizpah to meet them, weeping all along as he went: and it happened, as he met them, he said to them, "Come to Gedaliah the son of Ahikam."* [7] *It was so, when they came into the midst of the city, that Ishmael the son of Nethaniah killed them, and cast them into the midst of the pit, he, and the men who were with him.* [8] *But ten men were found among those who said to Ishmael, "Do not kill us; for we have stores hidden in the field, of wheat, and of barley, and of oil, and of honey. So he stopped, and did not kill them among their brothers.* [9] *Now the pit in which Ishmael cast all the dead bodies of the men whom he had killed, by the side of Gedaliah (the same was who which Asa the king had*

made for fear of Baasha king of Israel), Ishmael the son of Nethaniah filled it with those who were killed. [10] Then Ishmael carried away captive all the residue of the people who were in Mizpah, even the king's daughters, and all the people who remained in Mizpah, whom Nebuzaradan the captain of the guard had committed to Gedaliah the son of Ahikam; Ishmael the son of Nethaniah carried them away captive, and departed to go over to the children of Ammon. [11] But when Johanan the son of Kareah, and all the captains of the forces who were with him, heard of all the evil that Ishmael the son of Nethaniah had done, [12] then they took all the men, and went to fight with Ishmael the son of Nethaniah, and found him by the great waters that are in Gibeon. [13] Now it happened that, when all the people who were with Ishmael saw Johanan the son of Kareah, and all the captains of the forces who were with him, then they were glad. [14] So all the people who Ishmael had carried away captive from Mizpah turned about and came back, and went to Johanan the son of Kareah. [15] But Ishmael the son of Nethaniah escaped from Johanan with eight men, and went to the children of Ammon. [16] Then took Johanan the son of Kareah, and all the captains of the forces who were with him, all the remnant of the people whom he had recovered from Ishmael the son of Nethaniah, from Mizpah, after that he had killed Gedaliah the son of Ahikam, the men of war, and the women, and the children, and the eunuchs, whom he had brought back from Gibeon: [17] and they departed, and lived in Geruth Chimham, which is by Bethlehem, to go to enter into Egypt, [18] because of the Chaldeans; for they were afraid of them, because Ishmael the son of Nethaniah had killed Gedaliah the son of Ahikam, whom the king of Babylon made governor over the land."

QUESTIONS

QUESTION 1   a

According to Jeremiah chapter 41:

At what time of the year was Gedaliah killed?

QUESTION 2   **b**

According to Jeremiah chapter 41:

Who was the son of Nethaniah, and what office did he hold in Judah?

QUESTION 3   **b**

According to Jeremiah chapter 41:

Who killed Gedaliah, and what is the name of the place where he was killed?

QUESTION 4   **a**

According to Jeremiah chapter 41:

What was Gedaliah doing when he was killed?

QUESTION 5   **a**

According to Jeremiah chapter 41:

How many men were in the group that killed Gedaliah?

QUESTION 6   **b**

According to Jeremiah chapter 41:

What group of people were killed along with Gedaliah?

QUESTION 7   **b**

According to Jeremiah chapter 41, after the death of Gedaliah, the Bible records that eighty men who had shaved their beards, torn their clothes and cut themselves arrived in the city:

Where did they come from?

QUESTION 8   **a**

According to Jeremiah chapter 41, the next day after the death of Gedaliah, some men went into the city of Mizpah:

What two things did they carry along with them?

QUESTION 9 b

According to Jeremiah chapter 41:

How many men went to Mizpah the day after Gedaliah was killed, how many of them were killed and how many survived?

QUESTION 10 b

According to Jeremiah chapter 41, some men went into the city after the death of Gedaliah, some were killed, but some were not killed:

Who killed them, and why were some of the men not killed?

QUESTION 11 b

According to Jeremiah chapter 41, some men who came into the city after the death of Gedaliah were killed:

How were their bodies disposed of?

QUESTION 12 b1

In Jeremiah chapter 41, King Asa was mentioned:

What was said about him?

QUESTION 13 b

According to Jeremiah chapter 41, immediately after the death of Gedaliah:

What happened to the people in Mizpah who were left in Gedaliah's care by Nebuzaradan?

QUESTION 14 a

According to Jeremiah chapter 41, when Johanan and the other military leaders heard about all the atrocities that Gedaliah's murderers had done:

What did they do?

QUESTION 15 a

According to Jeremiah chapter 41:

Where did Johanan catch up with Gedaliah's murderers?

QUESTION 16 a

According to Jeremiah chapter 41, when Johanan caught up with Gedaliah's murderers:

What did the people who were captured by Gedaliah's murderers do?

QUESTION 17 b

According to Jeremiah chapter 41, when Johanan caught up with Gedaliah's murderers, some of the murderers escaped:

How many of them escaped, and where did they escape to?

QUESTION 18 b

According to Jeremiah chapter 41:

Mention three categories of people who were among the people Johanan and his men rescued from Gedaliah's murderers.

QUESTION 19 b1

According to Jeremiah chapter 41:

To where did Johanan take the people he recovered from Gedaliah's murderers, and why did he take them there?

QUESTION 20 CMC

Read Jeremiah chapter 41:1–3, preach or write a commentary on the passage with emphasis on salvation.

ANSWERS

ANSWER TO QUESTION 1 a

The seventh month (Jeremiah 41:1).

ANSWER TO QUESTION 2 b

- Ishmael
- He was one of the chief officers of the king or princes or officials in Judah (Jeremiah 41:1).

ANSWER TO QUESTION 3   b

- Ishmael and his ten men
- Mizpah (Jeremiah 41:1–2).

ANSWER TO QUESTION 4   a

He was eating (Jeremiah 41:1–2).

ANSWER TO QUESTION 5   a

Eleven (11) men (Jeremiah 41:2).

ANSWER TO QUESTION 6   b

The Jews and the Chaldean (Babylonian) soldiers who were with Gedaliah (Jeremiah 41:2–3).

ANSWER TO QUESTION 7   b

Shechem, Shiloh and Samaria (Jeremiah 41:4–5).

ANSWER TO QUESTION 8   a

- Meal or grain offerings or offerings
- Frankincense or incense (Jeremiah 41:5).

ANSWER TO QUESTION 9   b

- Eighty men
- Seventy were killed
- Ten survived (Jeremiah 41:7–8).

ANSWER TO QUESTION 10   b

- Ishmael
- Because they told Ishmael that they had stores of wheat, barley, oil and honey hidden in the field (Jeremiah 41:7–8).

ANSWER TO QUESTION 11   b

They were thrown into a pit or cistern (dug by King Asa) (Jeremiah 41:9).

ANSWER TO QUESTION 12   b1

King Asa dug the pit in which Ishmael cast the bodies of the men he killed. He made the pit or cistern as a defence against King Baasha of Israel (Jeremiah 41:9).

ANSWER TO QUESTION 13   b

Ishmael took them captives and departed for Ammon (Jeremiah 41:10).

ANSWER TO QUESTION 14   a

They took all their men and went to fight Ishmael (Jeremiah 41:11–12).

ANSWER TO QUESTION 15   a

By the great waters that are in Gibeon

Or

At the large pool near Gibeon (Jeremiah 41:12).

ANSWER TO QUESTION 16   a

They turned from Ishmael and followed Johanan (Jeremiah 41:14).

ANSWER TO QUESTION 17   b

- Nine (9)
- Ammon (Jeremiah 41:15).

ANSWER TO QUESTION 18   b

- The men of war or Soldiers
- Women
- Children
- Eunuchs or Court officials (Jeremiah 41:16).

ANSWER TO QUESTION 19   b1

- He took them to Geruth Chimham or Kimham near Bethlehem

- To prepare to leave for Egypt because they were afraid of what the Chaldeans or Babylonians would do when they heard that Gedaliah, whom the king of Babylon appointed as governor, was killed (Jeremiah 41:17–18).

HINT TO QUESTION 20   CMC

Gedaliah trivialised the information Johanan gave him concerning the threat to his life (Jeremiah 40:13–16), and he faced the consequences. Though we are commanded to love our enemies, we should not throw caution to the wind in our relationship with people. We should be wise as serpents but harmless as doves.

CHAPTER 42

JEREMIAH CHAPTER 42

"Then all the captains of the forces, and Johanan the son of Kareah, and Jezaniah the son of Hoshaiah, and all the people from the least even to the greatest, came near, [2] and said to Jeremiah the prophet, "Please let our petition be presented before you, and pray for us to the LORD your God, even for all this remnant; for we are left but a few of many, as your eyes do see us: [3] that the LORD your God may show us the way in which we should walk, and the thing that we should do." [4] Then Jeremiah the prophet said to them, "I have heard you; look, I will pray to the LORD your God according to your words; and it shall happen that whatever thing the LORD shall answer you, I will declare it to you; I will keep nothing back from you." [5] Then they said to Jeremiah, "The LORD be a true and faithful witness among us, if we do not do according to all the word with which the LORD your God shall send you to us. [6] Whether it be good, or whether it be evil, we will obey the voice of the LORD our God, to whom we send you; that it may be well with us, when we obey the voice of the LORD our God." [7] It happened after ten days, that the word of the LORD came to Jeremiah. [8] Then called he Johanan the son of Kareah, and all the captains of the forces who were with him, and all the people from the least even to the greatest, [9] and said to them, "Thus says the LORD, the God of Israel, to whom you sent me to present your petition before him: [10] 'If you will still live in this land, then will I build you, and not pull you down, and I will plant you, and not pluck you up; for I grieve over the distress that I have brought on you. [11] Do not be afraid of the king of Babylon, of whom you are

afraid; do not be afraid of him, says the LORD: for I am with you to save you, and to deliver you from his hand. ^{12}I will grant you mercy, that he may have mercy on you, and cause you to return to your own land.' ^{13}But if you say, 'We will not dwell in this land'; so that you do not obey the voice of the LORD your God, ^{14}saying, 'No; but we will go into the land of Egypt, where we shall see no war, nor hear the sound of the trumpet, nor have hunger of bread; and there will we dwell': ^{15}now therefore hear the word of the LORD, O remnant of Judah: Thus says the LORD of hosts, the God of Israel, 'If you indeed set your faces to enter into Egypt, and go to live there; ^{16}then it shall happen, that the sword, which you fear, shall overtake you there in the land of Egypt; and the famine, about which you are afraid, shall follow close behind you there in Egypt; and there you shall die. ^{17}So shall it be with all the men who set their faces to go into Egypt to live there: they shall die by the sword, by the famine, and by the pestilence; and none of them shall remain or escape from the evil that I will bring on them.' ^{18}For thus says the LORD of hosts, the God of Israel: 'As my anger and my wrath has been poured forth on the inhabitants of Jerusalem, so shall my wrath be poured forth on you, when you shall enter into Egypt; and you shall be an object of horror, and an astonishment, and a curse, and a reproach; and you shall see this place no more.' ^{19}The LORD has spoken concerning you, remnant of Judah, 'Do not go into Egypt': know certainly that I have testified to you this day. ^{20}For you have dealt deceitfully against your own souls; for you sent me to the LORD your God, saying, 'Pray for us to the LORD our God; and according to all that the LORD our God shall say, so declare to us, and we will do it': ^{21}and I have this day declared it to you; but you have not obeyed the voice of the LORD your God in anything for which he has sent me to you. ^{22}Now therefore know certainly that you shall die by the sword, by the famine, and by the pestilence, in the place where you desire to go to live there."

CHAPTER 42

QUESTIONS

QUESTION 1   b1

According to Jeremiah chapter 42:

Who were the fathers of Johanan and Jezaniah, and what were Johanan and Jezaniah's positions in the army?

QUESTION 2   a

According to Jeremiah chapter 42, when the people that were remaining in Judah came to meet Jeremiah to pray for them:

What was their prayer request?

QUESTION 3   b

According to Jeremiah chapter 42, when the people came to meet Jeremiah requesting that he should pray to the Lord on their behalf:

What was Jeremiah's response?

QUESTION 4   b

According to Jeremiah chapter 42, when Jeremiah assured the remnants of the people of Judah that he would pray to the Lord on their behalf:

What was the people's response to Jeremiah?

QUESTION 5   a

According to Jeremiah chapter 42, when the people came to meet Jeremiah requesting that he should pray to the Lord on their behalf:

How many days did it take before God gave them a response?

QUESTION 6   CPC

Jeremiah chapter 42:10–11 says,

"If you will still live in this land, then will I build you, and not pull you down, and I will plant you, and not pluck you up; for I grieve over the distress that I have brought on you."

Complete verse 11.

QUESTION 7   b

According to Jeremiah chapter 42:

What did God say was the reason the remnants of Judah wanted to go to Egypt?

QUESTION 8   CPC

Jeremiah chapter 42:15–16 says,

"now therefore hear the word of the LORD, O remnant of Judah: Thus says the LORD of hosts, the God of Israel, 'If you indeed set your faces to enter into Egypt, and go to live there."

Complete verse 16.

QUESTION 9   b

According to Jeremiah chapter 42:

What did Jeremiah tell the remnants of Judah who refused to obey God's command after they had asked him to pray to the Lord for them?

QUESTION 10   CMC

Read Jeremiah chapter 42:1–22, preach or write a commentary on the passage with focus on verses 10–12 and with emphasis on salvation.

QUESTION 11   CMB

Read Jeremiah chapter 42:10–17, preach or write a commentary on the passage with emphasis on salvation.

ANSWERS

ANSWER TO QUESTION 1   b1

- Kareah was Johanan's father

Hoshaiah was Jezeniah's father

- They were both captains of the forces (Jeremiah 42:1).

ANSWER TO QUESTION 2   a

To pray so that the Lord may tell them the way to walk or where they should go and the things they should do (Jeremiah 42:2–3).

ANSWER TO QUESTION 3   b

He said he would pray to the Lord as they requested, and whatever the Lord responded, he would tell them everything, not keeping anything from them (Jeremiah 42:4).

ANSWER TO QUESTION 4   b

That the Lord will be a witness against them if they would not do all that the Lord will say. They would do everything God says, whether good or evil, so that it may be well with them (Jeremiah 42:5–6).

ANSWER TO QUESTION 5   a

Ten days (Jeremiah 42:7).

ANSWER TO QUESTION 6   CPC

"¹¹Do not be afraid of the king of Babylon, of whom you are afraid; do not be afraid of him, says the LORD: for I am with you to save you, and to deliver you from his hand." (Jeremiah 42:11.)

ANSWER TO QUESTION 7   b

To be free from war, the sound of the trumpets and hunger (Jeremiah 42:13–14).

ANSWER TO QUESTION 8   CPC

"16then it shall happen, that the sword, which you fear, shall overtake you there in the land of Egypt; and the famine, about which you are afraid, shall follow close behind you there in Egypt; and there you shall die." (Jeremiah 42:16.)

ANSWER TO QUESTION 9   b

That they would surely die by sword or war, famine and disease or pestilence in the land (Egypt) where they desire to go (Jeremiah 42:22).

HINTS TO QUESTION 10   CMC

- God is the epitome of fatherhood. He is a loving Father who disciplines us when we err, intending to draw us back to Himself but not to destroy us.
- We should emulate God by always disciplining our children to correct them, but not in a manner that will sever our relationship with them and send them to take counsel from the world.

HINT TO QUESTION 11   CMB

God required the people of Judah to remain in the land despite their fears of the king of Babylon. If we trust in God and put away all fears, God will come through for us no matter the circumstances. Our obedience to God lies at the end of our fears; this means that our fears hinder our total obedience to God's instruction. Obedience to the instructions of God is what brings peace and prosperity. Our progress depends not entirely on where we are but on our obedience to God.

CHAPTER 43

"It happened that, when Jeremiah had made an end of speaking to all the people all the words of the LORD their God, with which the LORD their God had sent him to them, even all these words, ²then spoke Azariah the son of Hoshaiah, and Johanan the son of Kareah, and all the proud men, saying to Jeremiah, "You speak falsely. The LORD our God has not sent you to say, 'You shall not go into Egypt to live there'; ³but Baruch the son of Neriah sets you on against us, to deliver us into the hand of the Chaldeans, that they may put us to death, and carry us away captive to Babylon." ⁴So Johanan the son of Kareah, and all the captains of the forces, and all the people, did not obey the voice of the LORD, to dwell in the land of Judah. ⁵But Johanan the son of Kareah, and all the captains of the forces, took all the remnant of Judah, who were returned from all the nations where they had been driven, to live in the land of Judah; ⁶the men, and the women, and the children, and the king's daughters, and every person who Nebuzaradan the captain of the guard had left with Gedaliah the son of Ahikam, the son of Shaphan; and Jeremiah the prophet, and Baruch the son of Neriah; ⁷and they came into the land of Egypt; for they did not obey the voice of the LORD: and they came to Tahpanhes. ⁸Then came the word of the LORD to Jeremiah in Tahpanhes, saying, ⁹"Take great stones in your hand, and hide them in mortar in the brick work, which is at the entry of Pharaoh's house in Tahpanhes, in the sight of the men of Judah; ¹⁰and tell them, 'Thus says the LORD of hosts, the God of Israel: "Look, I will send and take Nebuchadnezzar the king of

Babylon, my servant, and will set his throne on these stones that I have hidden; and he shall spread his royal pavilion over them. ¹¹He shall come, and shall strike the land of Egypt; such as are for death shall be put to death, and such as are for captivity to captivity, and such as are for the sword to the sword. ¹²I will kindle a fire in the houses of the gods of Egypt; and he shall burn them, and carry them away captive: and he shall array himself with the land of Egypt, as a shepherd puts on his garment; and he shall go forth from there in peace. ¹³He shall also break the pillars of Beth Shemesh, that is in the land of Egypt; and the houses of the gods of Egypt shall he burn with fire."""

QUESTIONS

QUESTION 1   b

According to Jeremiah chapter 43:

Name two persons who said Jeremiah was lying when he told the Judeans that God would prosper them if they remained in the land of Judah.

QUESTION 2   a

According to Jeremiah chapter 43, when the proud men of Judah said that Jeremiah was lying:

What did they say he was lying about?

QUESTION 3   b

According to Jeremiah chapter 43, when the remnants of Judah rejected Jeremiah's message from the Lord:

Who did they say incited Jeremiah to tell them the message which they said was false, and what did they say was the person's intention?

QUESTION 4   b

According to Jeremiah chapter 43, Johanan and other military leaders took away the remnants of Judah after they rejected Jeremiah's message from the Lord:

Mention two notable people that were among the remnants.

QUESTION 5   b

According to Jeremiah chapter 43, after the remnants of Judah rejected Jeremiah's message from the Lord:

Which city did Johanan and the other military leaders take them to?

QUESTION 6   b1

According to Jeremiah chapter 43, when the Judeans who left Judah with Johanan arrived at their destination:

What did God ask Jeremiah to do and what did He ask him to say to the people?

QUESTION 7   CMC

Read Jeremiah chapter 43:1–7, preach or write a commentary on the passage with emphasis on salvation.

ANSWERS

ANSWER TO QUESTION 1   b

- Johanan (son of Kareah)
- Azariah (son of Hoshaiah) (Jeremiah 43:2).

ANSWER TO QUESTION 2   a

That God said they should remain in Judah and not go to Egypt (Jeremiah 43:2).

ANSWER TO QUESTION 3   b

- Baruch (son of Neriah).

- They said he intended they remain in Judah and either be killed or carried to exile by the Chaldeans or Babylonians (Jeremiah 43:3).

ANSWER TO QUESTION 4   b

Baruch and Jeremiah (Jeremiah 43:6).

ANSWER TO QUESTION 5   b

Tahpanhes (Jeremiah 43:7).

ANSWER TO QUESTION 6   b1

God instructed Jeremiah to:

- Bury some large stones at the entrance of Pharoah's palace while the people were watching.
- Tell the people that He would certainly bring the king of Babylon to Egypt to set his royal pavilion or throne over those stones and destroy the land and temple of Egypt. Those who are for death will die, those who are for captivity will be taken captive, and those who are for sword or war will meet the sword or war (Jeremiah 43:9–11).

HINT TO QUESTION 7   CMC

Jeremiah delivered the word of the Lord to the people of Judah as they had requested, but they failed to obey the words as they had promised. Like these people, many people often show enthusiasm in their expectations of what God has to say, but when faced with the actual demands from God, they fail to keep their end of the bargain.

CHAPTER 44

"The word that came to Jeremiah concerning all the Jews who lived in the land of Egypt, who lived at Migdol, and at Tahpanhes, and at Memphis, and in the country of Pathros, saying, ²"Thus says the LORD of hosts, the God of Israel: 'You have seen all the evil that I have brought on Jerusalem, and on all the cities of Judah; and look, this day they are a desolation, and no man dwells in them, ³because of their wickedness which they have committed to provoke me to anger, in that they went to burn incense, to serve other gods, that they did not know, neither they, nor you, nor your fathers. ⁴However I sent to you all my servants the prophets, rising up early and sending them, saying, 'Oh, do not do this abominable thing that I hate.' ⁵But they did not listen, nor inclined their ear to turn from their wickedness, to burn no incense to other gods. ⁶Therefore my wrath and my anger was poured forth, and was kindled in the cities of Judah and in the streets of Jerusalem; and they are wasted and desolate, as it is this day.' ⁷Therefore now thus says the LORD, the God of hosts, the God of Israel: 'Why do you commit great evil against your own souls, to cut off from yourselves man and woman, infant and nursing child out of the midst of Judah, to leave yourselves none remaining; ⁸in that you provoke me to anger with the works of your hands, burning incense to other gods in the land of Egypt, where you have gone to live; that you may be cut off, and that you may be a curse and a reproach among all the nations of the earth? ⁹Have you forgotten the wickedness of your fathers, and the wickedness of the kings of Judah, and the wickedness of their wives, and your own wickedness, and the wickedness of your wives which they committed in the land of

Judah, and in the streets of Jerusalem? [10]*They are not humbled even to this day, neither have they feared, nor walked in my law, nor in my statutes, that I set before you and before your fathers.'* [11]*Therefore thus says the LORD of hosts, the God of Israel: 'Look, I will set my face against you for evil, even to cut off all Judah.* [12]*I will take the remnant of Judah, that have set their faces to go into the land of Egypt to live there, and they shall all be consumed; in the land of Egypt shall they fall; they shall be consumed by the sword and by the famine; they shall die, from the least even to the greatest, by the sword and by the famine; and they shall be an object of horror, an astonishment, and a curse, and a reproach.* [13]*For I will punish those who dwell in the land of Egypt, as I have punished Jerusalem, by the sword, by the famine, and by the pestilence;* [14]*so that none of the remnant of Judah, who have gone into the land of Egypt to live there, shall escape or be left, to return into the land of Judah, to which they have a desire to return to dwell there: for none shall return save such as shall escape.'"* [15]*Then all the men who knew that their wives burned incense to other gods, and all the women who stood by, a great assembly, even all the people who lived in the land of Egypt, in Pathros, answered Jeremiah, saying,* [16]*"As for the word that you have spoken to us in the name of the LORD, we will not listen to you.* [17]*But we will certainly perform every word that is gone forth out of our mouth, to burn incense to the queen of heaven, and to pour out drink offerings to her, as we have done, we and our fathers, our kings and our leaders, in the cities of Judah, and in the streets of Jerusalem; for then had we plenty of food, and were well, and saw no evil.* [18]*But since we left off burning incense to the queen of heaven, and pouring out drink offerings to her, we have wanted all things, and have been consumed by the sword and by the famine."* [19]*And the woman said, "When we burned incense to the queen of heaven, and poured out drink offerings to her, did we make her cakes to worship her, and pour out drink offerings to her, without our husbands?"* [20]*Then Jeremiah said to all the people, to the men, and to the women, even to all the people who had given him an answer, saying,* [21]*"The incense that you burned in the cities of*

Judah, and in the streets of Jerusalem, you and your fathers, your kings and your leaders, and the people of the land. Did not the LORD remember them, and did not it come into his mind, ²²so that the LORD could no longer bear because of the evil of your doings, and because of the abominations which you have committed? Therefore your land has become a desolation, and an astonishment, and a curse, without inhabitant, as it is this day. ²³Because you have burned incense, and because you have sinned against the LORD, and have not obeyed the voice of the LORD, nor walked in his law, nor in his statutes, nor in his testimonies; therefore this evil has happened to you, as it is this day." ²⁴*Moreover Jeremiah said to all the people, and to all the women, "Hear the word of the LORD, all Judah who are in the land of Egypt:* ²⁵*Thus says the LORD of hosts, the God of Israel, saying, 'You and your wives have both spoken with your mouths, and with your hands have fulfilled it, saying, "We will surely perform our vows that we have vowed, to burn incense to the queen of heaven, and to pour out drink offerings to her": establish then your vows, and perform your vows.'* ²⁶*Therefore hear the word of the LORD, all Judah who dwell in the land of Egypt: 'Look, I have sworn by my great name,' says the Lord, 'that my name shall no more be named in the mouth of any man of Judah in all the land of Egypt, saying, "As the Lord GOD lives."* ²⁷*Look, I watch over them for disaster, and not for good; and all the men of Judah who are in the land of Egypt shall be consumed by the sword and by the famine, until they are all gone.* ²⁸*Those who escape the sword shall return out of the land of Egypt into the land of Judah, few in number; and all the remnant of Judah, who have gone into the land of Egypt to live there, shall know whose word shall stand, mine, or theirs.* ²⁹*This shall be the sign to you,' says the LORD, 'that I will punish you in this place, that you may know that my words shall surely stand against you for evil':* ³⁰*Thus says the LORD, 'Look, I will give Pharaoh Hophra king of Egypt into the hand of his enemies, and into the hand of those who seek his life; as I gave Zedekiah king of Judah into the hand of Nebuchadnezzar king of Babylon, who was his enemy, and sought his life.'"*

QUESTIONS

QUESTION 1   b1

According to Jeremiah chapter 44, God sent a message to the Judeans living in Egypt:

Mention three of the Egyptian cities He sent messages to.

QUESTION 2   CPB

Jeremiah chapter 44:4–5 says,

"However I sent to you all my servants the prophets, rising up early and sending them, saying, 'Oh, do not do this abominable thing that I hate.'"

Complete verse 5.

QUESTION 3   CPC

Jeremiah chapter 44:9–10 says,

"Have you forgotten the wickedness of your fathers, and the wickedness of the kings of Judah, and the wickedness of their wives, and your own wickedness, and the wickedness of your wives which they committed in the land of Judah, and in the streets of Jerusalem?"

Complete verse 10.

QUESTION 4   CTX

"for then had we plenty of food, and were well, and saw no evil."

Give the context of the above quote:

Who said it, to who, and under what circumstance?

QUESTION 5   a

According to Jeremiah chapter 44:

Who was the king of Egypt when Jeremiah was forcefully taken to Egypt?

QUESTION 6   a

According to Jeremiah chapter 44, when God was talking about the fate of the king of Egypt while the remnants of Judah were in Egypt:

Which Judean king did He compare the fate of the king of Egypt to?

QUESTION 7   CMB

Read Jeremiah chapter 44:1–19, preach or write a commentary on the passage with focus on verses 15–19 and with emphasis on salvation.

QUESTION 8   CMC

Read Jeremiah chapter 44:20–22, preach or write a commentary on the passage with emphasis on salvation.

ANSWERS

ANSWER TO QUESTION 1   b1

- Migdol
- Tahpanhes
- Memphis or Noph
- Pathros or upper Egypt or Southern Egypt (Jeremiah 44:1).

ANSWER TO QUESTION 2   CPB

"⁵But they did not listen, nor inclined their ear to turn from their wickedness, to burn no incense to other gods." (Jeremiah 43:5.)

ANSWER TO QUESTION 3   CPC

"¹⁰They are not humbled even to this day, neither have they feared, nor walked in my law, nor in my statutes, that I set before you and before your fathers."' (Jeremiah 44:10.)

ANSWER TO QUESTION 4   CTX

- The men and women of Judah in Egypt (who worshipped idols).

- To Prophet Jeremiah
- When they were telling Jeremiah that when they worshipped the 'queen of heaven,' they prospered, but when they stopped, they suffered troubles, famine and wars (Jeremiah 44:17–18).

ANSWER TO QUESTION 5   a

Pharoah Hophra (Jeremiah 44:30).

ANSWER TO QUESTION 6   a

King Zedekiah (Jeremiah 44:30).

HINTS TO QUESTION 7   CMB

- The Judeans said to Jeremiah that when they worshipped their idols, all went well, but things began to fall apart when they stopped worshipping them. The possible reasons for things going difficult when one turns to God are either it is a period of trial or a time God is preparing them for His purpose, or they did not turn to God with all their hearts. Also, people who follow God's commandments solely with an expectation of earthly reward may feel disappointed when there is a delay or when God chooses not to grant what they were expecting. The Bible did not state why it happened to the Judeans like that, but when we turn to God, our faith should be unto death.
- The erroneous belief of the people of Judah that there is more gain in serving idols is similar to the belief of some people today who think that there is more gain in following the ways of the world than towing the path of righteousness. We should know that serving God entails the sacrifice of saying no to all pleasures of sin. Deciding to live for God ensures the salvation of our souls, which outweighs whatever benefits the world has to offer.

HINT TO QUESTION 8   CMC

When the people of Judah told Jeremiah that they prospered when they were burning incense to the queen of heaven, Jeremiah told them that even at that time, God saw them. The fact that they were not punished at the time they burned incense to the queen of heaven does not mean that God overlooked it. People continue in sin when they do not see God's punishment come on them immediately, not knowing that God is being patient with them, giving them time to repent.

CHAPTER 45

JEREMIAH CHAPTER 45

"The message that Jeremiah the prophet spoke to Baruch the son of Neriah, when he wrote these words in a scroll at the mouth of Jeremiah, in the fourth year of Jehoiakim the son of Josiah, king of Judah, saying, ^{2}"Thus says the LORD, the God of Israel, to you, Baruch: ^{3}'You said, "Woe is me now. For the LORD has added sorrow to my pain; I am weary with my groaning, and I find no rest."'" ^{4}"You shall tell him, 'Thus says the LORD: "Look, that which I have built will I break down, and that which I have planted I will pluck up; and this in the whole land. ^{5}Do you seek great things for yourself? Do not seek them; for, look, I will bring disaster on all flesh, says the LORD; but your life will I give to you for a reward in all places where you go."'"

QUESTIONS

QUESTION 1   b

According to Jeremiah chapter 45:

Who was king in Judah when God gave Baruch a message through Jeremiah, and in what year of his reign did this happen?

QUESTION 2   CTX

"Do you seek great things for yourself?..."

Give the context of the above quote:

Who said it, to who, and under what circumstance?

QUESTION 3   **b**

According to Jeremiah chapter 45:

What was Baruch's complaint to God?

QUESTION 4   **a**

According to Jeremiah chapter 45:

What was God's promise to Baruch?

QUESTION 5   **b**

According to Jeremiah chapter 45:

What did God say Baruch should not seek after, and why?

ANSWERS

ANSWER TO QUESTION 1   **b**

- King Jehoiakim
- Fourth year (Jeremiah 45:1–2).

ANSWER TO QUESTION 2   **CTX**

- God, through Prophet Jeremiah
- To Baruch
- When Baruch complained to God about his sorrow and God sent a message from Jeremiah to him not to seek great things that He (God) would destroy the land of Judah but would give Baruch his life as a reward, that is, preserve him wherever he will be (Jeremiah 45:1–5).

ANSWER TO QUESTION 3   **b**

His complaint was that God had added more sorrow to his pain, that he was weary with his groaning and found no rest (Jeremiah 45:3).

ANSWER TO QUESTION 4   a

That He (God) will give Baruch his life as a reward wherever he goes (Jeremiah 45:5).

ANSWER TO QUESTION 5   b

- Great things
- Because He will bring disaster on all flesh (Jeremiah 45:5).

CHAPTER 46

JEREMIAH CHAPTER 46

"The word of the LORD came to Jeremiah the prophet concerning the nations. ²Of Egypt: concerning the army of Pharaoh Necoh king of Egypt, which was by the river Perath in Carchemish, which Nebuchadnezzar king of Babylon struck in the fourth year of Jehoiakim the son of Josiah, king of Judah. ³"Prepare the buckler and shield, and draw near to battle. ⁴Harness the horses, and get up, you horsemen, and stand forth with your helmets; furbish the spears, put on the coats of mail. ⁵Why have I seen it? They are dismayed and are turned backward; and their mighty ones are beaten down, and have fled in haste, and do not look back: terror is on every side," says the LORD. ⁶"Do not let the swift flee away, nor the mighty man escape; in the north by the river Perath have they stumbled and fallen. ⁷Who is this who rises up like the Nile, whose waters toss themselves like the rivers? ⁸Egypt rises up like the Nile, and his waters toss themselves like the rivers: and he says, 'I will rise up, I will cover the earth; I will destroy cities and its inhabitants.' ⁹Go up, you horses; and rage, you chariots; and let the mighty men go forth: Cush and Put, who handle the shield; and the Ludim, who handle and bend the bow. ¹⁰For that day is of the Lord, the LORD of hosts, a day of vengeance, that he may avenge him of his adversaries: and the sword shall devour and be satiate, and shall drink its fill of their blood; for the Lord, the LORD of hosts, has a sacrifice in the north country by the river Perath. ¹¹Go up into Gilead, and take balm, virgin daughter of Egypt: in vain do you use many medicines; there is no healing for you. ¹²The nations have heard of your shame, and the earth is full of your cry;

for the mighty man has stumbled against the mighty, they are fallen both of them together." [13] *The word that the LORD spoke to Jeremiah the prophet, how that Nebuchadnezzar king of Babylon should come and strike the land of Egypt.* [14] *"Declare in Egypt, and publish in Migdol, and publish in Memphis and in Tahpanhes: say, 'Stand forth, and prepare; for the sword has devoured around you.'* [15] *Why are your strong ones swept away? They did not stand, because the LORD pushed them.* [16] *He made many to stumble, yes, they fell one on another: and they said, 'Arise, and let us go again to our own people, and to the land of our birth, from the oppressing sword.'* [17] *They cried there, 'Pharaoh king of Egypt is but a noise; he has let the appointed time pass by.'"* [18] *"As I live,"* says the King, *"whose name is the LORD of hosts, surely like Tabor among the mountains, and like Carmel by the sea, so shall he come.* [19] *You daughter who dwells in Egypt, furnish yourself to go into captivity; for Memphis shall become a desolation, and shall be burnt up, without inhabitant.* [20] *Egypt is a very beautiful heifer; but destruction out of the north has come, it has come.* [21] *Also her hired men in the midst of her are like calves of the stall; for they also are turned back, they are fled away together, they did not stand: for the day of their calamity has come on them, the time of their visitation.* [22] *The sound of it shall go like the serpent; for they shall march with an army, and come against her with axes, as wood cutters.* [23] *They shall cut down her forest, says the LORD, though it can't be searched; because they are more than the locusts, and are innumerable.* [24] *The daughter of Egypt shall be disappointed; she shall be delivered into the hand of the people of the north."* [25] *"The LORD of hosts, the God of Israel, says: 'Look, I will punish Amon of No, and Pharaoh, and Egypt, with her gods, and her kings; even Pharaoh, and those who trust in him:* [26] *and I will deliver them into the hand of those who seek their lives, and into the hand of Nebuchadnezzar king of Babylon, and into the hand of his servants; and afterwards it shall be inhabited, as in the days of old,' says the LORD.* [27] *'But do not be afraid, Jacob my servant, neither be dismayed, Israel: for, look, I will save you from afar, and your seed from the land of their captivity; and Jacob shall return, and shall be quiet and at ease, and none shall make him afraid.* ²⁸ *Do not be afraid, O Jacob my servant,' says the LORD; 'for I am with you: for I will make a full end of all the nations where I have driven you; but I will not make a full end of you, but I will correct you in measure, and will in no way leave you unpunished.'"*

QUESTIONS

QUESTION 1   a

According to Jeremiah chapter 46, God gave a message through Jeremiah to foreign nations:

Which nation was addressed in this chapter?

QUESTION 2   CTX

"Prepare the buckler and shield, and draw near to battle."

Give the context of the above quote:

Who said it, to who, and under what circumstance?

QUESTION 3   b1

According to Jeremiah chapter 46, when God gave Jeremiah a message to foreign nations, a battle between two kings was referenced:

What are the names of the kings involved in the battle, and where did the battle occur?

QUESTION 4   a

According to Jeremiah chapter 46:

Who or what was described as 'rising as the river Nile'?

QUESTION 5   a

Jeremiah chapter 46:11 says, *"Go up into Gilead, and take balm...."*

Who is the above scripture referring to?

QUESTION 6   **b1**

Jeremiah chapter 46:18 says, *"surely like Tabor among the mountains, and like Carmel by the sea, so shall he come."*

Who is the above scripture referring to?

QUESTION 7   **b1**

Jeremiah chapter 46:14 says, *"Stand forth, and prepare; for the sword has devoured around you."*

Mention three cities in Egypt to which the above quote was directed.

QUESTION 8   **CTX**

"Why are your strong ones swept away? They did not stand, because the LORD pushed them."

Give the context of the above quote:

Who said it, to who, and under what circumstance?

QUESTION 9   **CPC**

Jeremiah chapter 46:15–16 says,

"15 Why are your strong ones swept away? They did not stand, because the LORD pushed them."

Complete verse 16.

QUESTION 10   **b1**

Jeremiah chapter 46:25 says, *"The LORD of hosts, the God of Israel, says: 'Look, I will punish Amon....'"*

Who or what is Amon in the above scripture?

QUESTION 11   **CPC**

Jeremiah chapter 46:27–28 says,

"27 'But do not be afraid, Jacob my servant, neither be dismayed, Israel: for, look, I will save you from afar, and your seed from the

land of their captivity; and Jacob shall return, and shall be quiet and at ease, and none shall make him afraid."

Complete verse 28.

QUESTION 12   **CMB**

Read Jeremiah chapter 46:27–28, preach or write a commentary on the passage with emphasis on salvation.

ANSWERS

ANSWER TO QUESTION 1   **a**

Egypt (Jeremiah 46:1–2).

ANSWER TO QUESTION 2   **CTX**

- God, through Prophet Jeremiah
- To Egypt
- When He gave Jeremiah a message concerning Egypt's army (Jeremiah 46:1–3).

ANSWER TO QUESTION 3   **b1**

- Pharoah Necoh of Egypt and King Nebuchadnezzar of Babylon
- By the river Perath or Euphrates in Carchemish (Jeremiah 46:2).

ANSWER TO QUESTION 4   **a**

The Egyptian armies (Jeremiah 46:8).

ANSWER TO QUESTION 5   **a**

Virgin daughter of Egypt or Egypt (Jeremiah 46:11).

ANSWER TO QUESTION 6   **b1**

King Nebuchadnezzar (Jeremiah 46:13–18).

ANSWER TO QUESTION 7   b1

1. Migdol
2. Memphis
3. Tahpanhes (Jeremiah 46:14).

ANSWER TO QUESTION 8   CTX

- God, through Prophet Jeremiah
- To Egypt or Migdol, Memphis and Tahpanhes
- When He gave Jeremiah a message about King Nebuchadnezzar's plan to attack Egypt (Jeremiah 46:15).

ANSWER TO QUESTION 9   CPC

"16He made many to stumble, yes, they fell one on another: and they said, 'Arise, and let us go again to our own people, and to the land of our birth, from the oppressing sword.'" (Jeremiah 46:16.)

ANSWER TO QUESTION 10   b1

The god of No or Thebes in Egypt (Jeremiah 46:25).

ANSWER TO QUESTION 11   CPC

"28Do not be afraid, O Jacob my servant,' says the LORD; 'for I am with you: for I will make a full end of all the nations where I have driven you; but I will not make a full end of you, but I will correct you in measure, and will in no way leave you unpunished.'" (Jeremiah 46:28.)

HINT TO QUESTION 12   CMB

- God's love for His children was manifested in not correcting the Judeans beyond measure and His promise of protection amidst their discipline. Every act of discipline meted by God towards His children is out of love and with the goal to correct and restore them, and it will never be done out of proportion.

CHAPTER 47

JEREMIAH CHAPTER 47

"The word of the LORD that came to Jeremiah the prophet concerning the Philistines, before that Pharaoh struck Gaza. ²"Thus says the LORD: 'Look, waters rise up out of the north, and shall become an overflowing stream, and shall overflow the land and all that is in it, the city and those who dwell in it; and the men shall cry, and all the inhabitants of the land shall wail. ³At the noise of the stamping of the hoofs of his strong ones, at the rushing of his chariots, at the rumbling of his wheels, the fathers do not look back to their children for feebleness of hands; ⁴because of the day that comes to destroy all the Philistines, to cut off from Tyre and Sidon every helper who remains: for the LORD will destroy the Philistines, the remnant of the isle of Caphtor. ⁵Baldness has come on Gaza; Ashkelon is brought to nothing, the remnant of their valley: how long will you cut yourself? ⁶You sword of the LORD, "how long will it be before you be quiet? Put up yourself into your scabbard; rest, and be still." ⁷How can you be quiet, since the LORD has given you a command? Against Ashkelon, and against the seashore, there has he appointed it.'"

QUESTIONS

QUESTION 1   a

Jeremiah chapter 47:2 says, *"Look, waters rise up out of the north, and shall become an overflowing stream, and shall overflow the land and all that is in it...."*

Which people were the above message sent to, and who was it talking about?

QUESTION 2 **CPC**

Jeremiah chapter 47:6–7 says,

"You sword of the LORD, "how long will it be before you be quiet? Put up yourself into your scabbard; rest, and be still.""

Complete verse 7.

ANSWERS

ANSWER TO QUESTION 1 **a**

- The Philistines
- Egyptian army or Egypt (Jeremiah 47:1–2).

ANSWER TO QUESTION 2 **CPC**

"⁷How can you be quiet, since the LORD has given you a command? Against Ashkelon, and against the seashore, there has he appointed it." (Jeremiah 47:7.)

CHAPTER 48

JEREMIAH CHAPTER 48

"Of Moab. "Thus says the LORD of hosts, the God of Israel: 'Woe to Nebo. for it is laid waste; Kiriathaim is disappointed, it is taken; Misgab is put to shame and broken down. ²The praise of Moab is no more; in Heshbon they have devised evil against her: "Come, and let us cut her off from being a nation." You also, Madmen, shall be brought to silence: the sword shall pursue you. ³The sound of a cry from Horonaim, "destruction and great calamity." ⁴Moab is destroyed; her little ones have caused a cry to be heard. ⁵For by the ascent of Luhith with continual weeping shall they go up; for at the descent of Horonaim they have heard the distress of the cry of destruction. ⁶"Flee, save your lives, and be like a shrub in the wilderness." ⁷For, because you have trusted in your works and in your treasures, you also shall be taken: and Chemosh shall go forth into captivity, his priests and his officials together. ⁸The destroyer shall come on every city, and no city shall escape; the valley also shall perish, and the plain shall be destroyed; as the LORD has spoken. ⁹Give wings to Moab, that she may fly and get her away: and her cities shall become a desolation, without any to dwell in them.' ¹⁰Cursed is he who does the work of the LORD negligently; and cursed is he who keeps back his sword from blood. ¹¹'Moab has been at ease from his youth, and he has settled on his lees, and has not been emptied from vessel to vessel, neither has he gone into captivity: therefore his taste remains in him, and his scent is not changed. ¹²Therefore look, the days come,' says the LORD, 'that I will send to him those who pour off, and they shall pour him off; and they shall empty his vessels, and break their

bottles in pieces. ¹³Moab shall be ashamed of Chemosh, as the house of Israel was ashamed of Bethel their confidence. ¹⁴How can you say, "We are mighty men, and valiant men for the war?" ¹⁵Moab is laid waste, and they are gone up into his cities, and his chosen young men are gone down to the slaughter,' says the King, whose name is the LORD of hosts. ¹⁶The calamity of Moab is near to come, and his affliction hurries fast. ¹⁷All you who are around him, bemoan him, and all you who know his name; say, "How is the strong staff broken, the beautiful rod." ¹⁸You daughter who dwells in Dibon, come down from your glory, and sit in thirst; for the destroyer of Moab has come up against you, he has destroyed your strongholds. ¹⁹Inhabitant of Aroer, stand by the way, and watch: ask him who flees, and her who escapes; say, "What has been done?" ²⁰'Moab is disappointed; for it is broken down: wail and cry; tell it by the Arnon, that Moab is laid waste." ²¹Judgment has come on the plain country, on Holon, and on Jahzah, and on Mephaath, ²²and on Dibon, and on Nebo, and on Beth Diblathaim, ²³and on Kiriathaim, and on Beth Gamul, and on Beth Meon, ²⁴and on Kerioth, and on Bozrah, and on all the cities of the land of Moab, far or near. ²⁵The horn of Moab is cut off, and his arm is broken,' says the LORD. ²⁶'Make him drunk; for he magnified himself against the LORD: and Moab shall wallow in his vomit, and he also shall be in derision. ²⁷For wasn't Israel a derision to you? Was he found among thieves? For as often as you speak of him, you shake your head. ²⁸You inhabitants of Moab, leave the cities, and dwell in the rock; and be like the dove that makes her nest over the mouth of the abyss. ²⁹We have heard of the pride of Moab. He is very proud; his loftiness, and his pride, and his arrogance, and the haughtiness of his heart. ³⁰I know his wrath,' says the LORD, 'that it is nothing; his boastings have worked nothing. ³¹Therefore I will wail for Moab; yes, I will cry out for all Moab; I will mourn for the men of Kir Heres. ³²With more than the weeping of Jazer will I weep for you, vine of Sibmah: your branches passed over the sea, they reached even to the sea of Jazer: on your summer fruits and on your vintage the destroyer is fallen. ³³Gladness and joy is taken away from the fruitful field and *from the land of Moab; and I have caused wine to cease from the wine presses: none shall tread with shouting; the shouting shall be no shouting.* ³⁴*From the cry of Heshbon even to Elealeh, even to Jahaz have they uttered their voice, from Zoar even to Horonaim, to Eglath Shelishiyah: for the waters of Nimrim also shall become desolate.* ³⁵*Moreover I will cause to cease in Moab,' says the LORD, 'him who offers sacrifice in the high place, and him who burns incense to his gods.* ³⁶*Therefore my heart sounds for Moab like pipes, and my heart sounds like pipes for the men of Kir Heres: therefore the abundance that he has gotten is perished.* ³⁷*For every head is bald, and every beard clipped: on all the hands are cuttings, and on the waist sackcloth.* ³⁸*On all the housetops of Moab and in its streets there is lamentation every where; for I have broken Moab like a vessel in which none delights,' says the LORD.* ³⁹*How it is broken down. How they wail. How Moab has turned the back with shame. So shall Moab become a derision and a terror to all who are around him.'* ⁴⁰*For thus says the LORD: 'Look, he shall fly as an eagle, and shall spread out his wings against Moab.* ⁴¹*Kerioth is taken, and the strongholds are seized, and the heart of the mighty men of Moab at that day shall be as the heart of a woman in her pangs.* ⁴²*Moab shall be destroyed from being a people, because he has magnified himself against the LORD.* ⁴³*Fear, and the pit, and the snare, are on you, inhabitant of Moab, says the LORD.* ⁴⁴*He who flees from the fear shall fall into the pit; and he who gets up out of the pit shall be taken in the snare: for I will bring on him, even on Moab, the year of their visitation,' says the LORD.* ⁴⁵*'Those who fled stand without strength under the shadow of Heshbon; for a fire is gone forth out of Heshbon, and a flame from the midst of Sihon, and has devoured the corner of Moab, and the crown of the head of the tumultuous ones.* ⁴⁶*Woe to you, O Moab. The people of Chemosh is undone; for your sons are taken away captive, and your daughters into captivity.* ⁴⁷*Yet will I bring back the captivity of Moab in the latter days,' says the LORD. Thus far is the judgment of Moab."*

QUESTIONS

QUESTION 1 a

According to Jeremiah chapter 48:

In which nation is the city of Nebo?

QUESTION 2 b

Jeremiah chapter 48:2 mentions Madmen:

Who or what is Madmen?

QUESTION 3 a

According to Jeremiah chapter 48:

Which nation did Jeremiah say will no more be praised?

QUESTION 4 b

According to Jeremiah chapter 48:

What did Jeremiah say will happen to Madmen?

QUESTION 5 a

According to Jeremiah chapter 48:

In what city would people plot evil against Moab?

QUESTION 6 b

According to Jeremiah chapter 48:

From which city will cries of devastation and great destruction be heard?

QUESTION 7 a

According to Jeremiah chapter 48:

Who or what was Chemosh?

QUESTION 8   a

According to Jeremiah chapter 48:

How many cities of Moab did Jeremiah say would be spared or escape the coming destruction?

QUESTION 9   b

According to Jeremiah chapter 48:

What did God say would happen when He would send men to pour Moab out of her vessel?

QUESTION 10   b

According to Jeremiah chapter 48:

What comparison did Jeremiah draw between Chemosh and Bethel?

QUESTION 11   a

Jeremiah chapter 48:14 says, ***"How can you say, "We are mighty men, and valiant men for the war?""***

Who was the above verse referring to?

QUESTION 12   b

According to Jeremiah chapter 48:

Why did Jeremiah ask the inhabitants of Dibon to come down from their glory and sit in thirst or on the dust?

QUESTION 13   a

According to Jeremiah chapter 48:

Which people did Jeremiah say should stand by the road while the Moabites escaped and ask what happened?

QUESTION 14   CPB

Jeremiah chapter 48:25–26 says,

"The horn of Moab is cut off, and his arm is broken,' says the LORD."

Complete verse 26.

QUESTION 15   a

According to Jeremiah chapter 48:

Which people were asked to leave their cities and live in the rocks or cave?

QUESTION 16   a

According to Jeremiah chapter 48:

Which people were asked to be like doves that make their nest over the abyss?

QUESTION 17   c

Jeremiah chapter 48:34 says, *"From the cry of Heshbon even to Elealeh, even to Jahaz have they uttered their voice, from Zoar even to Horonaim...."*

What significant thing is recorded about Zoar in the Bible?

Give a Bible reference for your answer.

QUESTION 18   CPC

Jeremiah chapter 48:43–44 says,

"Fear, and the pit, and the snare, are on you, inhabitant of Moab, says the LORD."

Complete verse 44.

QUESTION 19   b2

Jeremiah chapter 48:45 says, *"for a fire is gone forth out of Heshbon, and a flame from the midst of Sihon...."*

In Bible history, who was King Sihon, and how did he die?

QUESTION 20   **CMB**

Read Jeremiah chapter 48:6–7, preach or write a commentary on the passage with emphasis on salvation.

QUESTION 21   **CMB**

Read Jeremiah chapter 48:29,42, preach or write a commentary on the passage with emphasis on salvation.

ANSWERS

ANSWER TO QUESTION 1   a

Moab (Jeremiah 48:1).

ANSWER TO QUESTION 2   b

It was a city or location in Moab (Jeremiah 48:1–2).

(It was once a city between the boundaries of the tribe of Gad and Reuben east of the Jordan River).

ANSWER TO QUESTION 3   a

Moab (Jeremiah 48:2).

ANSWER TO QUESTION 4   b

It shall be brought to silence, and the sword shall pursue it

Or

The sword shall pursue it (Jeremiah 48:2).

ANSWER TO QUESTION 5   a

Heshbon (Jeremiah 48:2).

ANSWER TO QUESTION 6   b

Horonaim (Jeremiah 48:3).

ANSWER TO QUESTION 7   a

The Moabites' god (Jeremiah 48:7).

ANSWER TO QUESTION 8   a

No city shall escape (Jeremiah 48:8).

ANSWER TO QUESTION 9   b

They will empty the vessel and break their bottles into pieces (Jeremiah 48:12).

ANSWER TO QUESTION 10   b

Moab will be ashamed of Chemosh just as Israel was ashamed of Bethel, their confidence

Or

Moab trusted in Chemosh just as Israel trusted in Bethel (Jeremiah 48:13).

ANSWER TO QUESTION 11   a

The Moabites or Moab (Jeremiah 48:14).

ANSWER TO QUESTION 12   b

Because the destroyer of Moab will destroy them also (Jeremiah 48:18).

ANSWER TO QUESTION 13   a

The inhabitants or people of Aroer (Jeremiah 48:19).

ANSWER TO QUESTION 14   CPB

"26'Make him drunk; for he magnified himself against the LORD: and Moab shall wallow in his vomit, and he also shall be in derision." (Jeremiah 48:26.)

ANSWER TO QUESTION 15   a

The inhabitants or people of Moab (Jeremiah 48:28).

ANSWER TO QUESTION 16   a

The inhabitants or people of Moab (Jeremiah 48:28).

ANSWER TO QUESTION 17   c

- It was the place Lot ran to during the destruction of Sodom and Gomorrah
- Genesis 19:17–22.

ANSWER TO QUESTION 18   CPC

"44He who flees from the fear shall fall into the pit; and he who gets up out of the pit shall be taken in the snare: for I will bring on him, even on Moab, the year of their visitation,' says the LORD." (Jeremiah 48:44.)

ANSWER TO QUESTION 19   b2

- He was a King of the Amorites
- He was killed when he waged war against the Israelites led by Moses as they journeyed to the Promised Land (Numbers 21:21–26).

HINT TO QUESTION 20   CMB

One of the things God held against Moab was their trust in their works, treasures and idols. Consequently, God declared that they would go into captivity. We should not put our trust in anything but the Lord.

HINT TO QUESTION 21   CMB

One of the things God held against Moab was their pride; they magnified themselves against the Lord. God is the creator of heaven and earth. We owe Him everything we have, whatever position or honour we attain. It is pride and rebellion when we take credit for anything we achieve in life and fail to give thanks to God or acknowledge Him.

CHAPTER 49

JEREMIAH CHAPTER 49

"Of the children of Ammon. "Thus says the LORD: 'Has Israel no sons? Has he no heir? Why then does Malcam possess Gad, and his people dwell in its cities? ² Therefore look, the days come,' says the LORD, 'that I will cause an alarm of war to be heard against Rabbah of the children of Ammon; and it shall become a desolate heap, and her daughters shall be burned with fire: then shall Israel possess those who possessed him,' says the LORD. ³ 'Wail, Heshbon, for Ai is laid waste; cry, you daughters of Rabbah, clothe yourself in sackcloth: lament, and run back and forth among the fences; for Malcam shall go into captivity, his priests and his officials together. ⁴ Why do you glory in the valleys, your flowing valley, backsliding daughter? You who trusted in her treasures, saying, "Who shall come to me?" ⁵ Look, I will bring a fear on you,' says the Lord, the LORD of hosts, 'from all who are around you; and you shall be driven out every man right forth, and there shall be none to gather together the fugitives. ⁶ But afterward I will bring back the captivity of the children of Ammon,' says the LORD." ⁷ Of Edom. "Thus says the LORD of hosts: 'Is wisdom no more in Teman? Is counsel perished from the prudent? Is their wisdom vanished? ⁸ Flee, turn back, dwell in the depths, inhabitants of Dedan; for I will bring the calamity of Esau on him, the time that I shall visit him. ⁹ If grape gatherers came to you, would they not leave some gleaning grapes? If thieves by night, wouldn't they destroy until they had enough? ¹⁰ But I have made Esau bare, I have uncovered his secret places, and he shall not be able to hide himself: his seed is destroyed, and his brothers, and his neighbors; and he is no more.

¹¹Leave your fatherless children, I will preserve them alive; and let your widows trust in me.' ¹²For thus says the LORD: 'Look, they to whom it did not pertain to drink of the cup shall certainly drink; and are you he who shall altogether go unpunished? You shall not go unpunished, but you shall surely drink. ¹³For I have sworn by myself,' says the LORD, 'that Bozrah shall become an astonishment, a reproach, a waste, and a curse; and all its cities shall be perpetual wastes.'" ¹⁴I have heard news from the LORD, and an ambassador is sent among the nations, saying, "Gather yourselves together, and come against her, and rise up to the battle." ¹⁵"For, look, I have made you small among the nations, and despised among men. ¹⁶As for your terror, the pride of your heart has deceived you, O you who dwell in the clefts of the rock, who hold the height of the hill: though you should make your nest as high as the eagle, I will bring you down from there," says the LORD. ¹⁷"Edom shall become an astonishment: everyone who passes by it shall be astonished, and shall hiss at all its plagues. ¹⁸As in the overthrow of Sodom and Gomorrah and the neighbor cities of it," says the LORD, "no man shall dwell there, neither shall any son of man live in it. ¹⁹Look, he shall come up like a lion from the pride of the Jordan against the strong habitation: for I will suddenly make them run away from it; and whoever is chosen, him will I appoint over it: for who is like me? And who will appoint me a time? And who is the shepherd who will stand before me? ²⁰Therefore hear the counsel of the LORD, that he has taken against Edom; and his purposes, that he has purposed against the inhabitants of Teman: Surely they shall drag them away, the little ones of the flock; surely he shall make their habitation desolate over them. ²¹The earth trembles at the noise of their fall; there is a cry, the noise which is heard in the Sea of Suf. ²²Look, he shall come up and fly as the eagle, and spread out his wings against Bozrah: and the heart of the mighty men of Edom at that day shall be as the heart of a woman in her pangs." ²³Of Damascus. "Hamath is confounded, and Arpad; for they have heard evil news, they are melted away: there is sorrow on the sea; it can't be quiet. ²⁴Damascus has grown feeble, she turns herself to flee, and trembling has seized on her: anguish and sorrows have

taken hold of her, as of a woman in travail. ^{25}*How is the city of praise not forsaken, the city of my joy?* ^{26}*Therefore her young men shall fall in her streets, and all the men of war shall be brought to silence in that day," says the LORD of hosts.* ^{27}*"I will kindle a fire in the wall of Damascus, and it shall devour the palaces of Ben Hadad."* ^{28}*Of Kedar, and of the kingdoms of Hazor, which Nebuchadnezzar king of Babylon struck. "Thus says the LORD: 'Arise, go up to Kedar, and destroy the children of the east.'* ^{29}*Their tents and their flocks shall they take; they shall carry away for themselves their curtains, and all their vessels, and their camels; and they shall cry to them, 'Terror on every side.'* ^{30}*Flee, wander far off, dwell in the depths, you inhabitants of Hazor," says the LORD; "for Nebuchadnezzar king of Babylon has taken counsel against you, and has conceived a purpose against you."* ^{31}*"Arise, go up to a nation that is at ease, that dwells without care, says the LORD; that have neither gates nor bars, that dwell alone.* ^{32}*Their camels shall be a booty, and the multitude of their livestock a spoil: and I will scatter to all winds those who have the corners of their beards cut off; and I will bring their calamity from every side of them," says the LORD.* ^{33}*"Hazor shall be a dwelling place of jackals, a desolation forever: no man shall dwell there, neither shall any son of man live in it."* ^{34}*The word of the LORD that came to Jeremiah the prophet concerning Elam, in the beginning of the reign of Zedekiah king of Judah, saying,* ^{35}*"Thus says the LORD of hosts: 'Look, I will break the bow of Elam, the chief of their might.* ^{36}*On Elam will I bring the four winds from the four quarters of the sky, and will scatter them toward all those winds; and there shall be no nation where the outcasts of Elam shall not come.* ^{37}*I will cause Elam to be dismayed before their enemies, and before those who seek their life; and I will bring evil on them, even my fierce anger,' says the LORD; 'and I will send the sword after them, until I have consumed them;* ^{38}*and I will set my throne in Elam, and will destroy from there king and officials,' says the LORD.* ^{39}*'But it shall happen in the latter days, that I will bring back the captivity of Elam,' says the LORD."*

CHAPTER 49

QUESTIONS

QUESTION 1   c

Jeremiah chapter 49:1 says, *"Has Israel no sons? Has he no heir? Why then does Malcam possess Gad, and his people dwell in its cities?"*

Who was the first king of Israel to be associated with Malcam (Molech), and mention the Bible portion where it can be found?

QUESTION 2   b1

Jeremiah chapter 49:1 says, *"Has Israel no sons? Has he no heir? Why then does Malcam possess Gad, and his people dwell in its cities?"*

What was God's first command to the people of Israel against Malcam (Molech) in the Bible?

QUESTION 3   c

Jeremiah chapter 49:1 says, *"Why then does Malcam possess Gad, and his people dwell in its cities?"*

Who or what is Malcam (Molech), and where was this name first mentioned in the Bible?

QUESTION 4   b

Jeremiah chapter 49:1 says, *"Of the children of Ammon. Thus says the LORD...."*

Whose descendants were the Ammonites?

QUESTION 5   a

According to Jeremiah chapter 49:

Where is Rabbah?

QUESTION 6   a

According to Jeremiah chapter 49:

Why did God ask Heshbon to wail or cry?

QUESTION 7   CPC

Jeremiah chapter 49:4–5 says,

"Why do you glory in the valleys, your flowing valley, backsliding daughter? You who trusted in her treasures, saying, "Who shall come to me?"

Complete verse 5.

QUESTION 8   a

According to Jeremiah chapter 49:

What did God say He would do to Ammon in the future after their captivity?

QUESTION 9   a

According to Jeremiah chapter 49:

Where is Teman located?

QUESTION 10   a

Jeremiah chapter 49 mentions Edom:

Whose descendants were the Edomites?

QUESTION 11   b

According to Jeremiah chapter 49, God said He would bring calamity upon Edom but asked certain people to flee:

Who did He say should flee?

QUESTION 12   CPB

Jeremiah chapter 49:10–11 says,

"But I have made Esau bare, I have uncovered his secret places, and he shall not be able to hide himself: his seed is destroyed, and his brothers, and his neighbors; and he is no more."

Complete verse 11.

QUESTION 13   b

According to Jeremiah chapter 49:

What message was an ambassador sent to tell the nations?

QUESTION 14   CPC

Jeremiah chapter 49:17–18 says,

"¹⁷Edom shall become an astonishment: everyone who passes by it shall be astonished, and shall hiss at all its plagues."

Complete verse 18.

QUESTION 15   Tie

Jeremiah chapter 49:23 says, *"Hamath is confounded, and Arpad; for they have heard evil news, they are melted away...."*

Where were Hamath and Arpad located?

QUESTION 16   a

According to Jeremiah chapter 49:

What did Jeremiah say the fire kindled in the wall of Damascus will consume?

QUESTION 17   a

According to Jeremiah chapter 49:

Which king attacked the kingdom of Hazor?

QUESTION 18   b

Jeremiah chapter 49:29 says, *"Their tents and their flocks shall they take...."*

Whose tents and flocks is the above quote referring to?

QUESTION 19   a

According to Jeremiah chapter 49:

What would inhabit Hazor after they are attacked?

QUESTION 20   **a**

According to Jeremiah chapter 49:

To where did God say He would scatter the people of Elam?

QUESTION 21   **CPB**

Jeremiah chapter 49:38–39 says,

"and I will set my throne in Elam, and will destroy from there king and officials,' says the LORD."

Complete verse 39.

QUESTION 22   **a**

Jeremiah chapter 49 mentions the city of Damascus:

Which nation is Damascus the capital of?

QUESTION 23   **CMB**

Read Jeremiah chapter 49:1–39, preach or write a commentary on the passage with emphasis on salvation.

ANSWERS

ANSWER TO QUESTION 1   **c**

- King Solomon
- 1 Kings 11:7.

ANSWER TO QUESTION 2   **b1**

You shall not give any of your children to be sacrificed to Molech (Malcam) (Leviticus 18:21).

ANSWER TO QUESTION 3   **c**

- Malcam or Molech or Moloch is the god of the Ammonites or a god worshipped in most of the surrounding nations of Israel (or the Canaanite nations)
- Leviticus 18:21

ANSWER TO QUESTION 4   b

Ben Ammi or Lot (Genesis 19:30–38).

ANSWER TO QUESTION 5   a

In Ammon (Jeremiah 49:2).

ANSWER TO QUESTION 6   a

Because Ai is laid waste or destroyed (Jeremiah 49:3).

ANSWER TO QUESTION 7   CPC

"⁵'Look, I will bring a fear on you,' says the Lord, the LORD of hosts, 'from all who are around you; and you shall be driven out every man right forth, and there shall be none to gather together the fugitives.'" (Jeremiah 49:5.)

ANSWER TO QUESTION 8   a

He would bring them from captivity

Or

He would restore their fortunes (Jeremiah 49:6).

ANSWER TO QUESTION 9   a

Edom (Jeremiah 49:7).

ANSWER TO QUESTION 10   a

Esau (Genesis 36:9).

ANSWER TO QUESTION 11   b

The inhabitants or people of Dedan (Jeremiah 49:8).

ANSWER TO QUESTION 12   CPB

"¹¹Leave your fatherless children, I will preserve them alive; and let your widows trust in me." (Jeremiah 49:11.)

ANSWER TO QUESTION 13   b

To gather together and prepare an attack against Edom (Jeremiah 49:14).

ANSWER TO QUESTION 14   CPC

"18 "As in the overthrow of Sodom and Gomorrah and the neighbor cities of it," says the LORD, "no man shall dwell there, neither shall any son of man live in it."" (Jeremiah 49:18.)

ANSWER TO QUESTION 15   Tie

Syria (Jeremiah 49:23).

ANSWER TO QUESTION 16   a

The palaces of Ben Hadad (Jeremiah 49:27).

ANSWER TO QUESTION 17   a

King Nebuchadnezzar (Jeremiah 49:28).

ANSWER TO QUESTION 18   b

Kedar (Jeremiah 49:28–29).

ANSWER TO QUESTION 19   a

Jackals or Dragons (Jeremiah 49:33).

ANSWER TO QUESTION 20   a

Winds from the four quarters of the sky

Or

The winds

Or

To every nation of the earth (Jeremiah 49:36).

ANSWER TO QUESTION 21   CPB

"39 'But it shall happen in the latter days, that I will bring back the captivity of Elam,' says the LORD." (Jeremiah 49:39.)

ANSWER TO QUESTION 22   a

Syria.

HINT TO QUESTION 23   CMB

In Jeremiah chapter 49, God made declarations against several nations like Ammon, Edom, Hazor and Damascus, that is, Syria. Many of those nations God spoke about were great nations, both in military and economic terms. But in the verses under consideration, we see God showing His sovereignty over those nations in determining their fate, pronouncing punishment for iniquities and even promising restoration for Ammon. This teaches us that all the nations of the world are under God's radar and sovereignty, and each is accountable to Him. Therefore everyone should live with this awareness because, in the end, it would not matter where a person comes from or what they choose to believe in. Everyone will give an account of themself to God at the end of time.

CHAPTER 50

JEREMIAH CHAPTER 50

"The word that the LORD spoke concerning Babylon, concerning the land of the Chaldeans, by Jeremiah the prophet. [2]"Declare among the nations and publish, and set up a standard; publish, and do not conceal: say, 'Babylon is taken, Bel is disappointed, Merodach is dismayed; her images are disappointed, her idols are dismayed. [3]For out of the north there comes up a nation against her, which shall make her land desolate, and none shall dwell in it: they are fled, they are gone, both man and animal. [4]In those days, and in that time,' says the LORD, 'the sons of Israel shall come, they and the children of Judah together; they shall go on their way weeping, and shall seek the LORD their God. [5]They shall inquire concerning Zion with their faces turned toward it, saying, "Come, and join yourselves to the LORD in an everlasting covenant that shall not be forgotten." [6]My people have been lost sheep: their shepherds have caused them to go astray; they have turned them away on the mountains; they have gone from mountain to hill; they have forgotten their resting place. [7]All who found them have devoured them; and their adversaries said, "We are not guilty, because they have sinned against the LORD, the habitation of righteousness, even the LORD, the hope of their fathers." [8]Flee out of the midst of Babylon, and go forth out of the land of the Chaldeans, and be as the male goats before the flocks. [9]For, look, I will stir up and cause to come up against Babylon a company of great nations from the north country; and they shall set themselves in array against her; from there she shall be taken: their arrows shall be as of an expert mighty man; none shall return in vain.

¹⁰*Chaldea shall be a prey: all who prey on her shall be satisfied,'
says the LORD.' ¹¹Because you are glad, because you rejoice, O you
who plunder my heritage, because you are wanton as a heifer that
treads out the grain, and neigh as strong horses; ¹²your mother
shall be utterly disappointed; she who bore you shall be confounded:
look, she shall be the least of the nations, a wilderness, a dry land,
and a desert. ¹³Because of the wrath of the LORD she shall not be
inhabited, but she shall be wholly desolate: everyone who goes by
Babylon shall be astonished, and hiss at all her plagues. ¹⁴"Set
yourselves in array against Babylon all around, all you who bend
the bow; shoot at her, spare no arrows: for she has sinned against
the LORD. ¹⁵Shout against her all around: she has submitted
herself; her towers are fallen, her walls are thrown down; for it is
the vengeance of the LORD: take vengeance on her; as she has
done, do to her. ¹⁶Cut off the sower from Babylon, and him who
handles the sickle in the time of harvest: for fear of the oppressing
sword they shall turn everyone to his people, and they shall flee
everyone to his own land."' ¹⁷'Israel is a hunted sheep; the lions
have driven him away: first, the king of Assyria devoured him; and
now at last Nebuchadnezzar king of Babylon has broken his bones.
¹⁸Therefore thus says the LORD of hosts, the God of Israel: "Look,
I will punish the king of Babylon and his land, as I have punished
the king of Assyria. ¹⁹I will bring Israel again to his pasture, and
he shall feed on Carmel and Bashan, and his soul shall be satisfied
on the hills of Ephraim and in Gilead. ²⁰In those days, and in that
time, says the LORD, the iniquity of Israel shall be sought for, and
there shall be none; and the sins of Judah, and they shall not be
found: for I will pardon them whom I leave as a remnant."'"
²¹"Go up against the land of Merathaim, even against it, and
against the inhabitants of Pekod: kill and utterly destroy after
them," says the LORD, "and do according to all that I have
commanded you. ²²A sound of battle is in the land, and of great
destruction. ²³How is the hammer of the whole earth cut apart and
broken. How is Babylon become a desolation among the nations.
²⁴I have laid a snare for you, and you are also taken, Babylon, and
you weren't aware: you are found, and also caught, because you

have striven against the LORD. ²⁵*The LORD has opened his armory, and has brought forth the weapons of his indignation; for the Lord, the LORD of hosts, has a work to do in the land of the Chaldeans. ²⁶Come against her from the utmost border; open her storehouses; cast her up as heaps, and destroy her utterly; let nothing of her be left. ²⁷Kill all her bulls; let them go down to the slaughter: woe to them. For their day has come, the time of their visitation." ²⁸The voice of those who flee and escape out of the land of Babylon, to declare in Zion the vengeance of the LORD our God, the vengeance of his temple. ²⁹"Call together the archers against Babylon, all those who bend the bow; camp against her all around; let none of it escape: recompense her according to her work; according to all that she has done, do to her; for she has been proud against the LORD, against the Holy One of Israel. ³⁰Therefore her young men will fall in her streets, and all her men of war will be brought to silence in that day," says the LORD. ³¹"Look, I am against you, you proud one," says the Lord, the LORD of hosts; for your day has come, the time that I will visit you. ³²The proud one shall stumble and fall, and none shall raise him up; and I will kindle a fire in his cities, and it shall devour all who are around him." ³³Thus says the LORD of hosts: "The sons of Israel and the children of Judah are oppressed together; and all who took them captive hold them fast; they refuse to let them go. ³⁴Their Redeemer is strong; the LORD of hosts is his name: he will thoroughly plead their cause, that he may give rest to the earth, and disquiet the inhabitants of Babylon. ³⁵A sword is on the Chaldeans," says the LORD, "and on the inhabitants of Babylon, and on her officials, and on her wise men. ³⁶A sword is on the boasters, and they shall become fools; a sword is on her mighty men, and they shall be dismayed. ³⁷A sword is on their horses, and on their chariots, and on all the mixed people who are in the midst of her; and they shall become as women: a sword is on her treasures, and they shall be robbed. ³⁸A drought is on her waters, and they shall be dried up; for it is a land of engraved images, and they glory over idols. ³⁹Therefore the wild animals of the desert with the wolves shall dwell there, and the ostriches shall dwell in it:*

*and it shall be no more inhabited forever; neither shall it be lived in from generation to generation. *⁴⁰*As when God overthrew Sodom and Gomorrah and the neighbor cities of it," says the LORD, "so shall no man dwell there, neither shall any son of man live in it." *⁴¹*"Look, a people comes from the north; and a great nation and many kings shall be stirred up from the uttermost parts of the earth. *⁴²*They lay hold on bow and spear; they are cruel, and have no mercy; their voice roars like the sea; and they ride on horses, everyone set in array, as a man to the battle, against you, daughter of Babylon. *⁴³*The king of Babylon has heard the news of them, and his hands wax feeble: anguish has taken hold of him, pains as of a woman in labor. *⁴⁴*Look, the enemy shall come up like a lion from the pride of the Jordan against the strong habitation: for I will suddenly make them run away from it; and whoever is chosen, him will I appoint over it: for who is like me? And who will appoint me a time? And who is the shepherd who can stand before me?" *⁴⁵*Therefore hear the counsel of the LORD, that he has taken against Babylon; and his purposes, that he has purposed against the land of the Chaldeans: "Surely they shall drag them away, even the little ones of the flock; surely he shall make their habitation desolate over them. *⁴⁶*At the noise of the taking of Babylon the earth trembles, and the cry is heard among the nations."*

QUESTIONS

QUESTION 1   **b**

According to Jeremiah chapter 50:

What were the names of the Babylonian gods?

QUESTION 2   **a**

According to Jeremiah chapter 50:

Which people will return home together with the Israelites?

QUESTION 3   CPC

Jeremiah chapter 50:6–7 says,

"My people have been lost sheep: their shepherds have caused them to go astray; they have turned them away on the mountains; they have gone from mountain to hill; they have forgotten their resting place."

Complete verse 7.

QUESTION 4   b

Jeremiah chapter 50:9 says, *"For, look, I will stir up and cause to come up against Babylon a company of great nations from the north country; and they shall set themselves in array against her...."*

Which nation is referred to as the north country in the above scripture?

QUESTION 5   b

Jeremiah chapter 50:12 says, *"your mother shall be utterly disappointed; she who bore you shall be confounded...."*

Who is the above verse addressed to?

QUESTION 6   b

In Jeremiah chapter 50, God said He would punish the king of Babylon as He punished a particular person:

Who did He say He would punish the king of Babylon as?

QUESTION 7   b1

Jeremiah chapter 50:21 says, *"Go up against the land of Merathaim, even against it, and against the inhabitants of Pekod...."*

In which nation are Merathaim and Pekod?

QUESTION 8   a

Jeremiah chapter 50:24 says, *"I have laid a snare for you, and you are also taken...."*

Who is the above verse talking about?

QUESTION 9   **b**

According to Jeremiah chapter 50:

Who were those who would declare in Jerusalem the vengeance of God against those who destroyed His temple?

QUESTION 10   **CPC**

Jeremiah chapter 50:31–32 says,

""Look, I am against you, you proud one," says the Lord, the LORD of hosts; for your day has come, the time that I will visit you."

Complete verse 32.

QUESTION 11   **a**

According to Jeremiah chapter 50:

Who did God say has been oppressed or wronged?

QUESTION 12   **b**

Jeremiah chapter 50:38 says that the waters of Babylon will be struck with draught, and they will be dried up.

Why did God say this would happen?

QUESTION 13   **a**

According to Jeremiah chapter 50:

To which cities did God liken the destruction that would come upon Babylon?

QUESTION 14   **a**

Jeremiah chapter 50:43 says, *"The king of Babylon has heard the news of them, and his hands wax feeble: anguish has taken hold of him...."*

What was his pain or anguish compared to?

QUESTION 15   **CMB**

Read Jeremiah chapter 50:1–46, preach or write a commentary on the passage with focus on verses 1–3, 7–16, and with emphasis on salvation.

QUESTION 16   **CMC**

Read Jeremiah chapter 50:19–20, preach or write a commentary on the passage with emphasis on salvation.

ANSWERS

ANSWER TO QUESTION 1   **b**

Bel and Merodach or Marduk (Jeremiah 50:2).

ANSWER TO QUESTION 2   **a**

The people of Judah (Jeremiah 50:4).

ANSWER TO QUESTION 3   **CPC**

"7All who found them have devoured them; and their adversaries said, "We are not guilty, because they have sinned against the LORD, the habitation of righteousness, even the LORD, the hope of their fathers." (Jeremiah 50:7.)

ANSWER TO QUESTION 4   **b**

Medes and Persia (Jeremiah 51:11; Daniel 5:30–31).

ANSWER TO QUESTION 5   **b**

Babylon (Jeremiah 50:1,9,12).

ANSWER TO QUESTION 6   **b**

The king of Assyria (Jeremiah 50:18).

ANSWER TO QUESTION 7   **b1**

Babylon (Jeremiah 50:21–23).

ANSWER TO QUESTION 8   a

Babylon (Jeremiah 50:24).

ANSWER TO QUESTION 9   b

Those who escaped from Babylon (Jeremiah 50:28).

ANSWER TO QUESTION 10   CPC

"32 The proud one shall stumble and fall, and none shall raise him up; and I will kindle a fire in his cities, and it shall devour all who are around him." (Jeremiah 50:32.)

ANSWER TO QUESTION 11   a

The people of Israel and Judah (Jeremiah 50:33).

ANSWER TO QUESTION 12   b

Because the land is full of engraved images or idols and the people glory over them (Jeremiah 50:38).

ANSWER TO QUESTION 13   a

Sodom and Gomorrah and their neighbouring cities (Jeremiah 50:40).

ANSWER TO QUESTION 14   a

A woman in labour (Jeremiah 50:43).

HINT TO QUESTION 15   CMB

UTENSILS: Jeremiah chapter 50 lets us know of God's intention to punish Babylon. It should be noted that God had severally portrayed Nebuchadnezzar, King of Babylon and his Chaldean army as His instruments of punishing the nations, including Judah. However, in the verses under consideration, we see God talking about raising another instrument as a utensil for punishing Babylon and her king. A person who is an instrument of recompensing the wicked with wickedness is also guilty of wickedness and would face God's judgement for the wicked, and the people that do good will also receive the reward of doing good. This is why the Bible advises us to make ourselves utensils for doing good so that after God might have used us for doing good, He will give us the reward that follows. Whatsoever a person sows, they shall reap. The standard you use against others will be used against you. God rewards the righteous and the wicked for their respective deeds in this life and after this life.

HINT TO QUESTION 16   CMC

At a time God was passing Israel and Judah through some punitive process, He spoke of a time of their restoration and when their sins would be wiped off. The purpose of God in disciplining His children is to make them retrace their steps and turn to Him. The experience of the people of Israel and Judah would have been futile if it did not culminate in God's forgiveness of their iniquity.

CHAPTER 51

JEREMIAH CHAPTER 51

"Thus says the LORD: "Look, I will raise up against Babylon, and against those who dwell in Lebkamai, a destroying wind. ²I will send to Babylon foreigners who shall winnow her; and they shall empty her land: for in the day of trouble they shall be against her around. ³Do not let him who bends the bow bend it; nor not let him rise up in his armor. And do not spare her young men; utterly destroy her entire army. ⁴They shall fall down slain in the land of the Chaldeans, and thrust through in her streets. ⁵"For Israel is not forsaken, nor Judah, of his God, of the LORD of hosts; though their land is full of guilt against the Holy One of Israel. ⁶Flee out of the midst of Babylon, and save every man his life; do not be cut off in her iniquity: for it is the time of the LORD's vengeance; he will render to her a recompense. ⁷Babylon has been a golden cup in the LORD's hand, who made all the earth drunk: the nations have drunk of her wine; therefore the nations are mad. ⁸Babylon is suddenly fallen and destroyed: wail for her; take balm for her pain, if so be she may be healed. ⁹'We would have healed Babylon, but she is not healed: forsake her, and let us go everyone into his own country; for her judgment reaches to heaven, and is lifted up even to the skies.' ¹⁰'The LORD has brought forth our righteousness: come, and let us declare in Zion the work of the LORD our God.' ¹¹Make sharp the arrows; hold firm the shields: the LORD has stirred up the spirit of the kings of the Medes; because his purpose is against Babylon, to destroy it: for it is the vengeance of the LORD, the vengeance of his temple. ¹²Set up a standard against the walls of Babylon, make the watch strong, set the watchmen,

prepare the ambushes; for the LORD has both purposed and done that which he spoke concerning the inhabitants of Babylon. ¹³ *You who dwell on many waters, abundant in treasures, your end has come, the measure of your covetousness.* ¹⁴ *The LORD of hosts has sworn by himself, saying, "Surely I will fill you with men, as with the canker worm; and they shall lift up a shout against you."* ¹⁵ *He has made the earth by his power, he has established the world by his wisdom, and by his understanding has he stretched out the heavens.* ¹⁶ *When he utters his voice, there is a tumult of waters in the heavens, and he causes the vapors to ascend from the farthest parts of the earth; he makes lightning for the rain, and brings forth the wind out of his treasuries.* ¹⁷ *Every man has become brutish without knowledge. Every goldsmith is disappointed by his image; for his molten image is falsehood, and there is no breath in them.* ¹⁸ *They are vanity, a work of delusion: in the time of their visitation they shall perish.* ¹⁹ *The portion of Jacob is not like these, for he is the maker of all things; and Israel is the tribe of his inheritance; the LORD of hosts is his name.* ²⁰ *"You are my battle axe and weapons of war: and with you will I break in pieces the nations; and with you will I destroy kingdoms;* ²¹ *and with you will I break in pieces the horse and his rider; and with you will I break in pieces the chariot and its rider.* ²² *And with you will I break in pieces man and woman; and with you will I break in pieces the old man and the youth; and with you will I break in pieces the young man and the virgin;* ²³ *and with you will I break in pieces the shepherd and his flock; and with you will I break in pieces the farmer and his yoke; and with you will I break in pieces governors and deputies.* ²⁴ *I will render to Babylon and to all the inhabitants of Chaldea all their evil that they have done in Zion in your sight,"* *says the LORD.* ²⁵ *"Look, I am against you, destroying mountain,"* *says the LORD, "which destroys all the earth; and I will stretch out my hand on you, and roll you down from the rocks, and will make you a burnt mountain.* ²⁶ *They shall not take of you a stone for a corner, nor a stone for foundations; but you shall be desolate for ever,"* *says the LORD.* ²⁷ *Set up a standard in the land, blow the trumpet among the nations, prepare the nations against her, call* together against her the kingdoms of Ararat, Minni, and Ashkenaz: appoint a marshal against her; cause the horses to come up as the rough canker worm. [28] Prepare against her the nations, the kings of the Medes, its governors, and all its deputies, and all the land of their dominion. [29] The land trembles and is in pain; for the purposes of the LORD against Babylon do stand, to make the land of Babylon a desolation, without inhabitant. [30] The mighty men of Babylon have forborne to fight, they remain in their strongholds; their might has failed; they are become as women: her dwelling places are set on fire; her bars are broken. [31] One runner will run to meet another, and one messenger to meet another, to show the king of Babylon that his city is taken on every quarter: [32] and the passages are seized, and the reeds they have burned with fire, and the men of war are frightened. [33] For thus says the LORD of hosts, the God of Israel: "The daughter of Babylon is like a threshing floor at the time when it is trodden; yet a little while, and the time of harvest shall come for her. [34] 'Nebuchadnezzar the king of Babylon has devoured me, he has crushed me, he has made me an empty vessel, he has, like a monster, swallowed me up, he has filled his maw with my delicacies; he has cast me out. [35] The violence done to me and to my flesh be on Babylon,' shall the inhabitant of Zion say; and, 'My blood be on the inhabitants of Chaldea,' shall Jerusalem say. [36] Therefore thus says the LORD: "Look, I will plead your cause, and take vengeance for you; and I will dry up her sea, and make her fountain dry. [37] Babylon shall become heaps, a dwelling place for jackals, an astonishment, and a hissing, without inhabitant. [38] They shall roar together like young lions; they shall growl as lions' cubs. [39] When they are heated, I will make their feast, and I will make them drunk, that they may rejoice, and sleep a perpetual sleep, and not wake," says the LORD. [40] "I will bring them down like lambs to the slaughter, like rams with male goats. [41] How is Sheshach taken. and the praise of the whole earth seized. How is Babylon become a desolation among the nations. [42] The sea has come up on Babylon; she is covered with the multitude of its waves. [43] Her cities are become a desolation, a dry land, and a desert, a land in which no man dwells, neither does any son of man pass thereby. ⁴⁴I will execute judgment on Bel in Babylon, and I will bring forth out of his mouth that which he has swallowed up; and the nations shall not flow any more to him: yes, the wall of Babylon shall fall." ⁴⁵"My people, go away from the midst of her, and save yourselves every man from the fierce anger of the LORD. ⁴⁶Do not let your heart faint, neither fear for the news that shall be heard in the land; for news shall come one year, and after that in another year shall come news, and violence in the land, ruler against ruler. ⁴⁷Therefore look, the days come, that I will execute judgment on the engraved images of Babylon; and her whole land shall be confounded; and all her slain shall fall in the midst of her. ⁴⁸Then the heavens and the earth, and all that is in them, shall sing for joy over Babylon; for the destroyers shall come to her from the north," says the LORD. ⁴⁹As Babylon has caused the slain of Israel to fall, so at Babylon shall fall the slain of all the land. ⁵⁰You who have escaped the sword, go, do not stand still; remember the LORD from afar, and let Jerusalem come into your mind. ⁵¹"We are confounded, because we have heard reproach; confusion has covered our faces: for strangers have come into the sanctuaries of the LORD's house." ⁵²"Therefore look, the days come," says the LORD, "that I will execute judgment on her engraved images; and through all her land the wounded shall groan. ⁵³Though Babylon should mount up to the sky, and though she should fortify the height of her strength, yet from me shall destroyers come to her," says the LORD. ⁵⁴"The sound of a cry from Babylon, and of great destruction from the land of the Chaldeans." ⁵⁵For the LORD lays Babylon waste, and destroys out of her the great voice; and their waves roar like many waters; the noise of their voice is uttered: ⁵⁶for the destroyer has come on her, even on Babylon, and her mighty men are taken, their bows are broken in pieces; for the LORD is a God of recompenses, he will surely requite. ⁵⁷"I will make drunk her officials and her wise men, her governors and her deputies, and her mighty men; and they shall sleep a perpetual sleep, and not wake up," says the King, whose name is the LORD of hosts. ⁵⁸Thus says the LORD of hosts: "The broad walls of Babylon shall be utterly overthrown, and her high gates shall be *burned with fire; and the peoples shall labor for vanity, and the nations for the fire; and they shall be weary."* [59]*The word which Jeremiah the prophet commanded Seraiah the son of Neriah, the son of Mahseiah, when he went with Zedekiah the king of Judah to Babylon in the fourth year of his reign. Now Seraiah was chief quartermaster.* [60]*Jeremiah wrote in a scroll all the evil that should come on Babylon, even all these words that are written concerning Babylon.* [61]*Jeremiah said to Seraiah, "When you come to Babylon, then see that you read all these words,* [62]*and say, 'LORD, you have spoken concerning this place, to cut it off, that none shall dwell in it, neither man nor animal, but that it shall be desolate forever.'* [63]*It shall be, when you have made an end of reading this scroll, that you shall bind a stone to it, and cast it into the midst of the Perath:* [64]*and you shall say, 'Thus shall Babylon sink, and shall not rise again because of the evil that I will bring on her; and they shall be weary.'" Thus far are the words of Jeremiah."*

QUESTIONS

QUESTION 1   a

Jeremiah chapter 51:3 says, *"Do not let him who bends the bow bend it; nor not let him rise up in his armor. And do not spare her young men; utterly destroy her entire army."*

Whose young men did the above quote say should not be spared and her army completely destroyed?

QUESTION 2   b

Jeremiah chapter 51:6 says, *"Flee out of the midst of Babylon, and save every man his life...."*

What was the reason for the above instruction?

QUESTION 3   b

According to Jeremiah chapter 51:

What did the Bible say Babylon had been in God's hand, and what did God use it for?

QUESTION 4   a

According to Jeremiah chapter 51:

Who did the Bible say will be stirred up by God to attack Babylon?

QUESTION 5   b1

According to Jeremiah chapter 51:

By what did God do the following:

1. Make the earth?
2. Establish or preserve the world?
3. Stretch out the heaven?

QUESTION 6   CPB

Jeremiah chapter 51:17–18 says,

"Every man has become brutish without knowledge. Every goldsmith is disappointed by his image; for his molten image is falsehood, and there is no breath in them."

Complete verse 18.

QUESTION 7   CPA

Jeremiah chapter 51:20–21 says,

"You are my battle axe and weapons of war: and with you will I break in pieces the nations; and with you will I destroy kingdoms;"

Complete verse 21.

QUESTION 8   b

Jeremiah chapter 51:25 says, *""Look, I am against you, destroying mountain," says the LORD, "which destroys all the earth...."""*

Who is the above passage talking about?

QUESTION 9   b

Jeremiah chapter 51:29 says, *"The land trembles and is in pain; for the purposes of the LORD against Babylon do stand...."*

What purpose is the above scripture talking about?

QUESTION 10   b

According to Jeremiah chapter 51:

What did God say the daughter of Babylon was like?

QUESTION 11   a

According to Jeremiah chapter 51:

Who did the Lord say He would make drunk that they may sleep, never to wake up again?

QUESTION 12   CPB

Jeremiah chapter 51:37–38 says,

"Babylon shall become heaps, a dwelling place for jackals, an astonishment, and a hissing, without inhabitant."

Complete verse 38.

QUESTION 13   a

According to Jeremiah chapter 51:

Who or what is 'Bel'?

QUESTION 14   CPC

Jeremiah chapter 51:47–48 says,

"Therefore look, the days come, that I will execute judgment on the engraved images of Babylon; and her whole land shall be confounded; and all her slain shall fall in the midst of her."

Complete verse 48.

QUESTION 15   a

According to Jeremiah chapter 51:

In what year of the reign of King Zedekiah did Jeremiah send a letter through king Zedekiah's companion to Babylon?

QUESTION 16   **b2**

According to Jeremiah chapter 51:

Who did Jeremiah send on an errand to Babylon, and what was the errand?

QUESTION 17   **CMB**

Read Jeremiah chapter 51:5, preach or write a commentary on the passage with emphasis on salvation.

QUESTION 18   **CMB**

Read Jeremiah chapter 51:15–19, preach or write a commentary on the passage with focus on verse 17 and with emphasis on salvation.

QUESTION 19   **CMC**

Read Jeremiah chapter 51:24–26, preach or write a commentary on the passage with emphasis on salvation.

ANSWERS

ANSWER TO QUESTION 1   **a**

Babylon (Jeremiah 51:2–3).

ANSWER TO QUESTION 2   **b**

Because it was the time of the Lord's vengeance; so that the people would not get destroyed when destruction came on Babylon because of her sins (Jeremiah 51:6).

ANSWER TO QUESTION 3   **b**

- A golden cup
- To make the whole earth drunk (Jeremiah 51:7).

ANSWER TO QUESTION 4   a

The Kings of Medes (and Persia) (Jeremiah 51:11).

ANSWER TO QUESTION 5   b1

- He made the earth by His power
- He established the world by His wisdom
- Stretch out the heaven by His understanding (Jeremiah 51:15).

ANSWER TO QUESTION 6   CPB

"18 They are vanity, a work of delusion: in the time of their visitation they shall perish." (Jeremiah 51:18.)

ANSWER TO QUESTION 7   CPA

"21 and with you will I break in pieces the horse and his rider; and with you will I break in pieces the chariot and its rider." (Jeremiah 51:21.)

ANSWER TO QUESTION 8   b

Babylon (Jeremiah 51:25).

ANSWER TO QUESTION 9   b

To make Babylon desolate without inhabitants (Jeremiah 51:29).

ANSWER TO QUESTION 10   b

A threshing floor that is trodden (Jeremiah 51:33)

ANSWER TO QUESTION 11   a

Babylon or the inhabitants of Babylon (Jeremiah 51:37–39).

ANSWER TO QUESTION 12   CPB

"38 They shall roar together like young lions; they shall growl as lions' cubs." (Jeremiah 51:38.)

ANSWER TO QUESTION 13   a

A god of Babylon (Jeremiah 51:44).

ANSWER TO QUESTION 14   CPC

"⁴⁸Then the heavens and the earth, and all that is in them, shall sing for joy over Babylon; for the destroyers shall come to her from the north," says the LORD." (Jeremiah 51:48.)

ANSWER TO QUESTION 15   a

Fourth year (Jeremiah 51:59).

ANSWER TO QUESTION 16   b2

- Seraiah (son of Neriah)
- He was sent to go and read all of Jeremiah's prophecy against Babylon written on the scroll he was given. Then, he was to proclaim that God had said He would destroy the nation of Babylon and that no man or animal would be left in the land. After that, he was to throw the scroll into the Perath or Euphrates with a stone tied to it and make a pronouncement that Babylon would sink, never to rise again, the same way the scroll sank (Jeremiah 51:59–64).

HINT TO QUESTION 17   CMB

In the verse under consideration, God assured His people that they would not be forsaken even as they were going through punishment for their sins. One of the privileges of being a child of God is that God is still our Father even when we sin; He does not drive us away or abandon us but will discipline us. When we acknowledge our sins by turning to God with a repentant heart, He is always glad to take us back and restore us.

HINT TO QUESTION 18   CMB

Amidst Prophet Jeremiah's declaration of God's words concerning the nations, the prophet took time to eulogise God. He went ahead to state that every man is brutish and without knowledge. The wisdom of the natural man is foolishness. It is the fear of God that brings about true wisdom. Every man who fears God has His Spirit and does not fall into the category of 'brutish without knowledge' spoken of by Prophet Jeremiah.

HINT TO QUESTION 19   CMC

Validity of God's word: Jeremiah prophesied the Babylonian invasion of Judah and the captivity by Nebuchadnezzar in Babylon, the fall of the king of Babylon and the destruction and desolation of the Babylonian empire. None of the words of God spoken through Jeremiah failed to come to pass. So God's word is true and reliable, and everyone must submit to God's word to be saved from the impending judgement coming on the world as a result of sin.

CHAPTER 52

JEREMIAH CHAPTER 52

"Zedekiah was twenty-one years old when he began to reign; and he reigned eleven years in Jerusalem: and his mother's name was Hamutal the daughter of Jeremiah of Libnah. ²He did that which was evil in the sight of the LORD, according to all that Jehoiakim had done. ³For through the anger of the LORD it happened in Jerusalem and Judah, until he had cast them out from his presence. Zedekiah rebelled against the king of Babylon. ⁴It happened in the ninth year of his reign, in the tenth month, in the tenth day of the month, that Nebuchadnezzar king of Babylon came, he and all his army, against Jerusalem, and camped against it; and they built forts against it round about. ⁵So the city was besieged to the eleventh year of king Zedekiah. ⁶In the fourth month, in the ninth day of the month, the famine was severe in the city, so that there was no bread for the people of the land. ⁷Then a breach was made in the city, and all the men of war fled, and went forth out of the city by night by the way of the gate between the two walls, which was by the king's garden; (now the Chaldeans were against the city all around;) and they went toward the Arabah. ⁸But the army of the Chaldeans pursued after the king, and overtook Zedekiah in the plains of Jericho; and all his army was scattered from him. ⁹Then they took the king, and carried him up to the king of Babylon to Riblah in the land of Hamath; and he gave judgment on him. ¹⁰The king of Babylon killed the sons of Zedekiah before his eyes: he killed also all the officials of Judah in Riblah. ¹¹He put out the eyes of Zedekiah; and the king of Babylon bound him in fetters, and carried him to Babylon, and put him in prison until

the day of his death. ¹²*Now in the fifth month, in the tenth day of the month, which was the nineteenth year of king Nebuchadnezzar, king of Babylon, came Nebuzaradan the captain of the guard, who stood before the king of Babylon, into Jerusalem:* ¹³*and he burned the house of the LORD, and the king's house; and all the houses of Jerusalem, even every great house, burned he with fire.* ¹⁴*All the army of the Chaldeans, who were with the captain of the guard, broke down all the walls of Jerusalem all around.* ¹⁵*Then Nebuzaradan the captain of the guard carried away captive of the poorest of the people, and the residue of the people who were left in the city, and those who fell away, who fell to the king of Babylon, and the residue of the multitude.* ¹⁶*But Nebuzaradan the captain of the guard left of the poorest of the land to be vineyard keepers and farmers.* ¹⁷*The Chaldeans broke the pillars of bronze that were in the house of the LORD, and the bases and the bronze sea that were in the house of the LORD in pieces, and carried all their bronze to Babylon.* ¹⁸*They also took away the pots, the shovels, the snuffers, the basins, the spoons, and all the vessels of bronze with which they ministered.* ¹⁹*The captain of the guard took away the cups, the fire pans, the basins, the pots, the lampstands, the spoons, and the bowls; that which was of gold, in gold, and that which was of silver, in silver.* ²⁰*They took the two pillars, the one sea, and the twelve bronze bulls that were under the sea, and the stands which king Solomon had made for the house of the LORD. The bronze of all these vessels was without weight.* ²¹*As for the pillars, the height of the one pillar was eighteen cubits; and a line of twelve cubits encircled it; and its thickness was four fingers. It was hollow.* ²²*A capital of bronze was on it; and the height of the one capital was five cubits, with network and pomegranates on the capital all around, all of bronze: and the second pillar also had like these, and pomegranates.* ²³*There were ninety-six pomegranates on the sides; all the pomegranates were one hundred on the network all around.* ²⁴*The captain of the guard took Seraiah the chief priest, and Zephaniah the second priest, and the three keepers of the threshold:* ²⁵*and out of the city he took an officer who was set over the men of war; and seven men of those who saw the king's face,* who were found in the city; and the scribe of the captain of the army, who mustered the people of the land; and sixty men of the people of the land, who were found in the midst of the city. [26]Nebuzaradan the captain of the guard took them, and brought them to the king of Babylon to Riblah. [27]The king of Babylon struck them, and put them to death at Riblah in the land of Hamath. So Judah was carried away captive out of his land. [28]This is the people whom Nebuchadnezzar carried away captive: in the seventh year three thousand twenty-three Jews; [29]in the eighteenth year of Nebuchadnezzar he carried away captive from Jerusalem eight hundred thirty-two persons; [30]in the three and twentieth year of Nebuchadnezzar Nebuzaradan the captain of the guard carried away captive of the Jews seven hundred forty-five persons: all the persons were four thousand and six hundred. [31]It happened in the seven and thirtieth year of the captivity of Jehoiachin king of Judah, in the twelfth month, in the five and twentieth day of the month, that Evilmerodach king of Babylon, in the first year of his reign, lifted up the head of Jehoiachin king of Judah, and brought him forth out of prison; [32]and he spoke kindly to him, and set his throne above the throne of the kings who were with him in Babylon, [33]and changed his prison garments. Jehoiachin ate bread before him continually all the days of his life: [34]and for his allowance, there was a continual allowance given him by the king of Babylon, every day a portion until the day of his death, all the days of his life."

QUESTIONS

QUESTION 1   a

According to Jeremiah chapter 52:

Who was Hamutal?

QUESTION 2   b1

According to Jeremiah chapter 52:

How old was King Zedekiah when he was taken to Babylon? Explain how you arrived at your answer.

QUESTION 3   **b**

According to Jeremiah chapter 52:

How old was Zedekiah when he became king, and how many years did he rule?

QUESTION 4   **b1**

According to Jeremiah chapter 52:

In what year of the reign of King Zedekiah did the king of Babylon begin the siege on Jerusalem, and in what year was the city overtaken?

QUESTION 5   **b1**

How are Jehoiakim and Zedekiah related?

QUESTION 6   **a**

According to Jeremiah chapter 52:

In what year of the reign of King Zedekiah did the famine in Judah become very severe?

QUESTION 7   **a**

According to Jeremiah chapter 52:

Where did the Babylonian troops catch up with King Zedekiah when he fled the city of Judea?

QUESTION 8   **b1**

According to Jeremiah chapter 52:

Mention three (3) things King Nebuchadnezzar did to King Zedekiah when the Babylonian armies caught up with him and brought him before King Nebuchadnezzar.

QUESTION 9   **b**

According to Jeremiah chapter 52:

In what year and month of King Nebuchadnezzar's reign was the temple in Jerusalem burnt down?

QUESTION 10   b

According to Jeremiah chapter 52:

Mention two significant buildings the captain of the guard of the king of Babylon burnt down when he arrived in Jerusalem.

QUESTION 11   b

According to Jeremiah chapter 52, when the Babylonian armies led by Nebuzaradan came to Jerusalem after king Zedekiah had been captured:

Which people did he leave to remain in Jerusalem, and why did he leave them behind?

QUESTION 12   b2

According to Jeremiah chapter 52:

What were the dimensions or measurements of the pillars in the Lord's temple that the Babylonians destroyed?

QUESTION 13   a

According to Jeremiah chapter 52:

Which king made the bronze bulls in the temple of God that the Babylonians plundered?

QUESTION 14   a

According to Jeremiah chapter 52:

What material was the pomegranate on the capital of the temple pillar made from?

QUESTION 15   b

According to Jeremiah chapter 52:

What was the height of the capital on the temple's pillar?

QUESTION 16   b

According to Jeremiah chapter 52:

What were Seraiah and Zephaniah's offices or positions?

QUESTION 17   b1

According to Jeremiah chapter 52:

How many captives in total were taken to Babylon, and in what years of King Nebuchadnezzar's reign were they taken?

QUESTION 18   b2

Jeremiah chapter 52 gives a summary of the number of captives that were taken from Judah to Babylon:

In how many batches were they taken to captivity, and how many were they per batch?

QUESTION 19   a

According to Jeremiah chapter 52:

For how many years was Jehoiachin or Coniah imprisoned in Babylon before being released?

QUESTION 20   b

According to Jeremiah chapter 52:

Who released King Jehoiachin or Coniah from prison in Babylon, and in which month was he released?

QUESTION 21   CMC

Read Jeremiah chapter 52:10–11, 31–34, preach or write a commentary on the passage with emphasis on salvation.

ANSWERS

ANSWER TO QUESTION 1   a

She was the mother of King Zedekiah

Or

She was the daughter of Jeremiah of Libnah (Jeremiah 52:1).

ANSWER TO QUESTION 2   b1

- 32 years
- He became king at the age of 21 and ruled for eleven years. Therefore, 21+11=32 (Jeremiah 52:1).

ANSWER TO QUESTION 3   b

- Twenty-one years
- Eleven years (Jeremiah 52:1).

ANSWER TO QUESTION 4   b1

- Ninth year
- Eleventh year (Jeremiah 52:4–5).

ANSWER TO QUESTION 5   b1

They were brothers (1 Chronicles 3:15 and 2 Kings 24:17).

ANSWER TO QUESTION 6   a

The eleventh year (Jeremiah 52:5–6).

ANSWER TO QUESTION 7   a

In the plains of Jericho or Jericho (Jeremiah 52:8).

ANSWER TO QUESTION 8   b

- He made King Zedekiah watch as he killed or slaughtered his sons and his officials
- Then he put out or gouged out Zedekiah's eyes
- Put him in bronze chains and sent him to prison in Babylon, where he remained till he died (Jeremiah 52:10–11).

ANSWER TO QUESTION 9   b

- In the 19th year
- Fifth month (Jeremiah 52:12).

ANSWER TO QUESTION 10   b

1. The house of the Lord or temple
2. The king's house or the royal palace (Jeremiah 52:13).

ANSWER TO QUESTION 11   b

- Some of the poorest of the people
- To take care of the vineyards and fields (Jeremiah 52:16).

ANSWER TO QUESTION 12   b2

Height: 18 cubits or 27 feet or 8 metres

Circumference: 12 cubits or 18 feet or 5.5 metres

Thickness: 4 fingers or 3 inches or 75 millimetres (Jeremiah 52:21).

ANSWER TO QUESTION 13   a

King Solomon (Jeremiah 52:20).

ANSWER TO QUESTION 14   a

Bronze or brass (Jeremiah 52:22).

ANSWER TO QUESTION 15   b

5 cubits or 7½ feet or 2.3 metres (Jeremiah 52:22)

ANSWER TO QUESTION 16   b

- Seraiah was the chief or high priest while
- Zephaniah was the second priest or priest (Jeremiah 52:24).

ANSWER TO QUESTION 17   b1

- 4,600
- The seventh, eighteenth, and twenty-third years (Jeremiah 52:28,30).

ANSWER TO QUESTION 18   b2

- 3 batches.
- First batch: 3,023

Second batch: 832

Third batch: 745 (Jeremiah 52:28–30).

ANSWER TO QUESTION 19   a

37 years (Jeremiah 52:31).

ANSWER TO QUESTION 20   b

- Evilmerodach
- The twelfth month (Jeremiah 52:31).

HINT TO QUESTION 21   CMC

Considering the horror King Zedekiah faced at the hands of King Nebuchadnezzar, his initial fear of surrendering to the king of Babylon seems to be justified, but looking at the fate of Jehoiachin, how God preserved him as He had promised to those who would surrender to the king of Babylon, we see that there is never a better option than obeying God. We should never feel that we are better off when we cut corners, acting against the word of God to achieve our desires, for we do not know the good which God intended to work out for us through our situations.